Students' Experiences of E-learning in Higher Education

C000121108

Students' Experiences of E-learning in Higher Education helps higher education instructors/teachers and university managers understand how e-learning relates to, and can be integrated with, other student experiences of learning. Grounded in relevant international research, the book is distinctive in that it foregrounds students' experiences of learning, emphasizing the importance of how students interpret the challenges set before them, along with their conceptions of learning and their approaches to learning. The way students interpret task requirements greatly affects learning outcomes, and those interpretations are in turn influenced by how students read the larger environment in which they study. The authors argue that a systemic understanding is necessary for the effective design and management of modern learning environments, whether lectures, seminars, laboratories or private study. This ecological understanding must also acknowledge, though, the agency of learners as active interpreters of their environment and its culture, values and challenges.

Students' Experiences of E-learning in Higher Education reports research outcomes that locate e-learning within the broader ecology of higher education, and:

- Offers a holistic treatment of e-learning in higher education, reflecting the need for integrating e-learning and other aspects of the student learning experience.
- Reports research on students' experiences with e-learning conducted by authors in the United States, Europe and Australia.
- Synthesises key themes in recent international research and summarises their implications for teachers and managers.

Robert A. Ellis is Associate Professor and Director of eLearning at the University of Sydney, Australia.

Peter Goodyear is Professor of Education and co-director of the CoCo Research Centre at the University of Sydney, Australia.

Open and Flexible Learning Series

Series Editors: Fred Lockwood, A.W. (Tony) Bates and Som Naidu

Activities in Self-Instructional Texts
Fred Lockwood

Assessing Open and Distance Learners
Chris Morgan and Meg O'Reilly

Changing University Teaching
Terry Evans and Daryl Nation

Contemporary Perspectives in E-Learning Research: Themes, Methods and Impact on Practice
Gráinne Conole and Martin Oliver

The Costs and Economics of Open and Distance Learning
Greville Rumble

Delivering Digitally: Managing the Transition to the Knowledge Media
Alistair Inglis, Peter Ling and Vera Joosten

Delivering Learning on the Net: The Why, What and How of Online Education
Martin Weller

The Design and Production of Self-Instructional Materials
Fred Lockwood

Designing Video and Multimedia for Open and Flexible Learning
Jack Koumi

Developing Innovation in Online Learning: An Action Research Framework
Maggie McPherson and Miguel Baptista Nunes

Distance and Blended Learning: Opening up Asian Education and Training
Colin Latchem and Insung Jung

Exploring Open and Distance Learning
Derek Rowntree

Flexible Learning in a Digital World
Bettery Collis and Jef Moonen

Improving Your Students' Learning
Alistair Morgan

Innovation in Open and Distance Learning
Fred Lockwood and Ann Gooley

Integrated E-Learning: Implications for Pedagogy, Technology and Organization
Win Jochems, Jeroen van Merriënboer and Rob Koper

Interactions in Online Education: Implications for Theory and Practice
Charles Juwah

'Ellis and Goodyear have produced that rare thing – a book that makes genuine advances in an area of real importance, achieving this in a way that is both scholarly and yet entirely practical. Their ecological perspective not only introduces some powerful new approaches – such as "teaching as design", or the relationship between virtual and physical spaces for learning – but offers something close to a new language in which to consider higher education policy in general. The book offers us a sustained attempt to bring the available evidence to bear on some of the most challenging issues facing universities, with a particular focus on technology. It is grounded in the practical experience of the authors in teaching, research and management in global higher education, informed by a deep respect for research evidence, and balanced by placing the nature of the student experience at the centre of the enquiry. It is also elegantly and clearly written. If I were asked to compile a reading list for a new PVC Learning and Teaching of the half dozen most important books published in the last five years, then this would certainly be on my list.'

Professor Terry Mayes, Emeritus Professor,
Caledonian Academy, Glasgow Caledonian University, Scotland

'Ellis and Goodyear use a powerful set of ecological metaphors to guide readers to understand the complex relationships between learning, uncertainty, environment and leadership in universities. Learning is neither merely local nor independent but is situated in interactions with others and relationships to the environment. This suggests a framework for rethinking and planning meaningful learning, teaching and information technology in contemporary higher education.'

Professor Chin-Chung Tsai, Chair,
Graduate School of Technological and Vocational Education,
National Taiwan University of Science and Technology, Taiwan

Students' Experiences of E-learning in Higher Education

The Ecology of Sustainable Innovation

Robert A. Ellis and Peter Goodyear

Routledge
Taylor & Francis Group

NEW YORK AND LONDON

First published 2010
by Routledge
270 Madison Ave, New York, NY 10016

Simultaneously published in the UK
by Routledge
2 Park Square, Milton Park, Abingdon, Oxon OX14 4RN

Routledge is an imprint of the Taylor & Francis Group, an informa business

© 2010 Taylor & Francis

Typeset in Minion by RefineCatch Limited, Bungay, Suffolk
Printed and bound in the United States of America on acid-free paper by
Walsworth Publishing Company, Marceline, MO

Library of Congress Cataloging-in-Publication Data
Ellis, Robert.
    Students' experiences of e-learning in higher education : the ecology of
    sustainable innovation / Robert Ellis & Peter Goodyear
        p. cm.—(Open and flexible learning series)
    Includes bibliographical references and index.
    Education, Higher—Computer-assisted instruction.   2. Computers and
    college students.   I. Goodyear, Peter, 1952– II. Title.
    LB2395.7.E46 2009
    378.1′7344678—dc22

                                                             2009011579

ISBN 10: 0–415–98935–3 (hbk)
ISBN 10: 0–415–98936–1 (pbk)
ISBN 10: 0–203–87297–5 (ebk)

ISBN 13: 978–0–415–98935–0 (hbk)
ISBN 13: 978–0–415–98936–7 (pbk)
ISBN 13: 978–0–203–87297–0 (ebk)

Contents

Figures

Tables

Foreword

In the last 40 years or so, universities have had to contend with many changes, political, social, cultural, economic and technological. The most dramatic of these is technological. In that time, a succession of educational technologies have been visited upon them, being the digital equivalents of all the educational technologies ever invented over the entire course of the history of education. The digital equivalents of slate (word processor), chalk (mouse and keyboard), library (websites), blackboard (interactive whiteboard), classroom (online forum), printing press (internet) and so on, have forced us to rethink the way we do teaching and learning. In a digitally-connected world, the physical boundaries of the lecture theatre dissolve into a hinterland of social and academic networking and global information access behind every student. In such a context, what must the physically-situated learning experience of a university become?

The response of university communities has been to embrace all these technology challenges, in the sense that these and others can all be found in active use on every campus now. But that is not quite the same as harnessing the technology to the educational ends and the fundamental values of academic life. We risk being led inexorably by the technology in its own ever-changing directions, as we pursue each new and intriguing invention. If we take this piecemeal approach to adopting each new invention as it becomes available, without a clear sense of the part it plays in the overall system, then we lose the power of the holistic approach, which knows why we are taking on a new technology, and what it means for it to succeed, and what counts as failure and the need for revision. The affordances of a new technology are not sufficient to judge its value. For example, online forums afford flexible student interaction, but the history of their research and evaluation is full of disappointment. They play a particular role within the rich mix of formal and informal learning experiences of a student, but without an appreciation of that, they fail. The decontextualised online forum is the digital equivalent of telling students to go to a seminar room at a particular time to discuss this week's topic, and doing nothing else to guide or support them. In the pre-digital world we would not have done that. Digital technologies need the same understanding of their place if we are to use them well.

But how complex it is to think this through. To become fully aware of what it takes for a university community to deal with new technologies, it can sometimes help to imagine the introduction of now familiar technologies. Consider, for example, trying to advise a university on how to make best use of the new technology of *paper*. We have the vantage point of our modern understanding of its multiple affordances, and the variety of ways it supports the process of teaching, learning, management and administration, and even with this we can see the difficulty of working out the optimal way to introduce it into the institution as a whole. And paper is just one of the conventional technologies that is mirrored in our digital world.

That is a thread that runs throughout this book: the importance of putting back together – conceptually, and in practice – what has been taken apart. The authors tackle the issue of how best to embrace digital technology by insisting that we must learn to understand its role, in all its complexity, in the internal relations within a university. Digital technology is sometimes described as 'disruptive', but education is one of the systems whose existing powerful ecology of conventional forces has most robustly resisted disruption of its working methods. It resists technology by compartmentalising it. Technology is made the responsibility of a department, a manager, a champion, an assistant, so that the rest of us do not have to worry about it. However, digital technology will not go away, and we cannot afford to separate it out. Its use in teaching and learning has to be woven into the fabric of the institution, manifested in every aspect of its activities, infrastructure and organisation, just as paper is. That is the most important message of this timely book, as we all try to face up to the onslaught of continual invention from the world of digital technology, learning as we go.

Diana Laurillard
London Knowledge Lab, Institute of Education

Acknowledgements

This book has grown directly out of our research collaboration at the University of Sydney, but has also been informed by many conversations with colleagues about the practical problems that the book sets out to address. It is a huge pleasure to be able to thank the people involved, for their stimulation and support, even if they may not endorse everything we say.

At the University of Sydney we have benefited immeasurably from the vibrant intellectual environments provided by CoCo (the Centre for Research on Computer Supported Learning and Cognition) and ITL (the Institute for Teaching and Learning). In particular, we thank Peter Reimann, Keith Trigwell, Paul Ginns, Angela Brew, Simon Barrie and Mike Prosser. Mike Prosser has been a partner investigator in many of our projects and we extend particular thanks to Mike for his wise counsel. Ana Maria Bliuc has worked with us on many of the projects reported in this book and we extend special thanks to Ana Maria for her assistance in the final stages of preparing this book. Agnieszka Bachfischer has provided valuable research assistance and Shannon Kennedy-Clark also helped with the production of the book in its final stages.

We have learned a great deal from our PhD students over the years, and particularly wish to thank Ann Applebee, Carlos Gonzalez, Susan Matthew, Karen Scott, Gillian Roberts, Daniel Sze and Dai Fei Yang, whose research has influenced our thinking in this book.

A number of the ideas developed in the book, and findings on which they are based, have been presented and explored at conferences, workshops and through institutional partnerships between the University of Sydney and other universities. We are glad to be able to acknowledge our debts to colleagues who have discussed these matters with us, especially when they disagreed. Some of these colleagues have also been our partners in research projects and/or in joint writing. We would especially like to thank Mireia Asensio, Sue Atkinson, Marie-Therese Barbaux, Brendan Barrett, Sue Bennett, Martha Brillant, Rafael Calvo, Gráinne Conole, Andrew Cooper, Charles Crook, James Dalziel, Steve Draper, Helen Drury, Pierre Dillenbourg, Mark Freeman, Oliver Fulton, Viv Hodgson, Linda Hort, Jane Hughes, Chris Jones, Nerida Jarkey, Marianna Koulias, Ray Land, Diana Laurillard, Colin Lowe, Mary Jane Mahony, Terry Mayes, David McConnell, Mike O'Donoghue, Agi O'Hara, Ron Oliver, Mary Peat, Brigitte Picot, Dave Riley, Roland Rosner, Roger Säljö, Murray Saunders, Stephen Sheely, Mike Spector, Christine Smith, Fiona Strawbridge, John Sweller, Charlotte Taylor, Rosanne Taylor, Sue Tickner, Paul Trowler, Mary Helen Ward, Mark Weyers, Helen Wozniak, Denis Wright and Maria Zenios.

Research reported in this book has been funded by the Australian Research Council (Grants DP0559282, LP0562146). We would also like to acknowledge the support of the Australian Learning and Teaching Council, whose award of a Senior Fellowship to Peter Goodyear helped accelerate the writing.

The book would not have come into being without the encouragement and support of the series editors, and we are glad to have been able to work with Som Naidu, Fred Lockwood and Tony Bates. Their feedback at the start of the project was especially helpful. Thanks also to Sarah Burrows at Routledge.

As is so often the case with the preparation of books of this kind, our partners and children have had to put up with our grumpiness and mental vacations. Special thanks, therefore, to Louise, Sonia, Jeremy, Emily and Michael. We promise not to do it again too soon.

Robert A. Ellis and Peter Goodyear
Sydney, December 2008.

Acknowledgement of Copyright Permissions

We are pleased to acknowledge the kind permissions of Taylor & Francis and the editor of the journal *Higher Education Research and Development*, Ian Macdonald, for Figure 2.1, originally published in Trigwell and Prosser (1997); Blackwell publishing and the editor of the journal *The British Journal of Educational Technology*, Nick Rushby, for Tables 4.4, 4.5 and 4.6, originally published in Ellis and Calvo (2006); Carlo Ratti and Francesco Calabre and the team at iSpots at the Massachusetts Institute of Technology for Figure 10.12; Professor Derrick Armstrong and the Chief Information Officer Bruce Meikle, both of the University of Sydney for the figures 10.2 through to 10.11; and Professor David Chiddick, chair of the UK Space Management Group for tables 10.5 and 10.6, originally published in SMG 2006a.

1
Introduction

Universities play a pivotal role in society. They are hubs of innovation. They attract and develop talent. They provide a free and critical voice. They create and share new knowledge and enrich the arts. They are crucial assets in many metropolitan and regional economies. They link the local and the global. They do all these things with varying degrees of commitment and success, depending, in part, on the political and financial contexts in which they find themselves. No other institution provides this array of social benefits and few have shown comparable ingenuity and determination to survive (Smith & Webster, 1997; Bowden & Marton, 1998; Florida, 1999, 2003; Barnett, 2005). Not everyone speaks about universities in this way. Universities are often chided for being complacent, elitist, self-serving and detached from reality.

There is more than a grain of truth in such criticisms. But there is no point in trying to arbitrate. There is very little value in saying or showing that universities are necessarily and essentially innovative or hidebound, useful or beyond use. Discourses of derision, just like complacency, obscure the view of what needs changing, and how it might be changed. And there is an emerging consensus, particularly visible in universities in the richer nations, about the necessity of certain kinds of change. Against a background of declining public funding and intensifying global competition for good staff and students, universities are asking how they can provide better support for the education of a growing, diversifying, time-poor student body. How can they enhance opportunities for *all* the students who might benefit from university education: helping to make wealth, class, gender and ethnicity irrelevant as predictors of educational attainment? How can they upgrade curricula, teaching methods, assessment regimes and course outcomes so that all students are equipped to meet the uncertain challenges of the 21st century? (Simons, Linden & Duffy, 2000; Barnett, 2007; Kalantzis & Cope, 2008).

1

New technology – especially information and communication technology (ICT) – plays a surprisingly important role in addressing these questions. ICT is intimately bound up with powerful processes of globalisation, as well as with re-engineering business processes, accelerating product cycles, breaking down the economics, practices and assumptions of mass production, shortening the distance between producer and consumer (cutting out intermediaries), etc. The influence of technology needs to be understood on two levels: it enables these changes to happen but it also affects people's expectations about what is normal and possible. For example, the use of ICT in higher education makes it *possible* for universities to offer students much more flexible access to learning resources, administrative services and academic staff, but it also encourages students to *expect* such flexibility.

Moreover, the use of ICT to increase educational flexibility raises fundamental questions about what is essential to a university. It raises questions about the value of having a physical campus. By allowing teaching to be casualised and outsourced, it raises questions about the links between research and teaching, and about who should be seen as core members of the academic body. Blurring the boundaries around distance-learning – what *is* the distance? – makes some universities footloose; less attached to place, they face huge questions about identity, brand, market, loyalty and competitive edge.

We have written this book to help sharpen thinking and discussion about technology and higher education. Like many people who research and write about this topic, we are fundamentally interested in the improvement of student learning through the enhancement of educational practice, including through better design and management of learning environments. But in tackling this we also raise questions about what 21st century students and teachers need and want, and about how universities should conceive of, and manage, their physical, digital and intellectual resources. ICT allows students and staff to change the ways they organise their activities in time and space. It is capable of supporting the development of new working relationships, from small groups to extensive learning networks and communities. Its management raises questions that are not merely technical: they go to the heart of what a university means to its students.

Two main themes are woven through the book. One is concerned with a richer conception of student learning; the other with part-whole relationships. We aim to help all those who are in a position to improve university education to discuss and co-ordinate their work, *based on a shared understanding* of good learning and of how it sits within a web of relationships – within an ecology of learning. It is neither practically useful nor intellectually defensible to see technology as separable from the normal, everyday activities of university students and staff. 'E-learning' is part of their workaday experience. It is also novel, complex, slippery and likely to present itself in surprising ways, as technological developments continue to accelerate.

Contemporary Pressures and Tensions

Most universities are finding it hard to protect the quality of students' learning experiences, especially when faced with worsening staff:student ratios and declining public sector investment. Yet defending the status quo is neither possible nor desirable. There are unacceptable differences in educational outcomes for students from different socio-economic backgrounds. The quality of educational provision, and outcome, varies substantially between universities that are notionally equal. Variations in provision and outcome can also be found between departments in the same university. But unacceptable variation in outcome, using traditional measures of attainment, is only part of the problem. Even if these various levels of performance were brought up to the standards set by the best, we would still have to recognise that higher education is rather poor at defining, teaching and testing skills and knowledge fit for the 21st century. There have been radical changes in the nature of graduate employment. Even if the scope and scale of the knowledge economy is hard to map (Blackler, 1995; Brown, Hesketh & Williams 2003; Fleming, Harley & Sewell, 2004; Kenway, 2006), it is clear that the ways of defining and assessing graduate capabilities that crystallised in the industrial age are obsolescent, at best (Bereiter, 2002).

Other powerful changes are at work. Student numbers have grown. Students' needs, expectations and demands have diversified. Students have become more assertive, especially when they see themselves as paying customers. They have less time available for study and they have become more savvy about technology, even if they are not sure how best to use it for learning purposes. Governments, through various agencies, have become more intimately involved in regulating the quality of educational provision and its intended outcomes.

In addition, academic work is changing. The processes of research, and knowledge-creation generally, have become more complex. University teachers, as researchers, perform on a global stage and engage, on a daily basis, with colleagues in other universities and other countries. Research for many academics, even in the humanities, is becoming more collaborative, team-based and dependent on technology. Disciplinary traditions have been challenged by society's demands for applicable knowledge that cuts across subject boundaries. Projects involving partnerships with non-academic users of research are becoming commonplace. Academics are under increasing pressure to carry out research that is judged to be of high intellectual quality *and* to be of demonstrable social or economic importance. Academic work is now more closely monitored and measured, and its pressures are more intense, than ever before. In the developed world, these pressures are being felt by an academic workforce whose average age has increased significantly in the last 30 years. It is becoming harder to attract good people into the academic profession and there is a global war for talent, being waged around PhD candidates, first appointments and star researchers.

Higher education is not collapsing under these pressures. For all its problems and weaknesses, the system is sustained by the ingenuity and passion of those who have chosen the academic life. Some would argue that more of this innovative spirit can be seen in research than in teaching. We would have to agree that universities tend to be better at recognising, rewarding and fostering excellence in research than excellence in teaching. In some institutions, it is possible to prosper as a good researcher while being only an adequate teacher. A good teacher who is only an adequate researcher is unlikely to make full professor. The cards are still stacked against teaching, but there are more opportunities for advancement through innovation in teaching than there used to be (Ramsden, 2008). It is becoming quite respectable to engage in researching one's own practice – contributing to the scholarship of teaching. Funding sources for educational innovation and quality enhancement have expanded and diversified in universities and HE systems around the world. There are vigorous, high-profile, politically astute organizations committed to the improvement of university teaching and learning, that can now provide funding, resources, recognition and validation for the innovative work of individual academics as well as for teams engaged in curriculum reform. (The Higher Education Academy in the UK, the Australian Learning and Teaching Council, Ako Aotearoa in New Zealand, Educause in North America, are examples that come to mind.)

This reading of the landscape of contemporary higher education sees:

- universities and their staff as under huge pressure to demonstrate improvements in performance, across the board (even with declining resources);
- employers expressing dissatisfaction with the knowledge, skills and attitudes of new graduates (even if they cannot say precisely what they need);
- students demanding vocational relevance, flexible provision, good access to staff, timely responses and efficient systems (even if no-one is willing to bear the true costs);
- university teachers as ingenious, committed, intrinsically innovative people (even though they are overstretched, prone to burn-out, quick to blame the system and suspicious of ideas from other disciplines).

A growing cadre of university specialists – including educational designers, staff developers, pro-vice-chancellors for learning and teaching – find themselves working in this complex landscape. They will recognise the problems that arise from the lack of a shared language for talking about the subtleties of learning and teaching (Hedberg, 2004). One of our goals is to help everyone engaged in the improvement of university education find ways to talk about what is important to them. Another is to help university leaders, at all levels, to develop strategies for the enhancement of learning and teaching that give due acknowledgement to the constraints mentioned above, and especially to the related constraints of burn-out and innovation fatigue.

Purpose and Perspective

This book will help to improve the quality of learning and teaching in higher education if it can convince you, the reader, of the following:

1. Enhancing student learning depends on understanding the relationship between the student experience of learning and the students' learning environment. It doesn't make sense to try to 'fix' the environment or 'fix' the students – they are not independent of each other.
2. Teachers can work themselves into exhaustion trying to help students find and persist with better ways of studying. A system which needs continuing inputs of energy is unsustainable.
3. Clever leadership, design and management can create an ecosystem which adapts to change, improves through learning, learns through experience and can bring itself back into balance through the efficient working of its own internal processes.

This book provides evidence for these claims and strategies for addressing the challenges they create. The evidence comes from a range of sources, including recent studies carried out by our research teams, including our graduate students. The strategy is really just a coherent way of thinking about a university as an educational ecosystem. Research involves learning. So do teaching, management and leadership. To understand a university is to understand an ecology of learning. Such systems can get out of balance, but with some careful attention to key internal processes, they are quite capable of looking after themselves.

This book is one of many that discuss e-learning. It differs from most of these books in two main ways. First, it offers a distinctive combination of ideas and evidence: some fresh ways of understanding ingrained and emerging issues in higher education. Second, while the book has a sharp focus on e-learning, we argue that e-learning *has* to be understood and managed as part of the broader ecology of learning and teaching. Each of these claims merits some unpacking.

Much of the evidence we present in this book comes from recent research into students' and teachers' experiences of using e-learning in situations where the use of technology is intended to be an integral part of the students' learning activity. Some of this research is our own. Some has been carried out with and by our research students. Some is reported in the literature.

Our own recent research – and much of the research by our students – has taken a particular approach to understanding educational experiences. We believe this approach has the merit of being able to provide a unified account of learning and teaching in higher education – one which avoids the problems of taking either an individualistic, psychologically-oriented perspective or a more structural, sociologically-oriented perspective.

The psychology of learning has made great strides in the last 60–70 years. It was particularly successful at modelling the acquisition of perceptual and motor skills (in the 1940s and 1950s) and of some cognitive skills (especially in the 1980s). Earlier work in the 20th century had provided a foundation for understanding the learning of simple concepts, factual knowledge and propositions. In the 1970s and 1980s, researchers using computer-based methods and analogies were able to model more complex cognitive achievements, introducing ideas such as mental schemata, mental models and rule-based production systems. Painstaking research on human response times, research involving attention to multiple tasks and information sources, and some elegant computer-based modelling allowed researchers in the emerging field of cognitive science to map the architecture of cognition: positing a set of mental processes and mental structures that could account for observed regularities in human performance. (For excellent, accessible overviews, see Ohlsson, 1995; Bransford, Brown & Cocking, 2000; Sawyer, 2006.)

Research on learning took a social or cultural turn in the early 1990s. In part, this was due to a drying-up of funding for computationally-oriented studies, especially in areas such as Artificial Intelligence, where some over-ambitious promises were made and not kept. In part, it was a response to a compelling critique of the computational, cognitivist approach, made most eloquently by Lucy Suchmann (1987/2007), Jean Lave and Etienne Wenger (e.g. 1991). We do not have space here to trace the arguments. Suffice to say that some of the high ground in research on learning was taken by scholars who evinced no particular interest in the capabilities of the lone human, taken outside the contexts in which work or learning could be said to occur. For much of the 1990s, it became quite uncouth – in some circles – to talk about what might or might not be going on between a person's ears. Learning came to be seen as a social or cultural practice. Competence came to be seen as situated in a context – emphasising that what one can do is very dependent on the tools and resources that come to hand, including the help available from other people. Alongside this socio-cultural work on learning, other researchers and commentators have continued to draw on broad areas of social theory and work out some of its implications for higher education. (Much of this writing has taken a critical stance, rather than engaging closely in the improvement of practice.)

Of course, work in the cognitive tradition has also continued and it is very lively and influential in some places. Critics might say that it is telling us more and more about less and less – that we are now getting some very detailed models of highly-specialised phenomena. But that would be to ignore the broad foundations provided by cognitively-inspired research of the last 30 years or so: foundations on which some influential ideas in the higher education literature are built. We will discuss these in more detail in Chapter 2, but should note, in passing, that we are thinking about such things as the significance of deep mental processing of information, making personal sense of information, the ability to monitor and manage one's own thought and study processes (known as 'metacognition' and 'self-regulation') and the ability to activate prior knowledge when it is needed.

In the last few years, it has been possible to detect an emerging consensus that neither psychological accounts of individual mental accomplishments nor the socio-cultural accounts that foreground social practice are – on their own – adequate ways of understanding learning (see e.g. Sfard, 1998; Shoenfeld, 1999). We need to be able to account for the characteristics and capabilities that someone can 'carry with them' from one context to another. We need a psychology that acknowledges the situatedness of human thought and action. We also need accounts of social practice that admit the importance of mental processes, mental structures and cognitive limitations. To say one understands learning, one needs an account which is cognitively plausible as well as rich enough to acknowledge the subtle influences of social and material context.

But our preferred approach goes further than acknowledging the importance of the psychological and the social. Rather, it focuses on *relations* between (what is conventionally conceived as) the psychological and the social.

This is easiest to explain by talking about our interest in *experiences* of learning and teaching. An experience is a relational concept. As Ference Marton and Shirley Booth observe, in talking about the dependence of learning on experience: an experience has to be an experience of something. An experience has to be somebody's experience. That is, an experience involves a relationship between a person and a phenomenon. It is neither mental nor physical but a relationship between the subject and the world (Marton & Booth, 1997). *What* is experienced is important, and the characteristics of *who* is doing the experiencing are also important in shaping the experience. (You and I will differ in how we make sense of things. But I also act and experience things differently in different contexts.)

This relational mode of thinking turns out to be very productive. It sheds light on some potentially important matters whose character can be obscured by dualistic thinking. (Dualistic thinking is predisposed to separating and contrasting things, rather than seeing their interdependence. It is good for the kinds of analysis that reduce a complex system into a set of simpler component parts. It is less good at helping us see how the nature of some taken-for-granted thing is conditioned by the web of relations in which that thing appears to sit.) We are not trying to insist that the world is constituted one way or another – real or imagined, objectively knowable or not – or even that one way of thinking is intrinsically superior to another. Our claims are more modest: that taking a hard look at how things are related offers insights that can sometimes be surprising, and often turn out to be useful.

In Chapter 2, we use a relational perspective to talk about the place of e-learning in the broader ecology of university learning and teaching. We find it a useful way of stepping outside the classic line of thought about technology in education: that technology should be seen as a *replacement* for some established way of doing things (assuming it can be shown to be superior). Relational thinking can help us move from a mindset that is stuck on issues of comparison (of rival treatments) to one that addresses the challenges of integration in complex systems.

The relational thinking exemplified by Marton and Booth can also be found in the work of the psychologist James Gibson. Neither refers to the other, though both are having a substantial influence on thinking about educational technology. Gibson's conception of ecological psychology (see e.g. Gibson, 1986) rejects the dualistic notion that perception is essentially a transfer of information from a world 'out there' to an inner world of the mind. Perception is not the work of a mind in a body but rather an intrinsic quality of the organism's engagement in the world – engagement which is more accurately characterised as exploratory movement than static observation. Gibson rejects the notion that perception is somehow separate from, and prior to, meaning-making and the attribution of value. Rather, he uses the notion of 'affordance' to link sensation and usefulness. Thus we see that a solid flat surface affords being walked upon. A handle on a cup affords picking up. YouTube affords browsing through popular videoclips. Gibson's notion of affordance is proving to be a powerful idea in educational technology, particularly since it offers a way of talking about the subtle influences of the features of a tool, resource, or environment without resorting to technological or environmental determinism (see e.g. Laurillard, 1987, 1993; Greeno, 1994; Norman, 1999; Turner, 2005; Conole & Dyke, 2004).

A third strand of relational thinking that we need to weave into our account is best articulated in the writing of the anthropologist Tim Ingold (e.g. Ingold, 2000), though it builds on the work of Gibson and also on Gregory Bateson's notion that 'the mental world – the mind – is not limited by the skin' (Bateson, 1973, p. 429). Over the last 20 years or so, Ingold has attempted to reconcile social and physical anthropology, with their separate concerns for mind-in-culture and evolutionary biology. He has achieved this in two steps: first, by showing that it is more productive to think of the (sociocultural) person as being simultaneously a (biological) organism, rather than the former being grafted onto the latter; second, by adopting a relational view of persons-organisms that sees them as nodes in fields of relationships rather than as discrete entities.

Instead of trying to reconstruct the complete human being from two separate but complementary components, respectively biophysical and sociocultural, held together with a film of psychological cement, it struck me that we should be trying to find a way of talking about human life that eliminates the need to slice it up into these different layers.

(Ingold, 2000, p. 3)

such a synthesis would start from a conception of the human being not as a composite entity made up of separable but complementary parts, such as body, mind and culture, but rather as a singular locus of creative growth within a continually unfolding field of relationships.

(Ingold, 2000, pp. 4–5)

Ingold's relational perspective is particularly useful in thinking about the term 'environment'. From a relational perspective, it does not make sense to talk of an environment without reference to an organism. An environment cannot exist without an organism – whose environment it is. Every organism has an environment. Organism shapes environment; environment shapes organism. So it helps to think of an indivisible totality of 'organism plus environment' – best seen as an ongoing process of growth and development. This perspective also discourages the conceit that one can sit 'outside' one's environment; adopting some dispassionate, objective, detached view (Ingold, p. 20). This has profound implications for how we think of leadership and management in relation to learning environments or to the broader ecology of a university.

Our fourth and final strand of relational thinking refers to social structures and human agency. The starting point for this is the work of the sociologist Anthony Giddens, who uses a relational approach when introducing his structuration theory. Some writers have argued that social and economic structures determine human action. Others see social structures as mere aggregations of a myriad, freely-chosen human actions. Giddens (see e.g. 1984) uses the relational concept of structuration to show how social structures shape *and are shaped by* human actions. As with the notion of affordance, the idea of structuration helps deal with issues of freedom and influence. It also draws attention to the way in which social structures are sedimented from human activity. From a technological perspective, recognising that much human activity leaves a digital trace, we can see how the contours of the digital world shape and are reshaped by the actions of myriad users. (Think of book recommendations in Amazon, or the growing array of social navigation and social networking technologies.) Similar arguments can be applied in thinking about students' use of learning technologies (e.g. Stubbs, Martin & Endlar, 2006), their use of built space and the various combinations of the physical and virtual with which they furnish their various learnplaces. We return to this in Chapters 7 to 10.

It should come as no surprise that Ference Marton's work has had a strong influence on our research into students' and teachers' experiences of learning and teaching with new technology. We have borrowed from a rich tradition of research on learning and teaching, inspired by Biggs, Booth, Entwistle, Kember, Laurillard, Marton, Prosser, Ramsden, Säljö, Svensson and Trigwell. We expand on some of the key ideas and insights from this body of work when we discuss conceptions of, and approaches to, learning and teaching in Chapters 2, 4, 5 and 6. What may be more surprising is that we are also able to make productive use of relational ideas from the work of Giddens, Gibson, Bateson and Ingold. In particular, they have helped us pursue some of the implications of adopting an ecological framework for understanding a university's teaching and learning activities.

These relational perspectives help us to emphasise

a. the centrality of experience (what phenomena students experience and how; how they interpret; what they decide to do);
b. the importance of what is in the environment (what phenomena are available to experience);
c. the fact that teachers, designers, managers and leaders – like students – are *in* the environment, not sitting (God like) above it. Hence sustainable innovation depends upon conditions of feedback and balance *within* the ecology. Innovation that depends upon regular injections of energy, funding, resources, etc., from outside the system will fail. Good design, teaching and leadership involve knowledgeable, *embedded* environmental management work.

This brings us to the second of our distinctive themes: the need to see e-learning in the broader ecology of learning and teaching. Computer technology presents opportunities and challenges for everyone working in higher education – whether they be students, teachers, specialist support staff, managers or leaders. As we noted above, there is a plethora of books on this topic – many of them having an evangelistic flavour. A new fleet of books appears with each new wave of technology. Most of these books are stronger on advice than evidence, and most focus on advancing claims for the potential benefits of a new technology, rather than on how it may become an integral part of the totality of provision for learning and teaching. The primary audience for these books consists, we suspect, of people who already specialise in educational technology rather than those who remain unconvinced.

It would be good to be able to draw on the 'mainstream' literature on learning and teaching in higher education for insights about the place of new technology. Sadly, few of the really influential books have much to say on the subject, despite the scale and complexity of technology's influence. This silence can be found in a lot of writing about education, in which technology is seen as separable from – and even a threat to – human nature. In contrast, we would want to argue that tools, mind, action and language have evolved together and cannot be understood in separation from one another (cf. Säljö, 1999; Gibson & Ingold, 1995; Ingold, 2000). This gap is a serious weakness in the higher education literature: a major obstacle for teachers and managers who are looking for guidance about how to think about and deal with new technology.

Studying the evolution and use of technology is difficult. It is easy to get things very wrong and for one's mistakes to be engraved in the literature for all time. But there *are* some emerging frameworks that look very promising. These tend to deal with the role and function of technology using a liberal dose of abstraction – thinking about higher-level needs and capabilities rather than the ephemeral minutiae of specific tools or products. They also tend to take a systemic view – looking at interacting networks of people, tasks and tools, for example. The best of this work, in our view, manages to combine insights at several levels – picturing the broad sweep and general contours but also offering subtle vignettes of individual experience. (For examples of what we mean, see Nardi & O'Day, 1999; Agostinho, Oliver, Harper, Hedberg & Wills, 2001; Kaptelinin & Nardi, 2006; Crook & Light, 1999, 2002.)

Our book is intended as a contribution to 'mainstream' thinking about learning and teaching in higher education. It is no longer defensible, if ever it was, to ignore the involvement of new technology in the reshaping of educational practices, expectations, assumptions and relationships. Technology is not going to go away. Nor is its use a solved problem.

Two Related Arguments about Learning

Threaded through the book are two intertwined arguments. One of these is concerned with what students do, with their conceptions of the learning affordances of each task they are tackling, and with their intentions and strategies for tackling these tasks. The second argument is also about learning, but it concerns learning at the various levels of an ecosystem. We argue that sustainable innovation in learning and teaching depends upon the existence of appropriate information flows within the educational ecosystem that is a modern university. An essential point to make here is that work on the design and management of learning environments – indeed all educational leadership activities – have to be seen as taking place *within* the ecosystem. Leadership and management are not command and control, or even coordination, activities located *above* the ecosystem. They can only be effective if they are part of, and contribute to, the healthy functioning of the system itself.

Let us look at each of these arguments in a little more detail. First, there is the argument about the importance of how students conceive of what they are doing.

1. The only thing that really matters in education is the quality of what learners do, including how they think. The actions, intentions, abilities and qualifications of the teaching staff are secondary. A good university library is valuable, but only if students use it. Opportunities should be provided for students to work with and learn from each other, but they can't be forced to do so. Curricula should be well-designed, relevant and up-to-date and they should offer appropriate levels of challenge. Assessment should support learning, rather than just attempt to measure its outcomes. Students should have access to the 'tools of the trade' and should not feel that there is an inexplicable discontinuity between their experience of technology in their studies and in the rest of their lives. *But none of these considerations matter much if students' activity does not result in useful learning. Outcomes depend on what students actually do.*

2. A student's activity is influenced by a number of forces. The most powerful of these is the student's conception of what they are setting out to do – their sense of what can be learnt and how they should go about their learning, in each specific case.

3. If you ask a number of students (10–20), who are tackling the same task on the same course, about what they expect they will learn, you will get a number of different answers. The answers may differ considerably in detail, but there will turn out to be a manageably small set of distinctly different conceptions – more than two and less than eight, in our experience. The same will be true if you investigate what students say about their intentions and their learning strategies.

4. Taken at a broad level, students' conceptions of learning, and their approaches to study, have a powerful influence on learning outcomes. (Looking at their activity in finer detail, the way they tackle a particular subtask, and especially the degree to which they are able to make connections with things they know already, have a strong effect on what they learn.)

5. Students' conceptions and approaches have to be understood in a relational way. They are not intrinsic to a student or determined by the context. How a student conceives of the learning opportunities afforded by their current task is a relation between the student and the task. Different students may see the same task in different ways. The same student will see different opportunities afforded by different tasks. A practical implication is that students can be helped to approach their learning in better ways, but this is unlikely to succeed if the problem is seen as residing in the student. Changing the environment may well be part of the

solution: the essential issue is the relationship between student and environment.

We will examine these matters in greater detail in Chapter 2 and will present and discuss relevant evidence in Chapters 4 and 5. Turning now to the argument about the broader ecology of learning, we need to make the following points:

6. The exercise of management and leadership in complex educational systems, such as universities, is fraught with uncertainty. The global environment within which the university sits is characterised by periods of rapid change. Levels of student demand are very volatile, especially in international markets. The composition of the student body is becoming more diverse; expectations are changing but are voiced with greater conviction. The pace, scale and nature of technological developments are hard to predict, but technology is increasingly implicated in changing work and study practices. This has implications for planning the use of space. IT expenditure continues to consume a significant slice of the university budget, yet most students are now taking responsibility for meeting some of their own IT needs. Easy access to university-provided IT remains a priority – but for how much longer? And what are managers to make of all the talk of digital natives, unmet expectations, clunky systems and recalcitrant teachers?

7. Managing risk in such a complex, changing environment cannot be done through command and control. More flexible, responsive, embedded approaches are needed. In an age of uncertainty, resilience depends upon organisational learning and on what Karl Weick describes as a *collective state of mindfulness* (Weick & Sutcliffe, 2007).

8. The best approach prioritises the long term sustainability of the system, and it does this by attending to the smooth flow of accurate, timely, actionable information at and between each key level in the system (course unit/module; programme; school; faculty; whole institution). Students, teachers, managers and leaders, individually and collectively, learn through experience and reflection. Things which are unavailable to their experience will not contribute to their learning.

9. A core task – perhaps *the* core task – for senior management is to attend to these flows of knowledge. It is to ensure that those best placed to take the action needed to keep the ecology in good heart are getting the information that they require. The essence of successful management is to create the conditions in which the

system can adapt, with minimum shock and effort, to each significant change in circumstances. In Chapter 7 we present a number of
these ideas about ecology and management in more detail: examining the notion of ecological balance, and its enabling constructs of
ecological self-awareness, feedback loops and self-correction.

We are aware of the dangers of romanticising the university and its management: ecological metaphors are powerful and seductive, especially in times of
environmental crisis. A naïve ecologist might ignore the role of competition,
predation of the weak, selection of the fittest, extinction of species. He might
also ignore the role of power and established interests in distorting ecological
relationships. That said, we remain convinced by the ideal of the university as a
learning organisation. We acknowledge that universities are good at learning
through experience – they have survived well beyond their expected life.
But they have not survived without some rude shocks and unforeseen adapta-
tions. They can be poor users of their own intelligence. We revisit some of this
argument in Chapters 9 and 10, where, among other things, we examine issues
of leadership and campus planning in relation to physical and virtual learning
spaces. Infrastructure turns out to be a trickier topic than it might first seem. It
can appear that infrastructure is a 'given' – when teachers, teaching teams and
students are working out what to do, infrastructure is taken for granted as
a source of constraints and enablers. But the question of what counts as
infrastructure turns out to be another question concerned with relationships –
infrastructure only has meaning in relation to concrete activities (Conole &
Jones, forthcoming). Chapter 10 examines this in more detail, for managing
the mix of virtual and physical spaces is not just a major challenge for university leaders; it raises deep questions about what a university *is* to its
students.

Overview of the Remaining Chapters

In Chapter 2, we develop the conceptual foundations of the book using the
umbrella concept of an ecology of learning. We examine a number of key ideas
concerned with learning, technology and learning environments. We also look
at uncertainty and risk, offering an ecological conception of leadership and
management as a way of managing uncertainty.

Chapter 3 surveys some recent research on students' use of, and expectations about, new technology. There has been a great deal of commentary, but
rather less empirical research, on the media habits of the incoming waves of
'digital natives'. Chapter 3 concludes that there is strong evidence that students, however media-savvy they may be, are keen to see a good balance struck
between face-to-face and technology-mediated activities. They are also looking to their teachers for guidance about effective ways to use technologies in
learning.

In Chapters 4 and 5, we introduce some of our own recent studies, carried out using qualitative and quantitative methodologies drawn from relational research on student learning. Chapter 4 examines students' conceptions of, and approaches to, learning through discussion. Chapter 5 summarises our initial research on learning through inquiry. Both chapters report research that we have carried out in settings where use of technology has been integrated with other forms of learning activity.

Chapter 6 turns to research on university teachers' conceptions of, and approaches to, teaching with the aid of technology. Once more, the focus is on situations where 'face-to-face' and technology-mediated learning activities are blended together.

Chapter 7 changes gear. We move from reporting empirical research to implications for policy and practice. Most of these implications are easier to explain if we have a shared way of conceptualising the problems and evidence. Chapter 7 does this by outlining some practical theory for management, leadership and educational design, picking up on the theme of design and management in an ecology of learning.

Chapters 8, 9 and 10 are concerned with educational leadership, but at different levels of the university.

Chapter 8 focuses on the work of teaching teams: groups of teachers who have a shared responsibility for a course or programme of study. While some of the issues covered in this chapter are of relevance to the solo teacher, we argue that *sustainable* development depends on collaboration in teaching teams. Lone enthusiasts can achieve a lot, at a local level, but the dangers of isolation and burn-out are ever present. Chapter 8 is about teaching as a design-like activity. We introduce the idea of 'teaching-as-design' and present some models and other intellectual tools that can help teachers and course teams to engage more efficiently and effectively in educational design.

Chapters 9 and 10 shift the focus to senior managers – thinking mainly of people who have institution-wide responsibilities, or who work in units that have such scope. Maintaining the theme of leadership in a learning ecology, Chapter 9 surveys the various leadership roles that have a stake in the health of a university's physical and virtual learning spaces. Chapter 10 outlines a principled approach to campus management for learning spaces, as a way of discussing the challenge of uncertainty that accompanies technological change.

Finally, in Chapter 11 we summarise core lessons and themes: students, teachers, managers and leaders learn best those things which are afforded in their environment; conceptions of learning influence what is likely to be learnt; the ability to persist in learning is the best way to deal with uncertainty and change.

2
Thinking Ecologically About E-learning

Introduction

Recent research on student learning in higher education highlights the need for a richer conception of the aims and nature of higher education and of the influences upon what and how students learn. The primary purpose of this chapter is to provide the theoretical underpinnings needed to understand the research outcomes we present in the early chapters of this book, and to make sense of the practical implications of this research discussed in the later chapters. Our argument connects ideas about learning, e-learning, ecology and the management of uncertainty.

It is important to avoid polarised thinking that makes apparently simple but logically indefensible contrasts: between 'the new' and 'the traditional', between cognitive and cultural, technical and human, etc. Indeed, as we will try to show, adopting a perspective that foregrounds *relationships* rather than *differences* turns out to yield clearer insights into a number of thorny issues about the place of e-learning in the student experience.

Helping students learn, in contemporary higher education, involves an understanding of the complex web of relationships that give shape and meaning to students' activity and experience. Much of the writing about the role of educational technology, and other pedagogical innovations, in higher education is based on a 'compare and replace' paradigm. In its discourse, if not in its routine practices, education has tended to deal with innovation by treating each new idea or technology as if it is a *challenger* – as if the new can only find a place by displacing something old. This competitive mindset of 'replace or perish' also encourages rituals of comparison: the new must be demonstrably better than the old or there is no rational basis for replacing the old with the new. Oddly, the educational technology literature is suffused with studies showing 'no significant differences' between old and new approaches, yet technologies and other innovations continue to be adopted (Clark, 1983; Phipps & Merisotis, 1999; Ng & Cheung, 2007; Goodyear, 2006; Goodyear & Ellis, 2008).

Kulik, Kulik and Cohen (1980) and Clark (1983) provide early, influential reviews and meta-analyses of the comparative benefits of ICT in learning. More recent data can be found in Ferrell et al. (2007). Clark is associated with the argument that 'media will never influence learning' – arguing that instructional treatments rather than instructional media are what influence learning. (On this point, see also Clark (1994), Kozma (1994), Phipps & Merisotis (1999), Conger (2005) and Oblinger & Hawkins (2006)). Taking this line of argument one step further, Goodyear (e.g. 2005, 2006) has suggested that instructional treatments (defined as 'tasks') do not directly influence learning either. Rather, students adapt task specifications in various ways and it is their actual activity which influences learning outcomes. This argument is developed further in Chapter 8.

It turns out to be more productive to shift the perspective to one in which new and old entities find ways of co-existing. The shift is away from thinking of progress as something we can achieve by selecting the better of two rival 'interventions' or 'treatments' and towards thinking in more systemic or holistic terms: in short, towards a more ecological way of thinking. But this ecological perspective also has its own distinctive character, since we focus on the ways in which entities achieve joint success and sustainability within an ecosystem by co-operation rather than by competition.

Overview of the Chapter

We start with ecological perspectives on education. Such perspectives are not entirely new. The next section reviews some of the ways in which ecological metaphors and lines of thought have informed discussion in the literature.

We then discuss learning itself. It is not hard to find agreement in universities for the proposition that pedagogy should drive technology, even though the reverse sometimes seems to apply in practice. It can sometimes be *very* hard to create a shared understanding of what good pedagogy consists of, and to get people engaged in carefully-worded discussions of what should be learnt and how (Goodyear, 2005). In the section on 21st century learning we offer some ways of thinking about 'good learning' – appropriate to the ambitions of forward-looking universities at the start of the 21st century (Brew & Sachs, 2007). We draw on ideas about *what* should be learnt, as well as *how* good learning occurs. We pay particular attention to graduate attributes and the nature of knowledge work. Knowledge work, taken seriously, must involve the ability to improve and apply complex ideas – working with what Carl Bereiter and Marlene Scardamalia call 'conceptual artefacts' (Bereiter, 2002; Bereiter & Scardamalia, 2003; Scardamalia & Bereiter, 2006). Learning to recognise, evaluate, improve and apply ideas is best done through direct experience – through apprenticeship in 'knowledge-building'. And given the need to work with different forms of knowledge and ways of knowing, graduates must – we argue – acquire a versatility in knowledge-building that can best be described as 'epistemic fluency' (Goodyear & Ellis, 2007; Goodyear & Zenios, 2007). We find this emphasis on the *skilful* side of knowing to be a useful complement to the emphasis on variations in *understanding* that have tended to preoccupy researchers in the mainstream of research on university students' learning. Understanding, in practice, is skilful.

In the section on research on student learning in higher education we introduce some key ideas from research into university student learning, summarising a line of work constructed by Entwistle and Ramsden (1983), Marton and Booth (1997), Prosser and Trigwell (1999), Laurillard (2002), Ramsden (2002) and Biggs and Tang (2007). This section also introduces *phenomenography*: an approach to educational research that focuses on qualitative variations in the ways that people experience phenomena in the world (Marton, 1981; Marton & Booth, 1997; Prosser & Trigwell, 1999). Phenomenographic research has been particularly productive in revealing the importance of variations in the ways that students conceive of, and approach, learning. We summarise some of the achievements of this body of research, which has been growing in scale, scope and influence over the last 30 years, and explain some of the key analytic tools that phenomenographic research provides. We also draw on some of the phenomenographic research literature that deals with e- learning, as a preface to the research results reported in Chapters 4 and 5.

The section on characteristics and affordances of e-learning shifts the focus to e-learning. Some people use this term in a very general way – to embrace all forms of technology-assisted learning. Others use it to denote something quite narrow, specific and rather routine. Our focus is specific, but ecological and, we believe, properly ambitious.

In the section on uncertainty, environment and leadership we make links between student experiences of e-learning, and the work and responsibilities of university leaders. Drawing on leaders' concerns about the management of uncertainty, especially in the light of rapid technological change, we begin to examine some of the issues involved in conceptualising the management of infrastructure. This introduces some of the ideas about co-ordinated planning of virtual and physical spaces that we examine in much more depth in Chapters 9 and 10.

Ecological Perspectives in Education

The science of ecology studies interactions between individual organisms and their environments. In ecological research, the environment is usually defined to mean both other individuals, of the same species and of different species, and non-living phenomena, such as the availability of food, water, shelter and sunlight. The environment includes living and non-living things. On this reading, you are part of my environment and I am part of yours. The etymological roots of the term are in Greek: *oikos* (household) and *logos* (knowledge). By implication, *oikos* suggests notions of dwelling or habitat (Ingold, 2000).

Ecological thinking also emphasises relationships and inter-dependence: fore-grounding the notion that a change in one part of a system can have unforseen consequences in other parts of a system, or for the system as a whole.

Ecological thinking and research are not restricted to what is sometimes called the 'natural' world. Over the years, serious attention has been paid to human ecology (Hawley, 1950; Duncan, 1964), social ecology (Alihan, 1939), to artificial or 'built' environments and to the role of culture in mediating interactions between people and their physical environment (e.g. Dogan & Rokkan, 1969; Steward, 2006). Ecological perspectives on human development have been particularly influential through the work of Urie Bronfenbrenner (e.g. 1979).

Research in higher education, as well as in education more generally, sometimes makes use of the term 'ecology' because of the availability of the term 'learning environment'. For example, Gale (2002) adopts an ecological perspective as a way of moving beyond what he sees as prevailing 'neuro-psychological' accounts of student abilities. He turns to ecological thinking as an approach which is 'mindful of individuals, but also of learning environments that frame both institutional practices and individual experiences' (p. 66). Taking an ecological perspective in this case can relocate students' difficulties so they are seen as arising from a mismatch with their environment rather than from intrinsic, persistent or context-free personal failings. (Gale's use of 'environment' is, therefore, broader than the usage we prefer. His includes culture, tasks and practices.)

Hannafin and Hannafin (1996) use the 'ecology/ecosystem' metaphor as a way of highlighting the complexity and interdependence of the many components and activities that make for success in a learning environment.

> Learning environments operate as ecosystems. Individual elements must function autonomously as well as interactively. In biological terms, each independent organism benefits from the mutualistic, symbiotic relationships among other organisms in the ecosystem in order to attain system homeostasis, or equilibrium. In learning environments, learners as well as facilitators observe, measure, test, listen and probe to assess the integrity and effectiveness of the environment and make needed changes. This may require the learner and facilitator to examine and adjust strategies, technologies or learning activities to achieve balance. It requires *active* teaching and learning to develop understandings of how each element, as well as the overall system, is functioning. . . . Ecosystems are judged successful when they promote equilibrium among their components and interact in ways that support their functions. Balance must be attained initially in order for the ecosystem to evolve, and must be maintained in order for it to survive and prosper.
>
> (Hannafin & Hannafin, 1996, pp. 52–3, our emphasis)

Two important sub-themes emerge in Hannafin and Hannafin's analysis: the importance of balance, sustainability and mutual independence; and the danger of seeking local solutions to problems that have systemic origins or consequences – of treating local symptoms as if they were root causes (see also Zhao & Frank, 2003).

The issue of balance or equilibrium is an important one. It presents itself as an awkward concept when one is considering the management of rapid change. Indeed, much of the discourse around the use of technology in higher education is about breaking out of a stable state and making radical structural and cultural changes (Bates, 2000; Laurillard, 2002; Oblinger & Oblinger, 2005). We address this in more detail below, and again in Chapter 7. For now, it is useful to clarify key aspects of an 'ecology of learning' and how the concept is used in this book. The key aspects of an ecology of learning in the arguments put forward here are: maintenance of an ecological balance; the development of self-awareness of how parts of the ecology are related to the whole; the ongoing pursuit of feedback to inform self-awareness, and the capacity of self correction required to ensure (re)alignment in a rapidly changing world. To elaborate a little:

- The point of *ecological balance* for a university most easily rests – amongst the trinity of learning and teaching, research and service – with *learning*, as it is in this concept that the other aspects of university work can find a home. Learning can enfold teaching, research and service to the community.
- Maintaining an ecological balance on learning requires all the parts of the university to act in ways that demonstrate *self-awareness* of their function and purpose in relation to the mission of the institution. Every part of the university needs to be imbued with an understanding of 'good learning'.
- In order for the parts of a university to understand how they are functioning, in relation to the work and purpose of the whole, they need to engage in systematic processes of collecting *feedback* from stakeholders about the effectiveness of their operations. Student feedback is central to this, but feedback from other internal and external stakeholders is important too.
- In a context of rapid change, *self-correction* by the parts of a university in order to align their operations to the mission of the university as a whole is constantly required in order to maintain an ecological balance focussed on learning.

These aspects of an ecology of learning are used as a framework in the later chapters of this book to discuss the implications of research findings about student experiences of e-learning. They help the reader to shift from looking at the phenomenon of learning through the eyes of the student (in Chapters 4 and 5), to considering the implications of the research for teachers who are designing learning tasks (in Chapter 8), and university leaders who are responsible for the campus investment supporting such experiences (in Chapters 9 and 10).

Twenty-first Century Learning

A number of commentators on the media habits of young people have argued that schools and universities will need to change to accommodate new learning styles (e.g. Prensky, 2001a; Oblinger & Oblinger, 2005). These new learning styles are held to involve a preference for multi-tasking, multimedia, bite-sized content and high levels of social interaction. As we will show in Chapter 3, there is actually rather a dearth of empirical research on the learning patterns and preferences of students who are making the transition to university. What we do see, from recent studies, is that students want their teachers to help them understand how best to use technology in their work as learners, and that many of the things that students have valued about good teaching in the past, continue to be of high value.

Prensky and others have argued, stretching rather scant neuropsychological evidence, that the brains of digital natives are different from those of the digital immigrants who teach them: that learning is different. Bereiter (2002) and Kress (2003), among others, have cautioned that there is no reason to think that learning itself is changing. Rather, there are changes to learning contexts, expectations and practices. The increasing availability of ICT has widened the range of places in which students can learn, and they now expect greater flexibility in educational provision. While they don't prioritise flexible access – anywhere, anytime learning – over the quality of interaction they can have with staff, students nevertheless express frustration if university processes are unnecessarily place- or time-bound.

In this section, we focus on two related sets of issues. The first set of issues is concerned with the changing goals for, or expectations of, higher education. What are society, employers and others looking for in new graduates? What are graduate attributes for the 21st century? *What* should students be learning? The second set of issues is concerned with changing conceptions of learning processes and learning activity – with *how* effective learning takes place. Following Peter Knight, we use the shorthand 'good learning' to capture the essence of what is important here.

What is Worth Learning in Twenty-first Century Higher Education?

Learning is a second-order effect . . . it transforms a system capable of certain performances into a system of additional ones. . . . The study of learning, if carried out with theoretical precision, must start with a model of a performing organism, so that one can represent, as learning,

the changes in the model. . . . If performance is not well understood, it
is somewhat premature to study learning.

(Newell & Simon, 1972, pp. 7–8)

What, then, should successful university graduates be able to do? Answers to
this question underpin much of the debate about graduate attributes (e.g.
Barrie, 2007) and about the nature and purposes of higher education (e.g.
Barnett, 1997, 2000a; 2000b; Brew, 2006; Taylor, Barr & Steele 2002). While it
is sometimes possible to build a consensus around some specific answers to
this question, for example, in relation to courses that are approved by an
external professional body, more general answers tend to dissolve into vague-
ness and ambiguity, offering little basis for serious discussion about capability
or curriculum.

This makes it particularly difficult to decide what learning activities are
most likely to be appropriate for the development of each attribute identified.
Since different kinds of knowledge are acquired in different ways, it is
necessary to have methods of classifying desired attributes that are both (a)
meaningful to the people concerned (employers, students, teachers, and so
on), and (b) pedagogically coherent. An example of where universities often
get this wrong is in their habitual talk about graduate *skills*. We have nothing
against the notion of skill – far from it. But skill is best acquired through
repeated practice with feedback and it takes a *lot* of time to acquire fluency.
Outside of some specialised areas of higher education, for example, in music
or language, it is very rare for there to be teaching activities that support
students in acquiring a skill through repeated practice and timely feedback. A
demonstration of the required performance and one or two supervised
attempts is about all that teaching resources typically allow. But this does not
dissuade those who write course outcome statements and lists of graduate
attributes from making unrealistic claims about the skills successful students
will acquire.

Our point is not to discourage talk of outcomes and skills, but to encourage
some pedagogical realism. Being able to talk with precision about the kind of
capability needed, and how it can be acquired, is at least half the battle.

We do not have space here to review all the kinds of things that employers,
governments and others say that graduates should know and be able to do.
Good summaries can be found in Knight and Yorke (2004) and Hager and
Holland (2006). In broad terms, one could say there is some agreement about
the importance of graduates who are taking up work in complex, knowledge-
intensive organisations having intellectual flexibility, powers of logical analysis
and an ability to conceptualise issues rapidly and to deal with large amounts of
information. In addition, they need to be able to manage time, cope with
pressure, understand organisational politics, forge effective working relationships with colleagues at all levels of seniority, listen critically and make a

persuasive case. These capabilities are rarely expressed with sufficient clarity and precision to allow confident design of appropriate learning activities or methods of assessment. Compounding the problem is the fact that employers underestimate the power of local knowledge and context. Their complaints about graduates not being 'workplace-ready' fail to acknowledge that capability has to be exercised in context – it needs to mould itself to the contours of each unique workplace, and this takes time. (Workplace capability is a relation between person and context.)

Characteristics of 'Good Learning' in Higher Education

Although there is considerable variation in the treatment of what constitutes 'good learning and teaching' in higher education, we think the propositions presented in Table 2.1 offer a reasonable summary.

Table 2.1 Propositions about Good Learning Appropriate to UK Higher Education

	Proposition	Explanation
1	Learning should be extensive	It is no longer defensible, if ever it was, to define the outcomes of higher education purely and simply in terms of mastery of a subject. Outcomes now also need to include more generally useful skills, including so-called transferable skills, the capacity to act as an autonomous lifelong learner, a belief in one's own efficacy, etc.
2	Learning involves constructing understandings that are acceptable within communities of practice	Learning involves acts of *sensemaking* within a community that shares common interests, practices, language and other cultural artefacts and tools. Access to disembodied information has little to do with real learning.
3	Learning is a natural outcome of the normal workings of communities of practice	Participation in the day-to-day life of a community of practice is inseparable from learning. If someone has a legitimised role within a community of practice – however peripheral that role may seem – they cannot help but learn. In HE, learning may best be seen as induction into one or more communities of practice.
4	Learning is situated and hard to transfer	What is learnt in one context tends to be hard to transfer to another – indeed the idea of 'transfer' may be suspect. However, learning in HE does require learners to be able to recognise community boundaries and shift between communities. It requires use of knowledge abstracted from specific contexts and the ability to work with different ways of knowing (epistemic fluency).
5	Engagement and practice make for good learning	Learning demands application (engagement in practice); skill-acquisition demands opportunities for repetition, feedback, fine-tuning, automation, etc.

(Continued Overleaf)

Table 2.1 Continued

	Proposition	Explanation
6	Learning involves challenge and scaffolding	Learning can be a by-product of taking on a challenging new task; challenge and learning go hand in hand but challenge should not overwhelm. What one can do with others is in advance of what one can do alone – the scaffolding they provide helps one accept and overcome challenges.
7	Learning must embody an idea of progression	Learning involves qualitative change in understandings rather than quantitative accumulation of factual knowledge. Learners in HE typically move from relatively simple to more complex beliefs about the nature of knowledge and learning. Curriculum challenges need to reflect this.
8	Learning is conversational and interactive	Learning and practice in communities is inseparable from discourse; generation of narratives and explanations are key to sense-making; understanding others' accounts of the world is an important aspect of academic learning; sharing in the construction of knowledge demands communication and other forms of social interaction.
9	Learning involves effective use of reflection	'Conversations' can be with others but they can also be with oneself; self-explanations and 'replaying' and analysing one's experiences are important parts of sense-making.
10	Learning is not significantly limited by fixed abilities	IQ and other claimants to be measures of 'general ability' are poor predictors of complex learning or of successful progression within a community of practice; engagement/application entail hard work not good genes and are cultural not inherited; specific knowledge rather than general ability is a potent influence on learning; other so-called stable traits (e.g., learning style) are more context-sensitive than is often acknowledged.
11	Motivation is something designed into the curriculum, not something added by charismatic teaching	People are motivated by goals they value, especially ones they have had chance to help shape; goals should be challenging but achievable; feedback aids persistence; intrinsic motivation accompanies a personal belief in the value of one's efforts – overuse of extrinsic motivators can undermine intrinsic motivation.
12	Teaching contributes to learning, but in various ways	Direct (didactic) teaching can be appropriate in helping learners reach mastery of tightly-structured subject matters – factual and rule-based material and skills coaching can be well served by direct teaching. But much of learning in HE involves uncertainty, complexity, ambiguity, weighing of evidence and judgement. Here, direct teaching is much less useful than designing appropriate learning tasks.

Source: Columns 1 and 2 adapted from Knight & Trowler, 2001, pp. 100–110, and Goodyear 2002.

There is a top-level view of 'good learning' that sees learning as a *guided process of knowledge-construction* (see e.g. Shuell, 1992; Biggs, 1999; Simons et al., 2000). In this process, the quality of what the learner *does* is all-important. Following Shuell (1992) and Goodyear (2002) we draw attention to the following characteristics of good learning: learning is active, cumulative, individual, self-regulated, goal-oriented, situated, and above all, an experience of the student.

Learning is active: A learner has to carry out a range of cognitive operations on new information, in order to make it personally meaningful, i.e. to understand it. The type of cognitive processing in which the learner engages will be the major determinant of what – how effectively – they learn. For example, one learner may approach a task in a way that involves 'deep processing', while another engages in 'shallow processing'. In the former, the learner expends considerable mental effort in making personal sense of new information, with the result that they can be said to understand it. In the latter, they may (at best) add the information to memory in such a way that they can repeat it word-for-word, but without any semblance of real understanding (Craik & Lockhart, 1972; Marton, Hounsell & Entwistle, 1997).

Learning is cumulative: What a learner already knows will play a large part in determining what sense they can make of new information. The extent of relevant prior knowledge – particularly knowledge activated during the learning process – is a major factor in determining the efficacy of a particular learning event (Tobias, 1994; Dochy, Segers & Sluijsmans, 1999).

Learning is individual: Every learner constructs their own knowledge in a unique way, using past experience and existing knowledge to make sense of new information. Since no two learners have the same knowledge and experience, all new information is dealt with in different ways by different learners. (This does *not* mean that we can have no insights into other people's ways of seeing the world.)

Learning is self-regulated: Effective learning is characterised by the learner's awareness of their own learning activity and their ability to take action based on this awareness. When a learner stands back from their current task, to consider how they are doing, they are said to be engaging in metacognitive activity. Metacognitive skills include reflectiveness and self-regulation. Effective learners often have a good idea about how they learn, and are able to use that knowledge to monitor and adjust their approach to problems (Vermunt & Rijswijk, 1988; Romainville, 1994; Vermunt, 1998).

Learning is goal-oriented: Clear goals are needed if learning is to be effective, and these goals need to be understood by the learner. These goals may be set by the learner, or the teacher, or through a process of negotiation involving both. The important thing is that the goals are and remain explicit.

Learning is situated: The more cognitively-oriented accounts of learning of the 1980s and early 1990s could be accused of over-playing the role and value of symbolic knowledge by drawing very close parallels between human cognition and computational processes. Seeing the human mind as a symbol-processing machine underplays the importance of the *situatedness* of human cognition. The work of Jean Lave, Lucy Suchman, Etienne Wenger, Jim Greeno, Allan Collins and others has been important in remedying this view. The social and physical context in which cognition (and learning) take place is usually very influential in shaping both processes and outcomes. Cognition can be distributed across individuals and artefacts, such that what a single individual can do on their own may be very different from what they can do when working with other people and/or with tools and other physical or digital resources (Pea, 1993; Salomon, 1993; Hutchins, 1995; Barab & Plucker, 2002). This impacts on learning with technology in three ways. First, it causes and helps us to understand the various forms of collaborative and co-operative learning: dwelling on learning as socially situated. Second, it causes and helps us to understand 'interactions' between individual learners and groups of learners and technological artefacts (thought of in the most general terms): dwelling on learning as physically/digitally situated. Third it introduces as important constructs the ideas of practice, culture and community. Learning can be understood as induction into a community of practice, in which appropriation of cultural tools and participation in cultural practices go hand in hand with increasing recognition and status in a community (Suchman, 1987; Brown, Collins & Duguid, 1989; Lave & Wenger, 1991). From a recognition of the importance of context in learning and action comes a growing emphasis, in educational design, upon the authenticity of learning tasks and learning contexts and upon the affordances of new technological resources (e.g. Goodyear, 1995; Wisner, 1995; Säljö, 1995; Oliver & Herrington, 2000).

Learning is an experience of the student: While it may seem obvious, the importance of recognising that learning is fundamentally about the learner has never been so important. Innovations in experiences of learning involving technology can threaten to divert the researcher's focus away from the development of student understanding and towards the technology. The investigations described in Chapters 4 and 5 adopt a student perspective on the experience of e-learning within a broader ecology of learning, one which acknowledges the role of technologies in the experience, but which focuses on student understanding.

Research on Student Learning in Higher Education

Research on student learning in higher education, over the last 30 years, has systematically explored the relational nature of key aspects of the student experience (Marton & Säljö, 1976a; 1976b; Entwistle & Ramsden, 1983; Biggs, 1987; Marton & Booth, 1997; Prosser & Trigwell, 1999; Biggs, Kember & Leung, 2001; Laurillard, 2002; Ramsden, 2002; Biggs and Tang, 2007). These aspects are shown in Figure 2.1.

The 3P model of student learning can be used to map relationships amongst research studies that have investigated aspects of university students' experiences of learning. Studies consistent with this model have shown that key aspects of the student learning experience in higher education include:

- student *perceptions* of the learning context, such as the clarity of the goals and standards of the course and the quality of teaching;
- students' *conceptions* of their learning – what they think they are learning;
- students' *approaches* to learning – what they do when they learn, encompassing both strategies and intent;
- characteristics of the students – including knowledge of prior experiences that they bring to learning;
- the course and departmental context – including course design, teaching methods, assessment and the like.

One strength of the model is that it can reveal connections between the work of researchers who may hold different epistemological and ontological beliefs about how to represent the experience of learning. In the research discussed in

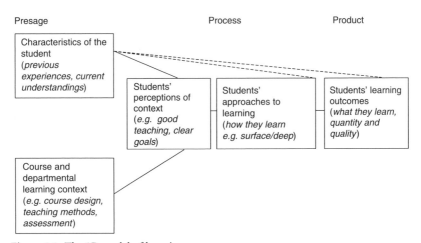

Figure 2.1 The 3P model of learning.

Source: Trigwell & Prosser, 1997.

Chapters 4 and 5, the view of learning used to shape the research and interpret the model is one in which there is an internal relationship between the individual and the world: what is sometimes referred to as a constitutionalist perspective. In this matter we follow Prosser and Trigwell (1999) and Marton and Booth (1997). This relational (non-dualistic) approach means that while the researchers may analytically separate parts of the experience into conceptions, approaches, and perceptions, for example, these are nevertheless held to be simultaneously present and interwoven in the students' awareness (see e.g. Prosser & Trigwell, 1999, p. 13).

Research into student perceptions of their learning context has found logical associations between perceptions and the student experience (Entwistle & Ramsden, 1983; Ramsden, 1979, 1991). The way learners perceive and interpret their surroundings seems to encourage them to relate to their experiences of learning in different ways. Aspects of the context that have been focused on include outcome variables such as generic skills and overall satisfaction, and concurrent variables such as perceptions about the quality of teaching, the clarity of course goals and standards, workload and assessment. Positive student ratings of these aspects have been found to be related to relatively higher quality learning experiences, while lower ratings have been found to be related to relatively lower quality learning experiences.

Student conceptions of learning have been investigated in relation to students' prior experiences of learning as well as in relation to their subsequent experiences of learning (see e.g. Crawford, Gordon, Nicholas & Prosser, 1998; Prosser & Trigwell, 1999). One of the seminal studies focussed on variations in how adult students conceived of learning (Säljö, 1979). Five qualitatively different conceptions were identified: learning as 'increasing knowledge', 'memorisation', 'acquiring facts and procedures', 'abstracting meaning' and 'understanding reality'. Further studies showed that these qualitative differences were replicable. Marton and colleagues extended Säljö's findings some years later with a sixth conception of learning that identified learning in terms of 'changing as a person' (Marton, Dall'Alba & Beaty, 1993).

Related research has focused on a range of learning situations, including writing (Hounsell, 1984, 1997), discussions (Ellis, Steed & Applebee 2006), problem-based learning (Hendry, Lyon, Prosser and Sze, 2006) and mathematics (Crawford et al., 1994). The studies tend to identify qualitatively different categories of conceptions, which can be grouped into *cohesive conceptions* – those that are closely associated with the development of understanding – and *fragmented* or *multistructural conceptions* – those which do not link the ideas into a coherent whole (Prosser & Trigwell, 1999).

Research into student *approaches* to learning has also identified qualitatively different categories. Three broad categories of approach have been identified in this research: deep, surface and achieving (or strategic). *Deep* approaches to learning have an orientation towards engaging with the subject matter in ways that promote understanding. Deep approaches are often associated with higher order learning outcomes such as synthesis, integration, critical evaluation and reflection. *Surface* approaches to learning have an orientation towards reproduction (memorisation for the purposes of being able to reproduce the surface features of that which is being learned, rather than making personal sense of it). Surface approaches often focus on just one part of the whole phenomenon being studied. *Achieving* approaches can resemble deep approaches. However, since their focus is usually on short-term performance, an intention to understand deeply is usually absent. This may well mean that long-term knowledge retention rates are poor (Biggs, 1987) and/or that there are limited opportunities for the knowledge to become embedded in professional capabilities (Yinger & Hendricks-Lee, 1993; Sternberg & Horvath, 1999).

A significant part of this research tradition has been the development and use of closed-ended questions in questionnaires used to identify and probe these aspects of student learning. The Revised Study Process Questionnaire (Biggs et al., 2001), the Approaches to Study Inventory (Entwistle, Tate & McCune, 2000), the Course Experience Questionnaire (Ramsden, 1991) and Conceptions of Learning Questionnaires (Crawford et. al., 1998) are examples of instruments that have been used to investigate approaches, perceptions and conceptions, respectively. The quantitative survey methods used in Chapters 4 and 5, below, were informed by knowledge of the development processes and internal structure and characteristics of these instruments.

Numerous studies using the 3P model have shown that the way students report thinking about their learning is logically related to qualitatively different ways they approach their studies. In other words, the results have suggested that, broadly speaking, deep approaches to learning tend to be related to coherent conceptions. Similarly, surface approaches to learning tend to be related to multistructural or fragmented conceptions. Also, coherent conceptions and deep approaches tend to be associated with better performance on course assessments.

Complementing these quantitative studies, qualitative approaches have been used to provide rich descriptions of the structure and meaning of students' experiences of learning. The predominant approach is phenomenography (Marton & Booth, 1997).

A Phenomenographic Perspective

Phenomenography can be defined as the study of variations in the ways in which people experience the world. It is better to think of it as an *approach* to researching certain sorts of issues of relevance to learning and understanding in educational settings, rather than as a methodology or a theory of experience.

> At the root of phenomenography lies an interest in describing the phenomena in the world as others see them, and in revealing and describing the variation therein, especially in an educational context.
>
> (Marton & Booth, 1997, p. 111)

Phenomenographic research reveals inter-personal variations in ways of experiencing particular phenomena in the world. People differ in the ways they experience the world and their *capabilities* for experiencing particular phenomena also vary. These capabilities exhibit intra-individual differences (i.e., any one person may exhibit different capabilities in relation to different phenomena, and the capabilities may also change over time). Empirically, it turns out that there is a limited number of ways of experiencing any particular phenomenon; or, more accurately, that what people say about the ways they experience a phenomenon can usually be classified into a small number of categories. Looked at from a particular point of view, these categories can be ordered: from complex, powerful and encompassing to simple.

> The description we reach is a description of variation, a description on the collective level, and in that sense individual voices are not heard. Moreover, it is a *stripped description* in which the structure and essential meaning of the differing ways of experiencing the phenomenon are retained, while the specific flavours, the scents, and the colors of the worlds of the individuals have been abandoned.
>
> (Marton & Booth, 1997, p. 114, our emphasis)

Phenomenography defines its object of research – variations in human experience – in a way which sees experience as relational or 'non-dualistic'. In other words, an experience is not seen as a mental or a physical entity but as an internal relationship between a person and a phenomenon. It offers researchers a recursive structural/ referential model of learning (Marton & Booth, 1997, p. 84). It suggests that any phenomenon can be divided into structural aspects (the parts that make it up) and referential aspects (aspects that give it meaning). For the phenomenon of learning, over three decades of research has revealed the fundamental importance of *how* students approach their learning and *what* they think they are learning. Each of these aspects can be recursively re-expressed into structural and referential parts. For *approaches*, these can be identified as the strategies that students adopt in their learning (structure) and the intention underpinning their strategies (reference). For *conceptions*, what students learn can be divided into its parts (structure) and its meaning (reference).

One of the key outcomes from the research described in Chapters 4 and 5 is recognition that student approaches to learning become structurally more complex when e-learning is involved. This happens when students are asked to engage with learning tasks that start in a tutorial, seminar, laboratory, clinic or lecture, then continue in a technologically-mediated context (such as an online discussion). Complexity is also increased when tasks start online and continue face-to-face. We have also observed tasks which move back and forward between face-to-face and technology-mediated contexts, requiring students to adopt even more complex strategies. Figure 2.2 visually represents the structure of the student experience of learning when e-learning is part of the mix. The ideas in Figure 2.2 are informed by Marton and Booth (1997) and Prosser and Trigwell (1999).

The Structure of Student Approaches to Learning When E-learning is Part of the Mix

Reading Figure 2.2 from the top downwards, the experience of learning when e-learning is part of the mix can be divided into what students learn, including concepts, and how they approach learning. How students learn can be divided into the strategies and intentions implicated in their experience of e-learning, and the strategies and intentions implicated in the other (face-to-face) parts of their experience. This is an *analytic* distinction. We are not asserting that students' experiences of e-learning and face-to-face learning are actually integrated or fragmented. Rather, by making this analytic distinction, for the purposes of research, we can begin to detect whether or not strategies and intentions are consistent across face-to-face and e-learning contexts. As Chapters 4 and 5 reveal, there are some significant differences between effective strategies deployed in face-to-face and online settings. Before delving more

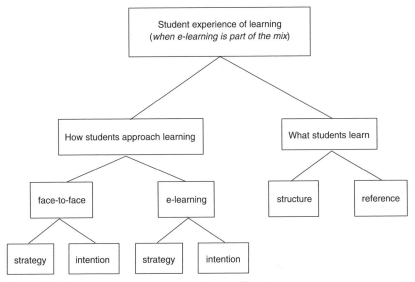

Figure 2.2 E-learning in the student experience of learning.

deeply into those findings, we need to sketch some of the key characteristics of e-learning.

E-learning: Characteristics and Affordances

We use the term e-learning to denote the systematic use of networked, multi-media computer technologies to

- improve learning;
- empower learners;
- connect learners to people and resources supportive of their needs;
- integrate learning with performance and
- link individual with organisational goals.

This view of e-learning, originally sketched in Goodyear (2001) has two main parts: a reference to technology (especially to the systematic use of technology), and a reference to purposes or goals. The purposes are most important, so we deal with them first.

Improving learning: E-learning needs to involve more than improving access and learner control. It also needs to improve the process and outcomes of learning. There are still very few studies in the research literature on e-learning that report clear measurable gains in learning outcomes. So any claims about the potential for improving learning outcomes need to be argued very carefully – with due reference to relevant models of 'good learning' and to the interactions between tools, tasks, activities and people.

Empowering learners: The empowerment of learners comes about through loosening of administrative and educational constraints. Administrative constraints include the location, timing, and cost of study. Educational constraints include the setting of learning objectives, methods of study, assessment methods, etc. Boot and Hodgson (1987) and Goodyear and Steeples (1992) refer to the relaxing of administrative constraints as increasing 'logistical independence', while relaxing educational constraints increases 'independence of mind'.

In the context of e-learning, these two aspects can be understood in terms of

- providing 24/7 or 'just in time' access to learning opportunities, from any networked 'learnplace'; reducing or removing administrative barriers (such as arise when 'providers' attempt to monopolise a learner); reducing costs of learning, etc.
- helping the learner take much more control over their own learning – setting goals, choosing study methods that suit them, choosing

whether to work independently or collaboratively, choosing between alternative assessment methods (or choosing whether to be assessed at all).

Learner empowerment is the most politically-charged part of this definition of e-learning, especially where it challenges the vested interests of existing providers and/or identifies tensions such as those that can arise between a learner's own goals and the goals of others. It is important that we don't ignore these kinds of tensions – something which is particularly easy to do if we only think about 24/7 access and the loosening of administrative rather than educational constraints.

Connecting learners to people and resources: Connecting learners to Web-based resources is part of most people's image of e-learning. Providing opportunities for groups of learners to interact with each other and/or with people in the role of tutor, teacher, trainer or mentor is another common image. Indeed much of the e-learning provision people have been developing in the recent past consists of either (a) placing learning materials on the web, and providing a space for some ancillary Web-based discussion activity, or (b) organising Web-based discussion activity, supported by Web-based learning materials. While there are sometimes good arguments for organising e-learning specifically to support individualised study by isolated learners, in the general case it makes sense to use the communication facilities of ICT to promote learning through human interaction. Indeed a strong theme emerging from much of the experimentation in e-learning builds on the idea of an ICT-supported 'learning community'. Some of the best learning communities are characterised by processes of shared knowledge creation – sometimes called the 'co-construction' of knowledge (Collins & Ferguson, 1993; Scardamalia & Bereiter, 1994; Morrison & Collins, 1996; McConnell, 2000; Strijbos, Kirschner & Martens, 2004).

Integration of learning with performance: E-learning methods and tools can usefully be deployed to support the practical and cognitive activities of learners as 'apprentice knowledge workers' working on authentic tasks; use of e-learning to provide 'just in time' support in the workplace is another aspect of integrating learning and performance. In workplace settings, or in relation to work-related learning more generally, learning is usually regarded as a means to an end rather than an end in itself. The goal of learning is to enable more efficient or effective job performance. Transfer of learning from the training classroom to the job is a well-recognised problem – learning outcomes rarely transfer to real-world task performance as completely or as frequently as employers and trainers would like (Singley & Anderson, 1989; Mayer & Wittrock, 1996; Robertson, 2000). This has two main implications for vocationally-oriented e-learning provided by higher education institutions. First, it makes sense to design vocational e-learning tasks and tools such that they align with the tasks and tools found in the workplace environment. Second, it may make sense to relocate learning from the classroom to the workplace – to support learning and performance improvement in the worker's workplace. This is where we see a potentially valuable convergence between the technologies of e-learning, knowledge management and performance support (Goodyear, 1995; Barron, 2000).

Integration of individual with organisational goals: This part of the definition has different resonances in different contexts. In university education for example, there is now a widely held view that some students adopt surface rather than deep approaches to learning because they misunderstand the value system of the academics teaching the course. This is a particularly severe problem when the academics' enacted values differ from their espoused ones – as when academics say they value exploratory learning but stick to tightly prescribed coursework assignments as their main form of assessment (see e.g., Biggs & Tang, 2007). If used to enable better communication between teachers and learners, e-learning can help break down such misunderstandings or misreadings and thereby promote a better integration of the goals of the learner and of the organisation in which they are learning.

Systematic use of networked multimedia computer technologies: What defining role does technology have in relation to e-learning? Is e-learning just the same as 'learning with computers' – something people have been doing for half a century? The current wave of interest in e-learning suggests that there must be something new which distinguishes it from earlier forms of Computer Assisted Learning or Computer Based Training. The parallel with e-commerce implies that the opening up of the internet and the exploitation of the World Wide Web are distinctive elements of e-learning – that e-learning ought to involve some significant use of internet technologies. But e-learning ought to be about more than just computer-mediated communication – more than just email or online chats. This means that we should take seriously both of the technological elements bound up in the acronym ICT – information *and* communications technologies. By this we mean that we should not underplay the power of computational devices or neglect their potential in the e-learning environment. There is – as we have seen – a tendency to regard Web-based learning (and even e-learning) as involving the use of human–human communication over the internet accompanied by access to hypermedia documents published via the World Wide Web. This conception involves only rather primitive interpretations of interactivity and neglects much of the progress that has been made in developing intelligently adaptive learning environments (see for example Jones & Winne, 1992; Lajoie & Derry, 1993;

Jonassen & Reeves, 1996; Lajoie, 2000). The 'information technology' part of ICT means that we have to treat computers seriously – they are more than presentational devices or conduits through which the streams of multimedia content are piped. So, computer simulations, modelling tools, exploratory environments, intelligent tutoring systems, etc., all potentially have a place in the e-learning world and to neglect them because of our current love affair with the World Wide Web would be a serious mistake. Table 2.2 may be useful in crystallising this issue. It has the failing that it turns fuzzy boundaries into sharp ones, but it does at least serve to emphasise two important dimensions of how e-learning environments can vary.

The 'ideal types' for each of these could be thought of in the following terms:

> *Type A* interactivity typically involves little or no human–human communication and access only to conventional web-based resources, rather than those which have been designed to support serious levels of interactivity.
>
> *Type B* interactivity like Type A, makes use of conventional web-based resources (limited interactivity) but is supplemented with human–human communication, e.g. through online discussion fora, chat rooms, etc. (see e.g., Salmon, 2000; McConnell, 2000; Strijbos et al., 2004).
>
> *Type C* interactivity involves little or no human–human communication but offers the learner access to learning resources which are capable of supporting more demanding forms of interactivity, e.g. through allowing high levels of learning control (as in exploratory learning environments or online case study packages) or through offering intelligent adaptation to the learner's actions. The kinds of computer-aided learning resource being described here were becoming common in stand-alone CAL applications during the 1990s but have been somewhat displaced with the headlong rush to the Web (see for example Lajoie, 2000).
>
> *Type D* interactivity involves both serious interactivity with online resources and good opportunities for rich human–human communication.

Table 2.2 Four Sub-classes or Types of Interactivity

		Degree of human–human interaction	
		Low	High
Degree of interactivity, adaptivity or 'intelligence' in the online resources used	Low	Type A	Type B
	High	Type C	Type D

Along with the potential benefits of e-learning comes uncertainty. Each new wave of technology, with its accompanying cacophony of claims about educational affordances, threatens to undermine prevailing practices and assumptions. No-one, whether they be teachers or university managers, has the energy to ride every wave.

Uncertainty, Environment, Leadership

At the risk of overstretching the metaphor, effective leadership can be seen as creating the conditions in which people can spot good waves in time to ride them, ignore the waves they can't catch, and cope with the uncertainty and frustration this necessarily entails.

We have seen that the possibilities for educational enrichment offered by the affordances of e-learning come with a cost. For students and teaching staff, these costs include the added complexity of learning and teaching strategies. For university managers who have to make decisions about investment in new infrastructure, and the maintenance and upgrading of existing infrastructure, the costs are also associated with risk and uncertainty. In Chapter 8 we will look at some of the implications for teaching teams. Chapters 9 and 10 focus on implications for managers who have to plan infrastructure.

From a relational perspective, university infrastructure can be seen as part of the learning environment. It consists of a complex mix of physical and virtual spaces, but might also be taken to include some of the shared resources that underpin university activities (e.g. the library's e-journals collection). It does not make sense to think of infrastructure on its own: it only becomes infrastructure in relation to human activity (Star & Ruhleder, 1996; Conole & Jones, forthcoming). Management of infrastructure therefore needs to be informed by an accurate understanding of good learning and of student and teacher activity patterns. In the absence of such an understanding, people are reduced to managing meaningless space when they should be managing (in) a learning environment. Echoing Bronfenbrenner (1979), Conole and Jones (forthcoming) make a useful distinction between micro, meso and macro levels in teaching, designing and managing infrastructure. This distinction – which we return to in Chapter 8 – makes it easier to see that infrastructure which is designed and managed by people at a macro level (say, across a whole university) comes to be taken-for-granted at the meso and micro levels where program teams and individual teachers and learners operate, within the constraints that derive from decisions taken 'above' them. This notion of levels also helps distinguish between infrastructure and tools. Something becomes a tool in relation to intentional activity at the micro level.

It can be argued that uncertainty and risk are felt most deeply in relation to the macro level. (In relation to university learning and teaching, most tools are cheap. It is often possible to substitute one tool for another quickly and with minimal cost. Changes to infrastructure are another matter. Planning cycles are necessarily longer; costs are greater; the risks of making strategic choices that turn out not to fit with the needs of valued educational activities become more serious.) For this reason, and because there is still not a great deal of guidance on such matters in the literature of higher education, we have chosen to devote a major part of the book (Chapters 9 and 10), to considerations of how to manage uncertainty in the planning of a university's learning spaces. In particular, we focus on the additional risks and complexity that flow from the need to integrate the management of virtual and physical spaces.

To make the scope of the problem clearer, we are not just thinking about formally designated learning spaces but the whole gamut of physical infrastructure, tools and resources, such as:

- the university library and the materials in it – including such things as catalogues and microfiche readers as well as journals and books;
- lecture theatres of various sizes and equipped with more or less sophisticated audio-visual equipment;
- laborator, studios and other specialised teaching-learning spaces;
- flexible spaces in which students can work collaboratively in small groups;
- cafés, restaurants, shops and childcare facilities, which influence both the pattern of the day (imposing constraints on students' use of time and space) and interaction with other students and teachers.

To this we can add what might be called the 'virtual spaces, tools and resources' provided in various ways by ICT: including 'office' or 'productivity' tools, instructional programs, wireless and wired network communications, learning management systems, websites, e-journal collections, databases, etc. The distinction between material and virtual is tricky to enforce. Computer hardware involves both, and as ICT becomes ever more ubiquitous we see an accelerating inter-penetration of the material and virtual worlds (think of data projectors, interactive whiteboards and iPhones, and then the emerging technologies of augmented reality).

Concluding Comments

While our basic premise about the ecology of learning may seem simple, the implications are profound – they require a university to have all of its learning and teaching activities and systems in balance. To achieve this, key parts of the university need to align their activities to the mission of the institution through the development of self-awareness and ongoing feedback. The process of self-correction brought about by these activities can be seen as an extension of Biggs' notion of constructive alignment (Biggs & Tang, 2007), moved up to the level of an ecology This includes the evaluation of student learning, the information and communication technology systems of a university, its approach to management of its learning and teaching spaces, library services and systems, policy development and appropriate leadership and management. We return to these issues in the closing chapters of this book.

3
New Students, New Technology

Introduction

As we noted in Chapter 2, there are several sets of changes upsetting the equilibrium of universities around the world. Of these, one of the changes attracting most comment is the shifting nature of student needs and expectations. In this chapter, we examine some of the evidence about students' use of IT and its implications for university education. We conclude that the story is far from simple. It soon becomes clear that there is no homogeneous 'net generation'. Universities and teachers should not let themselves be conned by pundits into believing that the incoming 'digital natives' know what they need, or that their needs are uniform or radically different from anything we have seen before. Technological change is accelerating and the ways in which people experience technology, and use it in their daily activities, are likely to diversify rather than converge. This puts a premium on evidence gathering: the well-prepared university will spend effort gathering data about the habits and expectations of its students. It will have the conceptual tools and self-belief needed to make sense of this evidence and use it to construct and monitor learning and teaching policies.

Chapter 3 is divided into two parts. First we scrutinise the line of argument that asserts that there is a new 'net generation' whose needs are not being met by formal education. This line of thinking has roots in some articles by Marc Prensky, but there are parallels in recent books by Tapscott (2008) and Palfrey and Gasser (2008). We end up agreeing with the sentiment that universities cannot afford to be complacent about their ability to understand and meet the needs of incoming students (Oblinger & Oblinger, 2005) but disagreeing profoundly with the view that there is a radical shift in needs or expectations.

Understanding these needs and expectations requires serious research. This research base is patchy, but in the second part of the chapter we distil some of the findings from recent survey-based studies in the UK, USA and Australia. This helps sketch a picture of how current university students in these countries are thinking about technology and learning. Students' access to technology, and their 'media habits', have been changing rapidly in recent years (Conole de Laat, Dillon & Darby, 2006). This has implications for teaching and also for university planning. For example, teachers benefit from knowing what students expect. They need to consider whether students' expectations about the use of technology in their courses are reasonable, and if they are reasonable, whether and how best those expectations can be met (Kirkwood & Price, 2005). Universities need to make forward plans for their IT infrastructure, as well as for the allocation, maintenance and upgrading of physical space. It is not so long ago that discussions of the use of IT in university teaching were dominated by considerations of the expense of providing sufficient numbers of computers and – even harder – sufficient space for computer labs, to allow students to access the technology. Now, in the USA, UK and a number of other well-resourced countries, over 95% of university students have their own computers. What do trends in student ownership and use of IT mean for university IT and estate planning in the next few years?

Understanding students' access to IT and their media habits is not the same as understanding how IT features in their learning. It turns out that there is little evidence to suggest that students understand, or are demanding access to, some of the more varied and powerful ways of learning that IT can open up. This provides a bridge to Chapter 4 of the book, in which we examine more closely the various ways in which students come to understand their learning, and what role IT can play in supporting their learning. It has to be said that much of the research reported in Chapter 3 is under-theorised, in the sense that many of the terms used in gathering data and reporting the research are rooted in everyday concepts, which may not be sharp enough to get below the surface of students' behaviour. We aim to remedy this in the research described in Chapters 4 and 5.

Do 'Net Generation' Learners Think Differently?

Much of the recent swathe of writing about the learning needs and preferences of the 'net generation' acknowledges the influence of Marc Prensky. Prensky, the CEO of a company specialising in educational computer games, wrote in 2001 of the gulf separating 'digital immigrants' from 'digital natives' (see especially Prensky, 2001a, b). Prensky defined as 'digital natives' those people who were born after digital technologies became widely available in their culture. That is, the digital natives have no knowledge of what it is like *not* to have near-ubiquitous IT. They have grown up regarding it as normal, unremarkable, to use computer games, email, surf the net, keep in touch via instant messaging, etc. They have spent more time reading screens than books. They carry their music with them on MP3 players. They organise their social lives using text messages on mobile phones. Prensky's catchy distinction between the fluent digital natives and their heavily accented immigrant elders

– whose clumsy, awkward use of technology betrays how far they are from home – is useful in drawing attention to some discontinuities in people's experience of technology. It has also been useful in causing people in education, especially higher education, to reflect upon how well the institutional provision of IT matches the needs and preferences of the students who are currently coming from school to university (see e.g. Herring, 2004; Oblinger & Oblinger, 2005). As should be clear by now, we are very much in favour of understanding what university students need, and how these needs are likely to change. However, we are particularly concerned that this understanding should be based on evidence, rather than speculation, and that assumptions about the carry over between media habits and learning needs should be scrutinised carefully. Prensky's position, in our view, does not withstand this scrutiny.

There are actually two versions of Prensky's main claim. The strong version is that children's experiences of growing up surrounded by digital media have led them to develop different brain structures. The weaker version is that their 'thinking patterns' have changed (Prensky, 2001b). In Prensky's view, digital natives prefer parallel processing, multitasking, graphics rather than text, random access (hypertext) rather than linear text, networking with their peers rather than working in isolation, instant gratification and frequent rewards (Prensky, 2001a, p. 2). This creates a mismatch when they encounter the formal structures of education. One can then ask whether the digital natives have to learn the successful habits of a formal education system that has been crafted by the digital immigrants or whether the education system has to change to meet the needs of the digital natives. Prensky is in no doubt. The fact that digital natives' brains are differently wired by the time they reach university means that it may simply be impossible to go back to the old ways. Prensky's evidence for the 'rewiring' of the brains of digital immigrants is presented in his second 2001 paper (Prensky, 2001b). It draws on accounts of neuroscientific research on (non-human) animals, but also mentions studies that have shown physically-detectable brain changes in humans, associated with specific experiences of learning. Examples would be the 5% increase in volume found in the cerebellum of musicians, associated with extended periods of musical training and practice, as well as the observation that the use of a language learned as an infant activates different areas of the brain than the use of a language learned in later life (Prensky, 2001b, p. 2).

While we are not qualified to evaluate the claims emerging from MRI-based studies of brain activity, we do want to acknowledge the growing literature on the implications of cognitive neuroscience for education, and especially the observations in that literature which emphasise the gulf between knowledge of brain structures and understanding of mental processes. John Geake, for example, has written very persuasively about 'neuromythologies' in education (Geake, 2008; see also Howard-Jones, 2007; Varma & Schwartz, 2008). With

Carl Bereiter (2002) we take the view that there is, as yet, no evidence of fundamentally new learning processes emerging from the so-called digital natives' lifelong encounters with IT. This is not to deny that people vary in their preferences for the use of technology, and in the ways that they like to work with information. What we do object to is the notion that is somehow 'hard-wired'. If anything, cognitive neuroscience emphasises the *plasticity* of neural connections (Mora, Segovia & del Arco, 2007).

Prensky's analysis also fails with respect to what we might call the *demographic fallacy*. By this we mean that it is dangerous to treat generations of people as if everyone in a generation shared the same characteristics, and to assume that there are sharp breaks between generations. The available survey data shows quite clearly that first year university students vary considerably in their experiences, habits and preferences (see next section). Moreover, the very idea of a generation is suspect. Access to IT in the last 20 years has been strongly associated with social class and wealth. 'Digital natives' began appearing in wealthy, well-educated, North American families significantly earlier than they began appearing in working class homes in Eastern Europe or in the homes of agricultural workers in China (Li & Kirkup, 2007). Mobile phones have played a stronger role in the adolescence of Japanese, Korean and Indian students than they have in the lives of North American students. In short, technology use has been, and will continue to be, varied and idiosyncratic rather than uniform (Kennedy, Judd, Churchward, Gray & Krause, 2008). It is, and will continue to be, dangerous to assert that new neural structures distinguish the first year students of each successive decade. This is especially the case in higher education systems, such as that of Australia, in which international students comprise a large section of the student population.

A final point is that there is, as yet, little or no evidence that says that the multitasking, rapid-cycle, link-hopping habits sketched by Prensky are associated with better learning outcomes than the more staid and focussed habits of the 'digital immigrants'. Research on the deleterious effects of excessive cognitive load would suggest the opposite (see e.g. Sweller, 1988, 2004). In the absence of evidence that the digital native (or anyone) learns well by studying à la Prensky, educational institutions that abandon the value of focussed study are shortchanging their students. We are especially worried by the suspicion that it is institutions that disproportionately cater for the children of the wealthy that will insist on focussed study, and that students from families new to higher education are vulnerable to being short-changed by institutions eager to flaunt their digital credentials.

University Students' Use of IT and their Changing Media Habits

In this section we present some recent data on university students' use of IT, drawing on surveys carried out in the USA, Australia and the UK. The material is presented on a country by country basis. *Some* comparable material is available for other countries but very few have established time-series of representative sample survey data (see e.g. Li, Kirkup & Hodgson, 2001; Tegegne & Chen, 2003; Spot+, 2004; Asgarali, Patel & Rajendran, 2007; Li & Kirkup, 2007; Fusilier & Durlabhji, 2008). Since access to IT, and associated media habits, appear to be changing very rapidly, it is hard to draw useful inferences from one-off surveys. What look like inter-country variations can turn out to be developmental differences. Conversely, national and cultural differences can be obscured by differences in the pace of change. The paucity of comparable international data about students' media habits, expectations and capabilities is particularly worrying – indeed a source of uncertainty and risk – for the many universities that are economically dependent on international students (OECD, 2005).

The United States

The largest regularly conducted survey of university students' use of IT is that organised by the Educause Center for Applied Research (ECAR) in the USA. The ECAR surveys began in 2004. The 2007 ECAR study (Salaway, Caruso & Nelson, 2007) surveyed almost 28,000 students from over 100 universities and colleges. This gives us some simple headline data which can be useful in considering university IT strategies, as well as assumptions about how IT might feature in teaching and learning.

Ninety-eight point four per cent of the 2007 ECAR survey respondents own a computer. Seventy-four per cent own a laptop (up from 53% in 2005). However, around 50% of all laptop owners never bring them to campus – because of weight and fear of theft – while around 25% bring their laptops to campus regularly (once a week or more). Lighter, cheaper, more portable and relatively less theft-prone laptops are likely to increase both the proportion of students bringing their computer with them to campus and the frequency with which they do so. However, at present, it is clear that on-campus use of IT still depends significantly on what the university provides. That said, students' use of IT is extensive and largely home-based.

Smartphone ownership is still quite low, with around 12% of students owning one. PDA ownership has dropped, and there are indications that the relatively slow growth in smartphone ownership will accelerate with the launch of models that take over more PDA functionality and with reductions in data transfer charges. This raises some important questions for universities planning IT provision. What assumptions should be made about the speed of introduction of educational applications on smartphones rather than laptops? What level of IT access does the university need to provide, given trends in laptop ownership and the portability of devices? What support models need to be in place for student laptop and PDA use in learning?

Reporting on home use of the internet, the ECAR respondents said that they spend an average of 18 hours per week online – for study but also for social and recreational purposes. Less than 9% are dependent on dial-up connections. The vast majority have highspeed internet access. Twenty-two per cent of students report using wireless as their main means of access to the internet (up from 12% in 2005).

For these US-based university students, IT is first and foremost a means of communication. Ninety-nine per cent use email; 84% use instant messaging. As one would hope, they also make use of institutional facilities for educational purposes. Ninety-five per cent report using IT to access institutional library resources; 83% access a course management system (CMS) of some kind. Eighty-two per cent report using social networking sites such as Facebook, most on a daily basis. Seventy-eight per cent play computer/video games but only 29% create their own web pages.

Eighty-three per cent of students said that they had a strong preference for the university to provide them with an email account (rather than depend on a commercial or other provider) and 85% expressed a preference for the university to use email – rather than, say instant messaging – for official communications. (There is some evidence to suggest that students do not want their university's official communications and related activities to encroach on what the students see as their own social technologies: Salaway et al., 2007, p. 14. We discuss this in more detail below.)

Most students report being very comfortable with their level of IT skills and only 25% of students want their university to provide them with upskilling in IT. The exception to this is where specialist IT tools are needed for a course. Students also mentioned – in relation to IT skills – that they would like their universities to provide the teaching staff with opportunities to upskill in the use of IT for teaching.

Australia

Closely comparable *national* data from Australia is not readily available. One useful source is the survey of 2,120 first year students' use of IT, conducted at the University of Melbourne in 2006 (Kennedy et al., 2007; 2008a, b). There are some reasons to believe that this data would somewhat *overestimate* the access to IT enjoyed by all Australian university students in 2006. In the Kennedy et al. data we find that 90% of students reported having unrestricted access to a desktop computer, with just 3.7% reporting 'no access' (cf. 98% of the US students owning a computer of some kind, in 2007). Sixty-three per cent of the Melbourne students reported having unrestricted access to a laptop (cf. 53% of the US students owning one in 2005; 74% owning one in 2007). Less than 1% of the Melbourne students reported having access to neither a desktop nor a laptop computer.

With respect to internet access, 14% of Melbourne students were restricted to dial-up connections (cf. 9% of the US students, one year later). One point four per cent of Melbourne students reported having no internet access at all.

Oliver and Goerke (2007) report two surveys carried out in 2005 and 2007 in a university in Western Australia with a less affluent demographic than the University of Melbourne. Samples were taken from 300–400 first year students in Business and Engineering. Forty-eight to forty-nine per cent reported owning a laptop (cf. 74% of the US students; 63% of the Melbourne students). Ninety-two to ninety four per cent reported having off-campus access to the internet (cf. 99% of the Melbourne students).

Turning to *uses* of IT, 78% of the Melbourne students reported using IT to access a course or learning management system (cf. 83% in the USA). Eighty per cent of students report using (offline) computer games; 50% play online games. The single biggest difference between the Melbourne students and the US students is in the reported use of social networking sites. In the 2006 Melbourne data, 63% of students said they never used social networking sites, and only 11% reported accessing social networking sites on a daily basis (cf. 82% of the US students). Given the very rapid growth of what is still quite a recent phenomenon, it is possible that the slightly later take-up of social networking in Australia, coupled with the year's difference in survey dates, may account for the apparent difference in use of social networking. (Kennedy et al. (2007), using data gathered from 2,588 students at Melbourne, Charles Sturt and Wollongong universities – but still mainly from Melbourne – in late 2006 found 57% of students still reported never using social networking sites and only 16% used them daily.)

The United Kingdom

The best broad-based UK data on university students' use of IT comes from a survey conducted for the Joint Information Systems Committee (the JISC) by the market research firm Ipsos MORI (see Ipsos MORI, 2008). This survey, conducted in March–April 2008, gathered data from a representative sample of 999 first year university students, as well as from a follow-up sample of 112 first year students who had taken part in an Ipsos MORI student expectations study, the year prior to starting university (Ipsos MORI, 2007). The survey data tell us more about students' use of IT than about raw levels of ownership, but it can be inferred from the 2008 data that fewer than 4% of the first year students do *not* have their own computer. About 21% have mobile phones on which they regularly access TV, email or GPS functions (cf. the 12% of US students owning a smartphone of some kind). Seventy-seven per cent of the students regularly access the internet from off-campus, though only 32% regularly do so for purposes specifically connected with their university work. When focussing on the use of the internet for university work purposes, 74% of students regularly access it from the university library, 41% regularly from other locations on campus and 28% during lectures or seminars (Ipsos MORI, 2008, Appendix Q4).

Turning to what the UK students use IT for, we find that 90% are users of social networking sites (80% of them claiming to be regular users). This is much closer to the US than to the Australian level of usage. Fifty-four per cent make some or regular use of wikis, blogs and online networks. Eighty-three per cent use instant messaging sometimes or regularly. They are regular but not daily users of CMS/LMS systems. Seventy-nine per cent access course-specific online materials at least once a week; 28% do this on a daily basis.

Learning with IT

Turning to what students do *educationally* with IT, we find that the landscape is dominated by: use of course/learning management systems; use of generic/productivity/office tools (email, presentation tools, word processing, spreadsheets); use of web searching tools for information discovery/research; and in some discipline areas, extensive use of specialised 'tools of the trade' (e.g. CAD software in architecture or statistical analysis software in psychology). While US and UK students – if not Australian ones – are making very frequent use of social networking tools (and IM), they exhibit a strong preference to keep these for social rather than educational purposes; or at least they may use them to help organise some aspects of their study, but they are wary of the idea that their teachers may 'invade' these spaces (Salaway et al., 2007, p. 14; Ipsos MORI, 2008 pp. 36–7; see also Creanor, Trinder, Gowan & Howells, 2006; Conole et al., 2006).

In relation to CMS/LMS use, the US data shows that the great majority of students have some experience of using these systems. Eighty-two per cent of the US student sample report having used a CMS at one time or another (up from 70% in 2005), and 46% report using a CMS several times a week (up from 40% in 2006). CMSs are also reported to be popular (59% of students saying they are positive, and 19% very positive about these systems). Less than 5% report having a negative experience with CMS/LMS systems. The US students particularly value keeping track of assignments and grades, and getting access to quiz or exam material.

As we observed, UK first year university students are regular but not daily users of CMS/LMS systems. Seventy-nine per cent access course-specific online materials at least once a week; 28% do this on a daily basis. This pattern of regular, but not daily, use is mirrored in some other aspects of IT use. For example, only 7% of students report using online library resources on a daily basis; 37% once a week or more (but less than daily); 32% once a month or more (but less than weekly). Put another way, 23% of the first year students report that they use online library resources less often than once a month. Twenty-two per cent of students report contacting their teachers/tutors by email or SMS at least once a week; 38% of students do this less than once a month. Table 3.1 provides an overview of IT uses, splitting between uses which might be said to be part of the fabric of students' lives (things they do at least

Table 3.1 UK First-year University Students' Use of IT for Course Purposes

How frequently, if at all, do you use or do each of the following, as part of your course?	At least once a week	Less than once a week	Never	% of those using, who found this very useful in enhancing their learning
Use online library resources	44%	51%	4%	44%
Use social networking sites to discuss coursework with others	27%	45%	25%	24%
Use other technologies (e.g., mobiles or email) to discuss coursework with others	45%	41%	13%	28%
Access course-specific materials online (e.g., lecture notes, slides, podcasts)	79%	19%	2%	74%
Access general course information online (e.g., timetables)	58%	39%	2%	62%
Take part in an online community, for example as 'virtual world' such as Second Life	8%	14%	74%	18%
Contact your tutor or lecturer online or by email or text	22%	74%	4%	52%
Search for papers/journals on non-university provided websites (e.g., Google Scholar)	28%	56%	15%	32%

Source: Ipsos MORI, 2008 (Appendix Q4 and Q5).

once a week) and those things which are part of the students' experience but not so frequent as to be a key part of how they do their work.

What stands out from Table 3.1 is the way in which course or learning management systems have become part of the valued fabric of students' lives. Contacting teachers by email (etc.), and online access to library resources, are also valued quite highly by those students who make use of these options. But they are not a weekly practice for the majority of students. Interestingly, the great majority of students do occasionally or regularly use some form of IT to talk about coursework with their peers, but less than 30% of those who do so say that they find this very useful in enhancing their learning.

A further point to make here concerns students' use of 'Web 2.0' technologies. As Kennedy et al. (2007) observed, it is not safe to assume that all students are heavy contributors to the Web. Moreover, Web 2.0 technologies are not a homogenous set. There is a great deal of difference between a student posting photos on their Facebook site and a team of students working together to produce or improve a Wikipedia entry. Facility with, and enthusiasm for, the social use of Facebook should not be taken to imply either a willingness to engage in the collaborative construction of knowledge or an understanding of why this might be valuable.

The Use of IT in Teaching and Learning: Students' Preferences for a Balanced Approach

Despite, or perhaps even because of, their facility with IT, newly arriving university students are not enthusiastic about the idea of technology replacing teachers. In general, the data from recent survey-based studies suggest that students are looking for a balanced use of technology. For example, the US data summarised by Salaway et al. (2007, pp. 13ff.) show that 60% of US university students are looking for 'moderate' amounts of IT use in their courses. This figure has been consistent across the last three years of ECAR surveys. In particular, students do not want to see IT displace face-to-face access to their teachers. Not all students are the same, of course. In the US 2007 data, engineering and business students, and students who define themselves as 'early adopters' of technology and as having above average skills in IT would be more content than other students to have greater use of IT in their courses. Female students, and younger students, expressed a preference for less use of IT, compared with the preferences of male and older students.

This preference for 'balance' in the use of IT is also echoed in UK data. For example, the Ipsos MORI data provides a consistent picture of student preferences for carefully integrated use of IT-based and face-to-face teaching methods. These students see face-to-face teaching as the best form of teaching but appreciate the application of IT *if it is used well*. 'Face to face interaction supported by inefficient or inept use of technology is worse than using none' (Ipsos MORI, 2008, p. 10). The more technically fluent students are the most critical when IT is used badly in their courses. An important point to make here, based on the qualitative data gathered by Ipsos MORI, is that when these first year students were talking about what they valued in teaching, they stressed formal teaching methods and talked about knowledge as something to be conveyed to them by a figure in authority (Ipsos MORI, 2008, p. 10).

The US data is generally positive about how students feel IT contributes to the quality of their educational experience, but the data do not amount to a wholehearted endorsement. For example, 61% of students agreed with the statement that IT improved their learning, but 9% disagreed with this statement and 30% felt neutral about it. As Salaway et al. (2007, p. 15) put it, 'a large minority of respondents chose not to assert that IT has a positive role in their learning'. The area where students felt most lukewarm was in relation to whether IT helped them to feel more *engaged* in their courses (only 40% said yes). They were more positive about the ways in which IT helped them collaborate and communicate with their colleagues (59% in the affirmative), and take control of their learning (60%), and more positive again about IT enabling them to do better research (71%) and to get faster feedback from their teachers (73%).

A theme that comes through clearly from the US survey data (Salaway et al., 2007, pp. 16–17) is that many students feel that their teachers do not recognise that IT has created a much more complex learning environment, and that teachers should make allowances for this complexity. Students also feel that some teachers do not recognise that there is a zone of IT use that students feel is appropriate. Students are critical if IT is underused, especially if teachers fail to use it for what the students see as basic provision, such as posting course grades, or overused, such as when the students think it is standing between them and the teacher. Students are also critical when they see IT used as a prop for poor teaching, such as when overuse of presentation software displaces more active teaching.

Students Vary in their Views on IT and Learning

The US data also shows that students are far from homogeneous with respect to their use of, and views on, IT in learning. Salaway et al. (2007, pp.15–16) characterise this difference as follows:

> Those who are high tech tell us they want much more technology; they experiment with new technologies and want to use these in courses. They are more engaged in sophisticated software such as that for creating graphics, video/audio and web pages. They spend a great deal of time online and like to learn through programs such as simulations and video games, and by contributing to web sites such as blogs and wikis. They report strong IT skills across the board, and may own PDAs or smartphones and are ready to use them for institutional applications. They are often found majoring in engineering or business and are more often males than females.

> At the other extreme is a class of students who through choice or circumstance make less use of technology. These respondents prefer limited or no technology in courses and adopt technologies only when they have to. Like others, they use IT for communicating with their peers, but they are far less likely to claim advanced IT skills in the basics required for courses – course management systems, presentation software and

spreadsheets. More often, members of this group are female and attend associate institutions. They do not spend as much time engaged in internet activities and more often depend on dial-up connections. The technology they own is often older, and some respondents do not even own a computer

Implications and Concluding Comments

As Helen Beetham and Rhona Sharpe have argued, universities need to change because ways of working with knowledge are changing, not because students learn differently (Beetham & Sharpe, 2007). Teaching methods and the provision of university infrastructure for learning need to be guided by a clear sense of how developments in knowledge work and innovations in technology play into each other. Modish reactions to each new media fashion will be expensive and miss the point.

Broadly speaking, students are with us in this. They are looking for guidance about good ways to learn. They do not expect universities to follow fashion. Indeed, they want some separation between social and educational uses of media. They see IT as a necessary tool for managing the complex activities of a complex organisation and they are understandably frustrated when universities fail to deliver. They like the flexibility IT offers, but hate it when IT is used badly. They do not want IT to reduce access to their teachers.

Much of the guidance we need to offer to students is concerned with helping them become more ambitious about learning and knowing. There is little evidence to suggest that they are drawn to high-stakes group-based tasks (as distinct from informal chats with friends about coursework), or that they picture themselves as apprentice knowledge workers. We need to help them become more adept at understanding their own learning needs and gain confidence and skill in managing their own learning. This includes the abilities they will need to learn from others – not just teachers – and to make efficient use of tools and media in their various 'learnplaces' (Goodyear, 2008; Goodyear & Ellis, 2008).

In order to tailor such guidance to the diverse needs of an increasingly diverse student body, we need to have a better understanding of students' own perspectives and experience. This is the goal of Chapters 4 and 5.

4
Student Experiences of E-learning in Higher Education
Learning through Discussion

Introduction

The context in which we are positioning e-learning in higher education is one in which it is part of a broader ecology of learning. We use the term 'ecology of learning' because we feel it best represents the nature of the phenomenon which has students at its centre, and includes all legitimate stakeholders including teachers, university service providers and university leaders. The associations amongst these stakeholders in relation to the student experience of e-learning is emphasised in the latter half of the book. For the moment we are turning the lens to view e-learning in higher education from the perspective of the student.

Our position is that to really understand the legitimate position of e-learning in higher education, we need to conceive of it as one that is integrated with learning activities that potentially traverse back and forward between face-to-face and e-learning contexts as students move towards a deeper understanding of the topics, issues and ideas valued by their disciplines. We argue this should be considered as the legitimate position of e-learning in higher education because, across universities internationally, it is far more common for e-learning to complement face-to-face experiences than replace them completely. This is not to say that there is no replacement of a portion of a face-to-face experience, but an effective replacement is one that seeks harmony of the parts, is integrated and ecologically balanced so as to focus students on learning outcomes and the development of understanding.

To understand the student experience of e-learning comprehensively within an ecological view of learning, we need to consider it from a number of perspectives. In Chapter 3, we considered student media habits in relation to new waves of technologies, such as Web 2.0 technologies. In the following chapters, we consider the student experience from the perspective of teaching, designing and visioning for campus-based universities. In this chapter, we focus squarely on the student experience of e-learning in a broader ecology of learning. The purpose of the chapter is to understand what aspects of learning come to the fore when e-learning is part of the overall teaching approach. We will not try to canvass every possible experience of e-learning in which a student might engage, but, rather, will consider how we can think about and discuss e-learning in a symbiotic relationship within a larger learning context.

How Students Learn through E-learning

There are many potential ways for students to learn through e-learning; however, two learning activities stand out as being particularly suitable for e-learning, as they are bound up with key affordances provided by the technology:

- *learning through discussion* as e-learning can be particularly effective in linking communities of learners together, and
- *learning through inquiry* as e-learning can be used to provide learners with a wealth of resources for research-based activities.

The question of how students learn through e-learning presupposes that e-learning is a meaningful part of the student learning experience. Research discussed here and in later chapters has identified that, too often, it is an afterthought, bolted on without much planning, or, worse, separated from the students' face-to-face experience and conceptualised as a course website 'over there'.

The way students learn through e-learning is linked to a key concept in research into student learning in higher education: approaches to learning.

Learning through Discussion

Learning through discussions has long been recognised as a fundamental part of the experience of learning. History tells us how Socrates helped students to learn through dialogic exchanges which attended to the student's powers of reasoning (Barr, 1968; Nussbaum, 1997), although some attribute the nature of a Socratic Dialogue to the ideas of German philosopher Leonard Nelson and his pupil Gustav Heckmann (van Hooft, 1999; 2005). In some ancient universities, such as Oxford and Cambridge, a small tutorial with one teacher and a few students is a preferred model of learning, based on intensive discussion and reflection.

One of the key changes reflected in late 20th century debates on the role of universities is referred to as the 'massification' of higher education (see e.g., Trow, 1973; Scott, 1995; NCIHE, 1997). A key idea associated with this shift is that universities have a responsibility to educate a broad range of people for a rapidly changing world. This is quite different from the 19th and early 20th century idea of a university, as groups of scholars guarding vaults of knowledge only accessible to those deemed worthy.

Larger numbers of students, in the absence of proportionally increased staffing resources, have resulted in larger class sizes. In this context, the potential benefits from learning activities such as discussion are threatened, simply because of the logistics involved. Large numbers of students are often an obstacle to teachers conceiving of, and trying, learning activities that are comparatively more intensive. It is for reasons such as these that teachers have turned to alternative solutions, such as the use of e-learning, to retain opportunities for learning through discussions.

Discussions using e-learning are still normally text-based and can be broadly divided into synchronous and asynchronous categories. Synchronous discussions require the participants to interact in real-time, and do not always leave a permanent record. Asynchronous discussions allow the participants to discuss issues over an extended period of time: the textual trace persists in virtual space, ready for the next 'speaker' to access when required in the course of a conversation.

Our preferred approach to researching learning through discussion is a relational one, which considers how students think about learning, how they approach it, how they perceive key aspects of the whole context and how these conceptions and approaches are related to their academic results. It is also important to take into account other kinds of research on learning through discussion.

Such studies have focussed on a number of different areas. Some have focussed on tools, particularly email (Geer, 2001; Lowry, 1994; Meacham, 1994; Zhang, 2002), some on critical thinking (Jeong, 2003; Fauske & Wade, 2003; Whipp, 2003) and some on synchronous discussion modes (Bump, 1990; Veerman, 2000; Burnett, 2003). The majority of the research, too extensive to deal with adequately here, has been on asynchronous online discussions. Relatively recent studies of asynchronous discussions have focussed on content analysis to evaluate postings (Weaver, 2006) collaboration (Kim & Sonnenwald, 2002; Clark, 2001; Baskin, 2001), knowledge-building (Tisdell et al., 2004; Schrire, 2006), and factors affecting learner participation (Dennan, 2005).

We now turn to our own research. The studies discussed in the next section were funded as part of, or were a precursor to, an Australian Research Council project we carried out between 2005 and 2008, in collaboration with Mike Prosser. They focus on learning through discussions that spanned face-to-face and online contexts.

Students' Approaches to, and Conceptions of, Learning through Discussions

Online discussions that complement discussions begun in class, or that continue and/or summarise ideas between classes, are potentially of great educational value and can support the development of student understanding, in certain circumstances. How these circumstances might be described is the focus of the following sections.

The studies used in the following section to examine student experiences of learning through discussion focus on situations in which:

- students were expected to discuss key topics in the course in and across face-to-face and online situations;
- evidence of qualitative variation in and across the face-to-face and online experiences of learning through discussion were captured;
- qualitative variation in the experience was related to key aspects of the learning context and course outcomes such as concepts and performance.

One of the first things to be aware of is that, when presented with similar opportunities, students report qualitatively different experiences. The material we present below is drawn from two related studies. We used the same methodology but on two contrasting courses. One course was an introduction to psychology for second year students of social work. The other course was about e-commerce and was for students studying Web-engineering. Face-to-face and online discussions played a significant role in both courses.

Methodology and Research Data

METHODS

The methodology used was primarily derived from research into university student learning, in the tradition of Marton and Säljö (1976a, 1976b), Entwistle and Ramsden (1983), Biggs (1987), Marton and Booth (1997), Prosser and Trigwell (1999), Biggs et al. (2001), Laurillard (2002), Ramsden (2002), Biggs and Tang (2007). A central place is given to the student perspective. Both qualitative and quantitative data are used.

The qualitative studies often involve *extensive* investigations with a relatively large sample of the population (of students on a course), and *intensive* investigations with a smaller sub-set of the population. The extensive studies typically use open-ended questionnaires in which students are invited to reflect on what they think they are learning (their conceptions of learning) and how they go about their learning (their approaches to learning), both in face-to-face and online contexts. The intensive investigations involve in-depth interviews, taking around 40 minutes or so per student. These interviews are semi-structured, audio-recorded and fully transcribed for the purpose of analysis. To triangulate the student ideas found in the extensive (questionnaire-based) investigations, and to probe many of them more deeply, the structure of the interviews is consistent with the questions in the questionnaire. Techniques adopted in the interview enable ideas and words used by the students to be recursively unpacked. For example, two students in two different interviews may use the word 'interactive'. After probing by the interviewer, one student may say for him it means doing what the teacher says in class, while another student might say for her it means clarifying the meaning behind a key idea the teacher is trying to explain. This type of interview strategy assists the researchers, when analysing the transcripts, to get below the surface of the students' words, and come closer to the students' intended meanings.

The analytic methods used in working with our qualitative data typically involve the researchers in several iterations. While precise details may vary from study to study, the analysis usually proceeds as follows.

Each of the researchers independently reads the student responses (interview transcript or responses to open-ended questions on the questionnaire) for the purpose of noting emerging patterns and structures of ideas in the data. The researchers then meet to share and make joint sense of the patterns they have independently found, in order to identify key themes common to all the analyses. Representative transcripts are chosen and the key themes are logically grouped into related areas, often in order to identify which themes seem to encompass other themes. These higher-level themes begin to form an *outcome space*. An outcome space in this methodology is comprised of categories of description which represent differing experiences of a phenomenon, logically related to each other, structured as a hierarchy in relation to a given criterion (Marton, 1992). In the research into student experience of learning below, the outcome spaces, their categories of description and representative quotations, draw on the SOLO taxonomy for their underlying structure and hierarchy (see e.g., Biggs & Tang, 2007).

During the development of the outcome space, the researchers iteratively clarify the categories of description in terms of their logical, structural and referential relationships. The process includes establishing the inter-rater agreement about the classification of transcript fragments. This provides a test of the *communicability* of the categories: similar to, but different from, a test of reliability (Johansson, Marton & Svensson, 1985). It is desirable to achieve inter-rater agreement for communicability of the categories of description somewhere between 80% and 90% (Säljö, 1988).

In most of the research reported below, a qualitative study, of the kind described above, usually precedes a quantitative study. However well-developed a researcher's intuitions may be, concerning key aspects of students' experiences of learning, it is much more sensible to proceed from more exploratory qualitative research towards the definition of quantitative instrumentation than to leap straight into constructing items for closed-ended questionnaires or rating scales.

The development of closed-ended items to investigate the student experience of learning across face-to-face and online contexts draws on previous quantitative research into student learning (e.g. Entwistle & Ramsden, 1982; Biggs, 1987; Ramsden, 1991; Prosser & Trigwell, 1999; Biggs et al., 2001). Methodological ideas and validated rating scales from these sources combined with insights from the rich descriptions of the students' experiences drawn from our qualitative studies, provide the basis for our own closed-ended questionnaires and associated rating scales.

Analysis of the quantitative data normally involves three levels of exploration: items, variables and groups of students. At the level of items, exploratory factor analyses have been used to look at the structural relationships amongst the items in the questionnaires, while Alpha coefficients have been used to test the reliability of the scales that are derived from the factor analyses. At the level of variables, Pearson correlation coefficients have been used to investigate the strength of the relationships between pairs of variables and exploratory factor analyses to investigate relationships amongst groups of variables. At the level of students, cluster analyses look for subgroups of students within each sample, identified on the basis of similarity in experiences of the variables being investigated.

Wherever possible, variations in the student experience of learning as measured by the student ratings of the closed-ended items are linked with overall student satisfaction and levels of achievement. The latter may be at the level of the course in which the student experience is investigated, or at the level of the task, whichever is the most meaningful in terms of understanding variations in the student experience.

DATA

In total, the samples used for the studies reported in this and the next chapter involved over 4,500 students, who between them completed over 5,000 closed-ended questionnaires, 400 open-ended questionnaires and 45 in-depth interviews. The nature of the studies determined the size of the samples, with larger numbers being used in the quantitative studies and smaller samples in the qualitative studies. The scale of the samples involved in the studies is at least sufficient for the purposes of discussion and exploration of the issues. More definitive conclusions could be drawn from replication of the studies in a wider range of universities and courses, though we have no reason to think that the conceptions and approaches uncovered in our research are unique to the settings we have studied. At a minimum, the data and initial conclusions help delineate an important, emerging area of research – one which has strong implications for people involved in understanding university learning environments, as well as for those who have to deal with the uncertainty that accompanies the introduction of technologies into an ecology of learning.

Approaches to Learning through Discussion in Social Work

To help the reader understand the main qualitative variations in student experiences of discussions, the following account begins by sharing excerpts from the student interviews and questionnaires that highlight some of the key aspects of the experiences. Later in the chapter we discuss quantitative results from analyses of the distributions and frequencies of the classifications of the qualitative data, and the student ratings of the closed-ended questionnaires. These provide a more broadly-based sense of the student experiences of learning through discussion.

In the social work course, students were studying psychology issues that related to the practice of social work. The students engaged in discussions across face-to-face and online contexts over a 14 week semester. The purpose of the discussions was to develop a sound understanding of the knowledge and theories encountered in the relevant psychology and social work literature, and to help students relate these ideas to their own experiences and to the experiences of other students. Much of the motivation for commencing discussions came from the course readings. The lecturer felt that this would help students to better understand how to relate key ideas to professional practice. Discussions in both large and small groups were used as a way of investigating the course readings and key ideas arising in other parts of the course. Students were required to participate in the (face-to-face) tutorials and to make a minimum of two online postings of 200 words each week, either beginning their own discussion thread, or continuing a thread created by another student. The discussions online often continued those in class. The online discussion was hosted on a WebCT 4.1 platform.

Towards the end of the semester, a subset of the students volunteered to take part in interviews about their experiences of learning through discussion on the course. Among other things, they were asked, 'How do you approach learning through discussions in class?' The following excerpts give a flavour of variations in students' responses to this question.

Student 1: I take, mostly what people say, I take down, and it is very varied what people come up with from the readings and also it is their point of view as well. So people have different points of view, but very different . . . I like the fact that we are all discussing the same thing but from different points of views, from different subjects. It's like you pick a question and you discuss a question, which means you are only getting that group's perspective on that question, whereas (in the bigger group) we are getting lots of people's perspectives on the same question. I think that is really good.

Student 1 provides a typical response consistent with a deep approach to learning through discussions. It suggests an approach that takes the discussions seriously, valuing the perspectives of others and using them to better understand the issues. The next extract is also consistent with a deep approach.

Student 2:   The small discussions you get more of a say because there is less people and you try to make that equal. What I actually do is I listen a lot. It is interesting. I don't zone out although I can't speak for everyone. So you listen and I write down a lot and if there is something that you want to address in the online discussions later, I will usually put a little asterisk next to it and then try and write after the tutorial. I will go down and write everything I think about that and then put that in an online discussion. Not only am I listening and thinking this is important now, I am thinking in the future for my online discussion and what do I want to address.

It is clear that student 2 is making a distinct connection between the face-to-face and online discussions. She adopts a strategy that she believes will help her to link the two to key ideas she wants to address.

In contrast, other students reported experiences of discussions in class that did not seem to indicate much awareness of the purpose of the discussions. The following extracts are taken from responses to the question 'How do you approach learning through discussions in class?'

Student 3:   I don't think there is that much learning. The most amount of learning would happen in lectures . . . I don't think there is that much learning, I think it's just embracing different ideas and I don't think you are actually learning something, I think what's in the readings it's not what you actually learn it's just stringing them all together and engaging, yeah.

Student 4:   Usually, like because we go around and usually by the last people your ideas and everything has been said you end up coming to basically the same sort of answer, give or take a few different sorts of points or once it gets around the last group doesn't usually have much to say because it is, you know everyone is coming to the same ideas.

The responses of students 3 and 4 are consistent with a surface approach to learning through discussions in this study. The responses do not indicate an approach that links the discussions with meaningful learning, understanding ideas from different perspectives or reflecting on them in the online discussions later on. Rather, there is an expectation that the discussions will not provide much help for learning.

Similar variation in the experience of students was reported in response to interview questions about their online discussions: 'How do you approach your discussions online?'

Student 5:   Benefits, I guess it's what I said earlier, it (online discussion) is about what these readings are saying and really reflecting on them seriously because I guess the tutorial you can quite easily get away without doing the reading, without thinking about them that much, so in that way I think online discussion is beneficial, it really makes me take the time to re-read and to consider it.

An approach to online discussion that emphasised reflection was one of the main benefits that students reported from the experience. Students seem to value being expected to reconsider some of the ideas outside class, in a way that will be visible to others.

Student 6:   It just makes me think, like the ideas, like someone today when a post I made this morning and one two days ago, which was about men in counselling and about how they just feel society pretty much pushed them out of it. It wasn't really that original but it was something which I hadn't thought of before. So I mean, I didn't respond to it because I didn't have much to say. It was just something for me to think about it as I come to university, and it will be something that I have already thought about and probably be able to apply it.

The quotations above (5 and 6) were considered to be consistent with a deep approach to discussions online. Not all the students reported experiences of online discussions that suggested deep learning.

Student 7:   I think a lot of people would like to write more, I probably wouldn't but a lot more opinions might come out if, I don't know, if the teacher wasn't reading it.

The above extract suggests an approach that does not embrace the nature of the whole context, one in which the teacher is playing a legitimate role. It is consistent with a surface approach to learning in online discussions suggesting an online experience with no real awareness of the benefits of reflection, receiving and giving feedback nor opening up a personal understanding of topics to new ideas and different perspectives.

Approaches to Learning through Discussion in Web-engineering

Variation in the student experience of learning through discussions has also been identified in more technically-oriented courses. In a third-year engineering course, students studied the basics of setting up an e-commerce business. They engaged in face-to-face discussions in a laboratory session and in discussions online over a 14 week semester. The purpose of the discussions was directly related to the ideas underpinning a written report, which the students were required to produce to demonstrate their understanding of the key stages of establishing a business. The students used an open-source software system, dotlrn (www.dotlrn.com) to facilitate their online discussions. The bulletin board tool within this system was used to support the asynchronous discussions.

Towards the end of the semester, the students reported qualitatively different experiences of the discussions in class. They were asked the same question as the students in social work: 'How do you approach learning through discussions in class?'

Student 1: With face-to-face discussions, we looked at what had to be achieved, i.e., what had to be completed in the tutorial. After looking at what was required, we discussed what we thought would be the question and why we thought (it). We then combined our answers to provide a thorough answer. These strategies got us thinking about the project and what we wanted to achieve.

Student 2: We were able to discuss various ways of tackling problems, not just going by the book, but rather thinking of 'real-world' issues. From our conversations, we were able to learn about e-businesses from another's perspective.

A deep approach to discussions in class included some of the aspects that are apparent in the above two extracts. Using the discussions to discover the intent underpinning the tutorial work, to integrate ideas and understanding into more thorough answers and to think about real-world issues were some of the key aspects. As with the social work course, class discussions were not experienced in the same way by all students.

Student 3: When I go to tutorials, waiting for all the tutors and stuff to turn up, well, we just do nothing. And then when the tutor comes, he talks about tutorial and what we do today. So what we do, is we go back and then read the tutorial on what we're supposed to do, just to do it step by step. We don't read the whole thing. We just do like the first question, and then we talk and after we talk about it, I

	type it up on the computer and just do every question step by step and one by one, that's all me and my friend do.
Student 4:	Nothing much was needed to engage in face-to-face discussions. One just talks and the other listens. And vice-versa.

Some students in engineering reported approaches in class that did not embrace any of the problem-solving, analysing strategies that were consistent with a deep approach. They tended to focus on superficial aspects of the process of discussions, almost as if it was a matter of going through a meaningless ritual.

In relation to the online discussions, a deep approach included seeking and providing feedback.

Student 5:	Online postings are really useful for me. By people looking through my posting, they can give me advice; indicate where I need to improve. The most important benefit is that they can find deficiencies in my posting that I am not able to see. This really helps me.
Student 6:	After reading the online discussions and analysing the problem, I asked the author about the disadvantages, provide constructive criticism and provide my own views.

The online discussions were used by students to gather views on their own postings in order to better understand what they might be missing. The more proactive students adopting a deep approach also returned the favour, testing their own views by providing feedback to their peers.

Some comparatively less useful approaches to the online discussions were adopted by students who seemed to be spurred on by things other than learning.

Student 7:	I read up on it, and usually I don't have time until the night before to actually post, yeah but that last one I actually posted to a wrong forum first.
Student 8:	Well other people's postings, that's the part I hate the most because I really don't like picking fault at other people's posts, unless, the thing I like, I like picking people's faults if they reply to my thread, but not the other way round. So sometimes when I reply I think I kind of like go off topic and I don't think my replies are helpful to them either way.

Characteristics of some approaches to online discussions included working in a rush – leaving insufficient time to engage properly – being reluctant to engage in discussions, not being able to distinguish between providing helpful feedback and being critical and not keeping to the topic under discussion. These characteristics were found to be part of a surface approach to online discussions.

Synthesising the Data on Approaches to Discussion

The above extracts, taken from interviews with undergraduate students on courses in social work and Web-engineering, illustrate some distinctive, qualitatively different approaches to discussions. Additional analysis and extracts can be found in Ellis, Goodyear, Prosser and O'Hara (2006) and in Ellis, Goodyear, Calvo and Prosser (2008). In the full set of extracts, key features consistent with a deep approach include:

- understanding the topic under consideration from a number of different perspectives;
- writing down ideas to follow-up online in the next stage of the discussion;
- understanding people who disagree and how they differ in their thinking;
- learning from the questions asked by other people;
- providing feedback to others about the relevance and usefulness of their ideas;
- integrating ideas with others in order to provide a more holistic answer to tutorial questions.

In contrast, interview responses consistent with a surface approach include:

- not having used the stimulus material or other online postings to engage meaningfully with the topic;
- posting at the last moment;
- not being willing to provide useful responses to other peoples' postings;
- confusing the idea of feedback with the idea of criticism;
- trying to save 'face' when engaging in a discussion rather than really engaging;
- being unwilling to take a lead in discussions from time to time.

Associations Between Approaches, Conceptions and Academic Outcomes

The developing argument here, about how learning can be supported, extended and elaborated by a mix of face-to-face and e-learning experiences, would be all for nought if there was no indication of associations between approaches to learning and other aspects of the experience of learning as

Table 4.1 Relationships Between Approaches to Face-to-Face and Online Discussion in Engineering

Face-to-face approaches	Online approaches		
	Deep approaches Categories C,D	Surface approaches Categories A,B	Totals
Deep approaches (C,D)	12	2	14
Surface approaches (A,B)	4	52	56
Total	16	54	70

$\chi^2 = 39.2$, phi = .75, p<0.001,

Source: Ellis, Goodyear, Calvo & Prosser, 2008.

indicated by Figure 2.2. Table 4.1 shows links between approaches to learning through online and face-to-face discussions.

Table 4.1 identifies the associations between face-to-face and online approaches that were reported by students in the Web-engineering course. Students whose comments were classified as surface approaches online, tended also to make comments that were classified as surface in face-to-face contexts. Similarly, students who reported approaches to discussion in class that were classified as deep, reported approaches online that were also classified as deep. In other words, in that study, there appears to be consistency of approach across online and face-to-face contexts.

The relatedness of different aspects of the experience of learning through discussions is not limited to approaches. Table 4.2 presents links between approaches and conceptions.

Notice Table 4.2 not only presents student *approaches* to discussions in face-to-face and online contexts, but also student *conceptions* of discussions. If you refer to Figure 2.2, you will see that the experience of learning can be usefully divided into how students approach learning and what they learn, their conceptions of learning. Research into student learning over many decades has shown that qualitatively different conceptions of learning are related in logically consistent ways to qualitatively different approaches to learning. In this case, deep and surface approaches to learning tend to be related to cohesive and multistructural (or fragmented) conceptions of learning respectively (Ramsden, 2002; Prosser & Trigwell, 1999).

In the studies referred to in this section, *cohesive conceptions* of learning through discussions are those that link the purpose of discussions to developing comprehension, understanding and a more complete picture of the topic under consideration. *Multistructural* (or *fragmented*) conceptions are those that conceive of only separate parts of the meaning of discussions. They tend

Table 4.2 Relationships Between Conceptions of, and Approaches to, Face-to-Face and Online Discussion in Social Work

Conceptions of learning through discussions		Approaches		
		Surface approaches Categories C,D	Deep approaches Categories A,B	Totals
Face-to-Face	Fragmented (C,D)	26	0	26
	Cohesive (A,B)	16	9	25
	Total	42	9	51
Online	Fragmented (C,D)	26	0	26
	Cohesive (A,B)	9	16	25
	Total	35	16	51

Face-to-face: $\chi^2 = 11.4$, phi = .47, p<0.001,
Online: $\chi^2 = 24.2$ phi = .69, p<0.001

Source: Ellis, Goodyear, Prosser & O'Hara, 2006.

to separate meaningful learning from the central idea behind the discussions. Table 4.3 presents categories of description of conceptions of discussions, as well as representative quotations.

Table 4.3 presents the outcome space from an analysis of how students reported conceiving of discussions in social work. In that study, the researchers felt that the students' conceptions of discussions could be usefully grouped into challenging and developing ideas, and acquiring and checking ideas.

The categories A–D in Table 4.3 can be described in hierarchical and relational terms. Referentially, categories C and D are simpler than categories A and B. In C and D, there is no indication that the conceptions of discussions include any ideas of challenging or developing ideas and understanding. These categories foreground relatively limited concepts of discussions that are primarily about checking and collecting ideas. In contrast, categories A and B are conceptions of discussions that emphasise how understanding is developed: discussions offer ways of delving more deeply into the ideas being discussed by analysing the perspectives of others and using these to test the ideas and beliefs held by oneself. Referentially, the categories can be considered to be hierarchical, with 'acquiring ideas' including the category of 'checking their accuracy' and with 'challenging ideas' including the category of 'developing ideas'. Structurally, the categories are not hierarchical, since fragmented and cohesive conceptions are mutually exclusive: that is, they cannot be held simultaneously.

Table 4.3 Categories of Conceptions of Learning through Discussions in Social Work

Category	Description	Representative quotation
A Challenging ideas	Discussions as a way of challenging ideas and beliefs in order to arrive at a more complete understanding	It (discussing) challenges my beliefs, which is always good . . . because a belief is something that is based on knowledge and experience and your understanding of the world, and if it is being challenged you are testing it. . . . If my beliefs are challenged, I believe that my understanding of concepts is more complete.
B Developing ideas	Discussions as a way of challenging and improving your ideas	It sort of gives you different views of what people are getting out of the readings and stuff . . . it helps me, I guess, just because I am not getting stuck in just this one mindset, it sort of makes me for a topic to go deeper, and just get other perspectives. . . . I guess it gives me an appreciation that people do see it differently, that it's not clear cut. It's one thing having my opinion, and it will mean different things to different people.
C Acquiring ideas	Discussions as a way of collecting ideas	It elaborates the readings even more like it sort of expands the readings out a bit . . . when you go to the tutorials and you express your ideas, it sort of makes them valid to yourself. Like you sort of remember it a bit more by the end of the tutorial . . . you just get to learn a bit more about the other people's ideas.
D Checking ideas	Discussions as a way of checking your ideas are right	Getting the teacher's point of view . . . it's good being able to talk and make sure you are really learning what you are supposed to be learning. It is just sort of reassuring.

Source: Ellis, Goodyear, Prosser & O'Hara, 2006.

Having understood some qualitative differences between the conceptions of learning through discussions, we are now in a better position to understand Table 4.3. This table suggests that cohesive conceptions of learning through discussions are related to deep approaches to discussion both in face-to-face and online contexts. Similarly, fragmented conceptions of learning through discussions are related to surface approaches to discussion in both face-to-face and online contexts.

Associations between aspects of the experience of learning through discussions are not limited to approaches and conceptions. Quantitative studies into student experiences of learning through discussions have identified the subtlety of some of these connections (Ellis & Calvo, 2004b, 2006; Ellis, Goodyear,

Prosser & O'Hara, 2006; Ellis, Goodyear, Calvo & Prosser, 2008). Some of this research has shown links between discussions and student perceptions of the context of learning. Perceptions in the student experience of learning have been shaped by the work of Paul Ramsden (1991, 2002). Variation in students' perceptions of key aspects of their context of learning (for example, student workload, the quality of teaching, an emphasis on independence) have been shown to be logically related to the quality of their experience of learning. Table 4.4 shows associations between approaches, conceptions and perceptions of learning in the same engineering course reported above, but conducted with an earlier cohort of students.

Cluster analyses interrogate data in ways that allow subgroups within a sample to be identified on the basis of similarities on the variables being investigated. In Table 4.4 cluster analysis has been used to investigate students' responses to closed-ended surveys. In addition to the variables interrogating approaches to, and conceptions of, learning through discussions, three additional variables from the Course Experience Questionnaire (Ramsden, 1991) were found to be significantly related to the experience. Two other variables, 'appropriate assessment' and 'clear goals and standards' were not found to be significantly associated. The three variables representing workload, independence and good teaching represent key aspects of the context of learning. A

Table 4.4 Cluster Analysis of Parts of the Experience of Learning through Discussions

Variable	Cluster (standardised mean)		Stat sig if $p<0.05$
	1, $n=97$ Reproducing	2, $n=18$ Understanding	
Approaches to learning through discussions			
Face-to-face surface approach	0.14	−0.76	<0.01
Face-to-face deep approach	−0.23	1.27	<0.01
Online surface approach	0.10	−0.54	0.01
Online deep approach	−0.11	0.57	0.01
Conceptions of learning through discussions			
Fragmented conception	0.14	−0.73	<0.01
Cohesive conception	−0.21	1.16	<0.01
Perceptions of learning through discussions			
Appropriate workload	−0.18	0.99	<0.01
Emphasis on independence	−0.17	0.92	<0.01
Good teaching	−0.19	1.04	<0.01
Performance			
Final mark	−0.10	0.55	0.01

n=115

Source: Ellis & Calvo, 2006.

positive score on 'appropriate workload' means that students did not feel over-burdened by the amount of work required to cope with the online part of the course; a positive score on the 'emphasis on independence' variable means that students perceived that they were encouraged to learn independently; and a positive score on the 'good teaching' variable means that students perceived the teacher to make an effort to understand things from the perspective of students, giving timely feedback and motivating students to do their best work.

The analysis in Table 4.4 identifies two clusters of students. The first cluster (n=97) is a group of students oriented towards a reproductive approach to learning through discussions, scoring positively on surface approaches to discussions, a fragmented conception of discussions and with negative scores on perceptions of appropriate workload, emphasis on independence, good teaching and performance. The second cluster (n=18) identifies a group of students oriented towards understanding, scoring positively on deep approaches to discussions, cohesive conceptions, and perceptions of appropriate workload, emphasis on independence, good teaching and performance. It is worth noting the differences in the size of the cluster, with cluster 1 being much larger than cluster 2. Teachers cannot assume most students will know how to carry on discussions effectively across face-to-face and online contexts. As a corollary, teachers need to know, and share, useful strategies that will help students.

In some of our quantitative studies of learning through discussions, cluster analyses have been complemented with factor and correlation analyses that are conducted at the level of variables. For the sake of coherence with the previous account, Tables 4.5 and 4.6 are taken from the same 2006 study.

Correlation analyses identify pairwise associations between variables. Factor analyses identify the structural relationships amongst groups of variables. Their use with correlation analyses helps by complementing evidence at the level of groups of students, with evidence of associations at the level of variables. Tables 4.5 and 4.6 provide evidence for our claim that e-learning needs to be understood in relation to other parts of the student learning experience; to be seen as part of the broader ecology of learning.

Table 4.5 shows that a high score on the face-to-face deep approach variable is positively and significantly associated with the cohesive conception variable (r=0.63, $p < 0.001$), the online deep approach variable (r=044, $p < 0.01$), the emphasis on independence variable (r=0.36, $p < 0.01$), the good teaching variable (r=0.44, $p < 0.01$), the appropriate workload variable (r=0.19, $p < 0.01$) and the overall satisfaction item (r=0.47, $p < 0.01$). There are other positive and significant associations, but perhaps the most important are those between the face-to-face surface approach variable and the fragmented conception variable ($r = 0.46$, $p < 0.01$), and with the online surface approach variable ($r = 0.39$, $p < 0.01$). Logically, there is a negative association between the face-to-face surface approach and the online deep variable ($r = 0.39$, $p < 0.01$), with the cohesive conceptions variable ($r = -0.24$, $p < 0.01$) and the

Table 4.5 Correlations Between Elements of the Experience of Learning through Discussions and Performance Outcomes

Variables	Variables									
	2 cc	3 fsa	4 fda	5 osa	6 oda	7 aws	8 esis	9 gts	10 osi	11 fm
Conceptions										
1 Fragmented conception (fc)	−.15	.46**	−.07	.51**	−.01	−.31**	.13	.10	−.01	−.33**
2 Cohesive conception (cc)		−.24*	.63**	−.05	.27**	.29**	.34**	.27**	.26*	.14
Approaches										
3 Face-to-face surface approach (fsa)			−.28**	.39**	−.09	−.47**	−.09	−.16	−.26*	−.22*
4 Face-to-face deep approach (fda)				−.04	.44**	.19*	.36**	.44**	.47**	.01
5 Online surface approach (osa)					−.13	−.36**	.09	.11	.03	−.22*
6 Online deep approach (oda)						.14	.22*	.07	.20*	−.01
Perceptions										
7 Appropriate workload (aws)							.15	.17	.26*	.23*
8 Emphasis on independence (esis)								.58**	.52**	−.14
9 Good teaching (gts)									.51**	−.03**
Overall satisfaction										
11 Overall satisfaction Item (osi)										−.12
Performance outcome										
12 Final mark (fm)										

* p<0.05, ** p<0.01, n=115

face-to-face deep approach variable ($r = -0.28$, $p < 0.01$), the overall satisfaction item ($r = -0.26$, $p < 0.01$), and the final mark ($r = -0.20$, $p < 0.01$).

Table 4.6 identifies two factors that emerged from the factor analysis. Factor 1 shows that a higher score on the face-to-face deep approach variable (0.78) is positively related to the online deep approach variable (0.37), the cohesive conceptions variable (0.60), the emphasis on independence variable (0.68) and the good teaching variable (0.70). Factor 2 reveals that a higher score on

Table 4.6 Principal Components of Factor Analyses of Conceptions, Approaches, Perceptions, Performance

Variables	Factors	
	1	*2*
Approaches		
Face-to-face surface approach		.62
Face-to-face deep approach	.74	
Online surface approach		.66
Online deep approach	.37	
Conceptions		
Fragmented conception		.75
Cohesive conception	.60	
Perceptions		
Appropriate workload		−.51
Emphasis on independence	.68	
Good teaching	.66	
Performance		
Final mark		−.41

Loadings of magnitude less than .4 omitted. Varimax Rotation, KMO=.68
Eigen-value 2.9 and 2.2, 51% variance explained, n=115

Source: Ellis & Calvo, 2006.

the face-to-face surface approach variable (0.62) is positively related to the online surface approach variable (0.66), the fragmented conception variable (0.75), and negatively related to the appropriate workload variable (−0.51) and the final mark (−0.41).

The results of the factor analysis suggest that the deep approach variables for the face-to-face and online contexts are strongly and positively associated with the cohesive conception variable, the emphasis on independence variable and the good teaching variable. Similarly, the surface approach variables for the face-to-face and online contexts are strongly positively associated with the fragmented conception variable (0.75), and negatively associated with the appropriate workload variable and the final mark (−0.41).

The Student Experience of E-learning and Discussions at the Level of the Whole Degree Programme

The preceding studies investigated discussions at the level of courses, where the term 'courses' refers to the units (or subjects) that make up a degree programme. Investigating the student experience of e-learning at a higher level within the structure of degree programmes is difficult because sufficiently common experiences across courses are often hard to identify.

Table 4.7 Items on the E-learning Scale

E-learning scale (E-LS)

---

14. Where it was used, information technology helped me to learn.

38. Resources on University of Sydney websites (e.g. WebCT, Blackboard, degree course sites, faculty sites, etc.) supported my learning.

41. Communicating online with students and staff helped my learning.

43. The online learning experiences of my degree course were well-integrated with my face-to-face learning.

45. My online experiences helped me engage actively in my learning.

One study (Ginns & Ellis, forthcoming) has examined student perceptions of e-learning at the degree level through the development of a student experience e-learning scale. The purpose of the e-learning scale was to investigate how key aspects of e-learning were related to the face-to-face experience at the level of the degree, across a large student population (n=3602) comprising many courses at the degree level. The e-learning scale linked how communicating online was related to other key aspects of e-learning and the student experience. The scale was developed in relation to a validated degree-level teaching evaluation instrument (Ginns, Prosser & Barrie, 2007): the student course experience questionnaire (SCEQ).

The design of the SCEQ represented key aspects of the students' face-to-face experience through the good teaching scale, the clear goals and standards scale, the appropriate assessment scale, the appropriate workload scale and the generic skills scale. The online part of the student experience was captured through the items in the (new) e-learning subscale. The items of the e-learning scale and its correlations with the other subscales are shown in Tables 4.7 and 4.8.

Table 4.8 Correlations Between the E-learning Scale and other Scales of the SCEQ

	GTS	CGS	AAS	AWS	E-LS	GSS
Factor correlations						
Good teaching scale α=.83	1					
Clear goals and standards scale α=.80	.64	1				
Appropriate assessment scale α=.71	.34	.38	1			
Appropriate workload scale α=.76	.38	.22	.45	1		
E-learning scale α=.81	.22	.23	.01	−.05	1	
Generic skills scale α=.78	.58	.38	.15	.27	.34	1
Correlations with overall satisfaction with degree quality item	.61	.47	.26	.27	.27	.53

n=3602

While this approach offers a complementary way into investigating the student experience of e-learning, at the level of the degree, some care needs to be taken with its interpretation. Reviews describing the uptake of e-learning across universities internationally, highlight the variation and differences in scale and scope of e-learning within universities (e.g. Hawkins & Rudy, 2004, 2007; Zastrocky, Harris & Lowendahl, 2007). Until we have more contextually-sensitive studies, at the level of degrees, across different types of campus-based universities internationally, the structure of scales intended to tap students' experiences of e-learning is likely to continue to shift (Ginns & Ellis, forthcoming).

Concluding Comments

Chapter 4 has considered the student experience of learning through discussions, drawing particularly on studies in social work and Web-engineering. Significant relationships can be observed between key aspects of the experience: logical relations between deep approaches, cohesive conceptions, positive perceptions of the learning context and relatively higher levels of performance are some of these. These have serious implications for people professionally involved in helping students and teachers to improve such experiences. We pick up on these points in our discussion of feedback for curriculum design in Chapter 8 and of campus design and planning in Chapter 10.

One of the purposes of presenting the cluster, correlation and factor analyses in the preceding discussion is to offer evidence for the proposition that students' experiences of e-learning need to be understood in relation to the whole of their experience of learning, whether at course or whole degree level. Clearly e-learning is part of a broader experience of learning. Its associations with other parts of the experience and the implications of these associations are only just beginning to be understood. We need more research-based evidence about the interrelatedness of the parts of the student experience in order to more deeply understand which aspects are likely to account for high quality learning outcomes.

The above studies have investigated only a few of the possible variables that might be considered. Other variables that are under, or which may merit, investigation include student experiences of design for learning, their perceptions of the resources of the internet, their role in a community of learners, and the like.

The benefits of e-learning for the development of student understanding are not limited to discussions. In the next chapter, we turn to students' experiences of learning through inquiry.

5

Student Experiences of
E-learning in Higher Education
Learning through Inquiry

Introduction

'Learning through inquiry' is an umbrella term that covers a range of pedagogical approaches united by the central place they give to students' investi-
gative work. Students independently or collaboratively research a topic or
problem and, in so doing, have the opportunity to gain a richer understanding of the area being researched, as well as greater proficiency in
research skills. Learning through inquiry is widely recognised as a pedagogical approach in higher education. One of its most common manifest-
ations is as problem-based learning (PBL), but there are a range of other
related methods, such as project-based learning, case-based learning and
collaborative knowledge construction (Scardamalia & Bereiter, 2006; Goodyear & Zenios, 2007). In addition to potential educational benefits of the
kind described above (deeper understanding of phenomena; honed inquiry
skills, etc.), learning through inquiry is often motivated by a desire to encourage more active, authentic and student-centred forms of learning, in which
students take more responsibility for the direction and management of
their own learning, acquiring useful metacognitive skills as they do so (e.g.
Vermunt, 1998; Herrington & Oliver, 2000; Loyens, Rikers & Schmidt, 2006).
Within this area of research, there is a sense that inquiry-based forms of
educational activity are particularly appropriate in a complex knowledge
society – that they are better aligned with the needs of knowledge work
than are forms of education that took shape in the industrial age (Goodyear
& Ellis, 2007).

   With the advent of the internet, the range of resources, and consequently
the range of strategies required to successfully search for, evaluate, identify and
integrate knowledge from a number of sources, has become more complex. We
believe that university teachers are currently at a disadvantage because they
lack understanding about (a) how students integrate internet-based inquiries
into their broader inquiries into problems, cases, and projects, and (b) why

students make the decisions they do during an inquiry process. This makes it harder to decide:

- how to design support for inquiry-based activities that traverse physical and online contexts, and
- how to approach teaching when students' inquiry-based activities traverse both of these contexts.

A description of the methodologies and data involved in the studies discussed below was provided in Chapter 4. As with our research on discussions, we suggest that a valuable starting point for improving our understanding of how students learn through inquiry is to begin by considering their *approaches*.

Learning through Inquiry: Case-based Experiences

The study reported here investigated the learning experiences of second and third year veterinary science students, who were required to investigate case studies of animals in poor health. With respect to their case-based learning, students were assessed in terms of the quality of the analysis evident in their written reports, as well as the value of their contributions in class. The case-based learning processes involved lectures, practical laboratory sessions and tutorials, revolving around the cases and making use of online case study activities and materials. The online materials for the case studies were substantial and provided the foundations for the students' case-based learning activities. The materials included:

- case scenarios giving authentic situations in which the students could orientate their discussions, conceptualisation and approaches;
- guidelines on how to complete case study reports, to structure findings in professionally appropriate ways;
- indicative commentary from personnel in the industry via audio/video clips;
- commentary from experts within the field via audio/video clips;
- annotated images of the animals showing symptoms or clinical signs for discussion;
- laboratory test results of the animals for the purpose of analysis;
- relevant library reference materials for background information on the theories and illnesses involved.

Students were offered background knowledge about the case in lectures. A practical class allowed them to relate the ideas in the lectures to hands-on veterinary activities. After these stages, the students worked on the case studies in small groups and then reflected on conclusions about the case studies in 'case resolutions' sessions. Considering the online resources more closely, issues that motivated discussion about each case were presented through a scenario. Each scenario provided case information about a sick or injured animal drawn from an authentic situation. The objectives of the case study were to encourage the students to integrate and analyse knowledge in a way that enabled them to demonstrate their understanding of the problems of an animal by completing a 'case report form'. The case report form underpinned a decision-making process used to get to the heart of the issues that were implicated in the illnesses of the animal.

In interviews at the end of the semester, students were asked how they approached learning through the case studies. Some students reported an awareness of aspects of a bigger context in which the veterinary cases sat. The following quotations are examples of comments made by one group of students.

Student 1: Visualise the case, what was happening, what was going on. Consider and think about the case, consider other differentials that could cause a disease. It encouraged broader thinking. Tried to fit this new knowledge and link it to past information to gain a wider picture.

Student 2: Lectures, learn, know about the stuff we need to know. Prac classes, learn what to do in practice. Self-study, reviewing the stuff we learnt in lectures. Reading books, as lectures may not be as detailed. Writing my own notes, I learn better this way. Jotting notes in lectures, helps do revision, integrates individual bits into a bigger picture.

From the extracts above, a deep approach to solving the case studies in face-to-face situations involved thinking about possible differential diagnoses behind the disease, engaging in broader thinking by relating the case information to other knowledge, by reviewing the knowledge from lectures and practical classes, often through writing and integrating the ideas into a bigger picture.

Another group of students reported approaching the case studies in class in a qualitatively different way.

Student 3: Did pracs, tutorials and lectures to get all sources of information that we would need to solve problems.

Student 4: So we'd get a problem, look at. The way it was assessed and the only thing we physically had to do was a presentation at the end of every week, so everything was geared towards the presentation, and who was going to speak and who was going to do what. So we'd look at a problem, try to work out what it was saying and we had a template sheet that we had to hand in, that prompted different questions that we had to answer and help us to overrule and help us come to terms with the case study, and usually each week, someone would get that sheet, write down the answers in the little boxes and submit it. So there wasn't a lot of coming together and trying to analyse it.

The comments made by students 3 and 4 are typical of a surface approach to learning through the case studies in class. Intending to find answers to problems without much real analysis of the case studies was a key characteristic of these approaches.

Similar variation was found amongst the students when asked about their approaches to learning through the online materials for the case studies.

Student 5:   We looked at all of the resources/data systematically (as we would have received them in an actual clinical situation) and discussed ideas as we went along. This helped us to develop our hypotheses differential diagnoses logically and ensured we didn't jump to conclusions.

Student 6:   I looked at the history, clinical signs, test results and used my knowledge and what I learnt in class to give a differential diagnosis.

Deep online approaches to investigating the case studies involved a significant engagement with the key data related to the state of the animals' health, such as the history, clinical reports, test outcomes. This type of approach seemed to involve an intent to hypothesise and test resolutions to the case studies.

An intent to engage in analysis and hypothesis appeared to be absent from the approaches reported by some other students.

Student 7:   Accessed the case from the website. Read the case so we know what is was about. Look at all the pictures and read the instructions for that task. Researched using links provided or just databases and search engines. Typed up our answers.

Some students reported trying to resolve the cases without using the online learning materials.

Student 8:   Didn't use anything on the website. Used text books and lecture notes.

Associations amongst Parts of the Experience of Case-based Learning

In this study, the researchers also identified qualitatively different *conceptions* of learning through case studies. There were key differences in how the students reported their conceptions of case studies. One was to use them as a way of recalling information – which was labelled a fragmented conception – the other was to use them to apply theory to practice, often in authentic situations – which was labelled a cohesive conception. Table 5.1 shows the associations amongst conceptions and approaches to case-based learning in this veterinary science study.

Table 5.1 shows that there is a positive and logical association between conceptions of case-based learning and both face-to-face and online approaches to case studies. In other words, a deep approach (in both face-to-face and online contexts) is related to a cohesive conception of learning through case studies. Similarly, a surface approach (both face-to-face and online) is related to a fragmented conception of learning through case studies. We will return to discuss the significance of this finding after we have presented some parallel data on problem-based learning in the next section.

The veterinary science study also revealed associations between the categories of conception and the marks achieved by the year 2 and 3 students.

Tables 5.2 and 5.3 show that cohesive conceptions of case-based learning were associated with higher final marks than were fragmented conceptions

Table 5.1 Associations Amongst Key Aspects of the Case-based Learning Experience

| Approaches to case-based learning | Conceptions of case-based learning | | |
| | Fragmented | Cohesive | |
	Categories A,B	Categories C,D	Totals
Face-to-face			
Surface			
(A,B)	56	44	100
Deep			
(C,D)	5	28	33
Total	61	72	133
Online			
Surface			
(A,B)	59	59	118
Deep			
(C,D)	2	13	15
Total	61	72	133

Face-to-face: chi^2 = 16.7, phi = .35, p<.001,
Online: chi^2 = 7.2, phi = .23, p<.01

Source: Ellis, Marcus & Taylor, 2006.

Table 5.2 Relationship Between Conceptions and Performance of Year 2 Students

Aspects of case-based learning	Final mark		
	Mean#	SD	Effect size (es=)
Conceptions			
Fragmented	65.23	10.33	0.82
Cohesive	73.47	9.77	
T test: T=	3.11*		

n=65, *p<.05, #=Mark out of 100

(year 2; t = 3.11, p < 0.05, es = 0.82; year 3, t = 2.15, p < 0.05, es = 0.50). These are large and medium effect sizes, similar to the effect sizes found in related studies (Crawford et. al, 1994; Ellis, Calvo, Levy & Tan, 2004).

Approaches to Learning through Inquiry: Problem-based Learning Methods

The study reported here involved pharmacy students. The field of pharmacy education is developing quite rapidly and one aspect of recent change is the range of professional online databases that are becoming regarded as essential for practitioners and students. Students engaging with these resources in a fourth year undergraduate course showed significant variation in how they approached their problem-based learning activities, including the various resources provided for them (Ellis et al., 2008a).

The students involved in the study attended two hours of lectures, four hours of tutorials and five hours of clinical placements (community or hospital pharmacy) each week. Over a semester of 14 weeks, they worked on eight or nine problem scenarios, each of which extended over a period of three tutorial sessions, during which students were guided by tutors. In the first session, a new scenario was given to each group. The scenario was designed to prompt students to hypothesise about, and research, the presenting signs, symptoms or product request of a patient and to determine what

Table 5.3 Relationship Between Conceptions and Performance of Year 3 Students

Aspects of case-based learning	Final mark		
	Mean#	SD	Effect size (es=)
Conceptions			
Fragmented	62.13	7.3	0.50
Cohesive	65.84	7.6	
T test: T=	2.15*		

n=77, *p<.05, #=Mark out of 100

further information they would require to identify any underlying issues or problems. In the second session, students were given more precise information upon request, such as the patient's medication history. Based on this information, students conducted further research, which allowed them to determine what further information they required or to identify specific problems and possible management options. In the final session, students presented their medication management plan and discussed this with another group of students.

During these problem-based learning activities, students were expected to make substantial use of the professional databases and texts, both during and between tutorial sessions. The online professional databases included: medication databases such as Australian Medicines Handbook, Micromedex, eMIMS, Therapeutic Guidelines; disease information such as the MERC manual, medical organisations such as the National Heart Foundation or Breast Cancer organisation, and bibliographic databases such as MedLine, EMBASE, IPA (International Pharmaceutical Abstracts) and PUBMED.

The following extracts are from interviews in response to questions asking students how they approached engaging with the problems face-to-face in class and online. The course required a very high entrance mark and there was a significant element of competitiveness apparent from the students' responses in the interviews. The researchers felt that this contributed to the emergence of a third category of approach in this study, referred to as an 'achieving' approach (Biggs, 1987).

Deep approaches to learning have an orientation towards engaging with the subject matter in ways that promote understanding. *Achieving* approaches can exhibit similar *strategies* to deep approaches. However, since their focus is often spurred on by a desire to excel in assessment, an *intention* to understand deeply is often absent. Researchers have suggested that, in this category of approach, long-term knowledge retention rates are poor (Biggs, 1987) and that there are limited opportunities for the knowledge to become embedded in professional capabilities (cf. Yinger & Hendricks-Lee, 1993; Sternberg & Horvath, 1999).

Students in the pharmacy course were asked how they approached learning through the case studies in class.

Student 1:   Through assessing the cues in the scenario, forming an inquiry plan, brainstorming hypotheses, further inquiry to narrow down possible hypotheses. We then split the topic areas/questions up, come together to discuss, go away, write up our sections plus email to the scribe. By hypothesising all possible causes/problems, it allows us to think 'outside the square' and not just jump up to obvious conclusions. This will hopefully encourage us to develop

> this process to use in practice to provide the best possible
> patient care.

Responses such as that of student 1 were identified as a deep face-to-face approach to problem-based learning in the pharmacy course. Key aspects of the approach included: refining the way inquiry-based activities were undertaken using cues, planning, hypothesising in order to narrow the possible options, resisting temptation to go for the most obvious answers in a context that focused on quality patient care.

The researchers felt that student 2 provided a similar response.

Student 2:   Initially it's almost like an upside-down pyramid where you're kind of trying to narrow down your options, down to that one final thing. And, so usually, the session one, they give you basic information, basic complaints. Go off and research based on those. You come back, they give you um, the current status, the medication that the patient's taking, the clinical pathology for the patient . . . even though you might fine tune it down to say ten options, OK, there could have been an option that you ruled out earlier but you kind of go, hold on a second, what's given here sounds more like that, you know. It could be . . . there's always like additional issues that you may consider.

Similarities in the approaches in the first and second quotations include the narrowing down of options to solve the problem, planning carefully by looking at the cues of the case through the pathology, and being careful about making a conclusion based on the evidence being presented. The difference between the two approaches was not apparent until students from each group were asked why they approached the cases in class the way they did. Student 3 reveals an intent consistent with a deep approach; student 4, consistent with an achieving approach.

Student 3:   I find that problem-based learning especially, like our PBLs are excellent in that, I think that when you research something yourself and you learn it that way, it stays with you for longer than someone telling you what the answer is. So I think that in that respect PBLs are really good and it makes me like want to do the work because, I mean, I know I have to do it and I know I have to know it. So that way I sort of remember it for longer.

Student 4:   Realistically, the fact that we had to hand it in. That

it's part of the process of getting the marks and the
reason.

The appearance of an achieving approach in the pharmacy course did not
mean that a surface approach was not also a feature of some students'
experience.

Student 5:   So basically, you know, someone would just be standing at
the whiteboard and various people would just say what's
sort of on their minds sort of. Yeah, what they think is
relevant to our case with that information presented . . . .
Well um I guess partly because with this, with the PBLs
um a report is written up at the end so. I guess it's compiling data for the report. So yeah, I guess the scribe is
mainly for information gathering so. And so everyone can
get down information . . . . So you're just getting – sort of
pooling information that everyone has so just basically,
yeah . . .

A surface approach to problem-based learning included approaching the
resolution of a problem as if it was an information collection exercise,
best realised by compiling data, by pooling it for distribution with little
concern for a deeper analysis of the data and how that might relate to
meaningful hypotheses.

The variation found in the students' face-to-face approaches to the problems
was consistent with the variation found when we looked at students' online
approaches to the problems.

Student 6:   Yeah when I'm um searching at home I'd probably use a
lot more online resources then text resources. That's
mainly to do the discussion questions. So looking up the
information to answer those it will be either um online
versions of the Therapeutic Guidelines, the MIMS online,
AMH, the and again probably using Google for some
broad information. Looking up health government health
websites like Health Insight or um other organisations
such um one called the Family Doctor. And also myself,
I look up original papers for MedLine . . . . Usually for,
if there's something in particular that I know there's
probably been research on. And that's probably conten-
tious issue – I'll use those so I can backup um general
information that you've found elsewhere.

Student 6's comments highlight some of the aspects of a deep approach to online inquiry. This included deliberate use of the professional resources in tandem with a generic search engine (Google) to provide a broader context of information, use of research-based information from professionally recognised sources (MedLine), and using all of the resources to triangulate ideas for the purposes of verification and strengthening of a position on important issues.

The approach reported by student 7 was classified as an achieving approach. Again, it is similar in nature to the deep approach, however the student (separately) reported engaging in these strategies mainly to maximise assessment grades.

Student 7:   (Google is) generally the first thing I do because it gives you a very basic understanding and it just sort of um guides you in the right direction and like it's not enough information, it never is, but it's sort of um sort of like what leads you in the right direction to you know find other information. And depending on what information I'm looking for, I'll go to different sources so (e.g., MERC, TG, AMH).

A surface approach to online inquiry about the problems was also a feature of some students' experience.

Student 8:   Initially I use the library website like the MedLine, PapMed(sic) or the journal. But after a few classes I found that using Google search is more easier, it's more easy than like usually there are more things to look at and also the thing is more appropriate – more general. Whereas the PapMed and MedLine usually regarding to research. I know these websites have very good evidence to support the things but it's just too scientific to read – too boring to read.

A surface approach to online inquiry about the problems included over-reliance on a generic search engine to source information and resolve inquiries. This was typically coupled with little in-depth searching of professionally-recognised sources, little critical evaluation of the information chosen, and no real awareness of a need to triangulate information.

The identification of three categories of approach in the pharmacy course increased the complexity of the associations amongst the key aspects of the experience of problem-based learning.

Associations amongst Parts of the Experience of Problem-based Learning

The study revealed associations (amongst the parts of the experience of problem-based learning) which were consistent in nature with those found in the case-based learning study described above, and with those found in the studies into learning through discussions described in Chapter 4.

Table 5.4 is a contingency table that shows associations amongst face-to-face and online approaches to problem-based learning. Overall, the associations amongst face-to-face and online approaches are significant. A series of 2×2 cross tabulations were conducted across the 3×3 table, sequentially excluding from the analysis deep, achieving and surface categories. This allowed the researchers to identify which were the significant associations amongst the approaches. The results reveal that a deep face-to-face approach to PBL tends to be associated with a deep online approach while a surface face-to-face approach to PBL tends to be associated with a surface online approach (for 2×2 table, $\chi^2 = 47.977$, phi $= .605$, $p < .001$).

Associations were also found with the students' course outcomes. Table 5.5 identifies associations between students' approaches to PBL and their final marks.

Table 5.5 shows that students who were classified as adopting a deep face-to-face approach to the problems tended to perform at a higher level than students who were classified as adopting achieving or surface face-to-face approaches ($t = 3.5$ $p < 0.05$, $es = 0.35$; $t = 2.2$, $p < 0.05$, $es = 0.28$). In addition, it shows that students who described taking a deep online approach to the problems tended to perform at a higher level than students adopting a surface online approach ($t = 2.5$, $p < 0.05$, $es = 0.28$). These are medium effect sizes. No significant difference in the final mark was found between deep and achieving approaches in the online context.

Table 5.4 Associations Amongst the Different Categories of Approaches to PBL in Pharmacy

	Face-to-face approaches			
	Deep (A)	*Achieving* (B)	*Surface* (C,D,E)	*Total*
Online approaches				
Deep (A)	14	2	3	19
Achieving (B)	0	7	4	11
Surface (C,D,E)	12	22	102	136
Total	26	31	109	166

Online: $\chi^2 = 70.1$, Cramer's phi$= .65$, $p < .001$

Table 5.5 Relationships Between Approaches and Performance

Aspects of PBL	Final mark		
	Mean[1]	SD	Effect size (s)
Approaches face-to-face			
Deep	74.5	8.5	
Surface	68.5	7.7	0.35
t =	3.5*		
Approaches face-to-face			
Deep	74.5	8.5	
Achieving	69.2	9.6	0.28
t =	2.2*		
Approaches online			
Deep	74.0	8.2	0.28
Surface	69.0	9.0	
t =	2.5*		

$n = 166$, *$p < .05$, **$p < .001$, [1]Mark out of 100.

The Student Experience of Internet Resources when Related to Learning Outcomes

One of the unanticipated insights of the pharmacy study was that many of the students did not understand the variable nature and quality of the resources available to them on the internet. Some internet-based resources and tools are consistently seen by pharmacy teachers and professionals as of high quality and high professional relevance. Others are seen as useful, but needing careful interpretation. Others again are seen as having dubious value. Students, in contrast, turn out to exhibit considerable variations in their sense of the quality and appropriateness of these various tools and resources.

We revisited the interviews to analyse how the students talked about the resources available to them via the internet, particularly in relation to the pharmacy problem scenarios. We looked for signs that students distinguished between different kinds of tools and resources and for evidence that they were mindful of the variable quality of the information to be found on the internet. It is hard to draw firm conclusions from the transcript data, but there are warning signs, as well as indications of promising directions for future research.

Broadly speaking, a significant subset of the pharmacy students experienced the online pharmaceutical resources as some kind of undifferentiated, amorphous mass, and were unable to discern any internal structure, or assign any distinctive purpose to its different parts. By contrast, other students were able to discern a structure to the internet resources, as they related to the PBL scenarios, showing awareness of the variable quality of the information and its usefulness.

Some students demonstrated an awareness of the internet resources that was comparatively elaborate and structured, in relation to the pharmacy problem scenarios.

> Student 1:   After class, I usually look up information of a disease and discussion points from the tutorial from the online environment. I always *use MERC for a basic disease and treatment* explanations. I like *eJournals from the library as they are evidence-based suggestions* and recommendations for different situations. I also like to readup from the *government websites as it gives us an idea of how a disease is perceived and managed* in different countries.

Student 1's account is consistent with seeing a logical structure for the internet resources, in relation to their experience of the pharmacy PBL scenarios. Three categories or sources of information are identified: MERC, eJournals and government websites. The student attributes a purpose related to learning to each of the categories: disease and treatment explanations, evidence-based suggestions for dealing with diseases in different situations and how diseases are perceived and managed in different countries. Student 2 below describes a similar experience of the online environment.

> Student 2:   Well, I usually tend to do – just to start with, I do a general Google – just a general Google search to see sort of what's out there and how much information is out there. If *it's a specific disease state, like if it's a cardiac thing, I'll go to the National Heart Foundation website because they've often got a lot of information that's also good to give to patients.* So I find that's good and tends to put everything in laymen's terms. As far as *research, I'd of course go, I like the um Australian Prescriber and National Prescriber,* I think it is. Because they tend to be a little bit more up-to-date and otherwise I'll use MedLine but, you often find that you'll get quite old articles and I don't like old Med. Other than that, if I can't get that information, I would just do a Google search and just start trying to refine my search so instead of just looking for one keyword, I'll give the disease state and something specific about that that I'm looking for. I do use the *AMH to remind sometimes . . . to look up just a quick overview of the drugs, adverse affects, and dosages to check the dosages.*

The comments made by Student 2 also indicate an awareness of some structure to the relevant internet-based resources. Four tools/sources of information are identified: search engines (in this case Google), government organisations, research sources and medication databases. The student attributes a purpose related to learning to each of the categories: general overview, disease states and non-technical language, research and dosages.

In contrast to students 1 and 2, some other students reported experiences that suggest they were not able to discern variations between different internet-based resources, as they related to learning.

> Student 3: Um Google is very convenient 'cause – sometimes there is heaps of information about one thing and I don't know what to choose. And I say oh my God, I can't put all this information in my discussion point or medication review but *Google gives the main point of the work.*

Like student 2, student 3 identifies a search engine as a source of information for the problem scenarios. Unlike the previous student however, the student does not indicate a more complex awareness that attributes a purpose to Google in relation to the pharmacy problem scenario (such as providing a general overview of the topic), nor an awareness of how other sources of information can provide a more structured and deeper understanding of the scenario. An 'unstructured' awareness of internet tools/resources is also demonstrated by student 4.

> Student 4: Google's fantastic . . . you type in define then colon and then you write down whatever word that needs to be defined. And it comes up with a whole list of definitions . . . I use that so – and that's really quick like during question time when the tutor asks what's this disease, I just type it in and oh it's this one . . . *Google's the main thing online.*

Comments made by student 4 suggest a lack of awareness of other key parts of the online environment for the pharmacy problem scenarios. The main source of information for this student is a generic search engine (Google). This contrasts significantly with students who have assigned a purpose to other professional sources of knowledge in the online environment for the different aspects of pharmacy problem scenarios, such as dosages, drug interactions and evidence-based practice.

While considering these comments, it was clear to the researchers that students reporting a more discriminating awareness of internet resources were also able to provide a reason for their choice of resource: they assigned distinct purposes to the different sites. The researchers looked at students who reported a less discriminating ('unstructured') awareness of the internet to see what they said about critical evaluation of the sites. Their strategies for evaluating the quality of information on sites provided by Google appeared relatively undeveloped.

Student 5:   I will choose the GOV which is the government website . . . .
              If there's no government website I'll go for the maybe
              ORG, the organisation Web. I know that information
              might not be correct but it's better than like advertising
              websites.

Student 6:   If it says DOT, GOV or like, if you know it's an
              organisation or if it's supported by the government
              – yeah.

Students with a limited awareness of the professional pharmacy sites and their purposes tended to display rudimentary strategies for evaluating the websites identified by the search engines they used. Not being aware of the professional standing of the pharmacy websites, they fell back on generic rules of thumb for assessing the veracity of information of websites (by URL). These heuristics are inappropriate for high stakes professional practice.

Further research is required to see whether and how variations in students' internet-based inquiry practices relate to their deeper conceptions about learning, information and knowledge.

Concluding Comments

Chapter 5 has reflected on student experiences of learning through inquiry. Particular examples chosen to frame the discussion were case-based learning and problem-based learning. In broad terms, the findings align with those we presented in Chapter 4, concerning learning through discussion. Two key points emerge. First, the introduction of e-learning tools, methods and resources add further complexity to the challenges students see themselves facing. (Students do not necessarily feel this is a bad thing in itself, but as we know from the data reported in Chapter 3, they want their teachers to acknowledge that there *is* additional complexity and act on the matter.) Second, students' intentions and strategies tend to be consistent across face-to-face and online contexts. If they adopt a deep approach in face-to-face learning they are often likely to adopt a deep approach when working online. The same is true with respect to the adoption of surface approaches.

There are several important practical implications. Perhaps the most important lesson to draw is that the introduction of e-learning, by itself, cannot be expected to shift students' approaches to learning. Students need to be helped to deal with the relatively novel challenges of e-learning in an integrated, coherent way. It will not be appropriate to have strategies for improving their approaches to e-learning that are disconnected from consideration of their learning more generally. In short, any initiatives teachers take to help students get more from their learning should address learning as a whole. There may be some detailed things to say specially about e-learning activities, but these detailed messages need to align with what is said and done more broadly about learning as a whole. The approach needs to be holistic, and consider the whole of the learning ecology.

We pick up some of these implications for more thorough consideration in the chapters on teaching-as-design and on the planning and management of learning spaces, in Chapters 8 and 9.

6
University Teachers' Experiences of E-learning in an Ecology

Introduction

The preceding chapters have largely adopted a student perspective on the experience of e-learning. In this chapter, we focus on e-learning from the teacher's point of view. This chapter summarises recent research on university teachers' experiences of teaching in situations where their students are expected to make significant use of e-learning, integrated with various face-to-face activities. The research we report is with colleagues in Australia and England, as well as some conducted by some of our research students. We draw out some of the implications of this research for thinking about the improvement of teaching and the design and management of courses.

The older literature on teaching with the aid of ICT over-represents experience drawn from distance-teaching universities. This is understandable, given that most of the early work carried out in more conventional universities typically involved just a few pioneers working on their own courses. Distance-teaching universities, when they decide to make serious use of ICT, tend to do so on a substantial scale. For example, the UK Open University has proved to be an extremely productive source of expertise concerning the use of e-learning in higher education (see e.g., Laurillard, 1993, 2002; Mason & Kaye, 1989; Salmon, 2001, 2002). However, this also underlines the point that our knowledge of comparable teaching experiences in conventional universities is relatively weak (Bliuc, Goodyear & Ellis, 2007).

In some ways, the contrast between distance and more conventional university teaching is too sharply drawn. The latter have, for a long time, experimented with forms of distance teaching and the distance teaching universities tend to use a mix of methods, including locally-based face-to-face tutorials (Guri-Rosenblit, 1999; Lewis, 2002). That said, our focus in this book is on situations in which e-learning is used as *part* of the teaching methodology: in the ideal case, e-learning is thoroughly integrated with all other aspects of the students' learning, both on-campus and off-campus. Understanding a successful integration of e-learning within an ecology of learning at all levels of a university is central to our aims.

Recognition of the complementary role of e-learning in a broader ecology enables us to discuss e-learning at university in a more nuanced and precise way. The ecological perspective also means that we will not be paying much attention to the myriad of studies that have tried to compare e-learning with some non-electronic alternatives. (Many of these studies end up finding no significant difference in outcomes – see e.g., Phipps & Merisotis, 1999 – or, when they do, they struggle to explain what exactly has caused the difference – see e.g., Goodyear & Ellis, 2008). Rather, we will focus on research that is trying to reveal what is happening when university teachers are aiming to combine their use of ICT with other, complementary, teaching strategies. There is still remarkably little literature on this topic.

Research into Conceptions of, and Approaches to, University Teaching

In Chapters 4 and 5, we provided an account of students' experiences of learning through discussion and learning through inquiry, in situations where their activity was spread across face-to-face and online contexts. This account drew its core concepts and methods from an established tradition of research on student learning, in which students' conceptions and approaches are fore-grounded. We draw upon similar methods and constructs here, reporting on what teachers say about learning and teaching when e-learning is part of the pedagogical mix.

There is a small body of research on teaching conceptions and approaches, which can be located in a broader field of research into university teachers' thinking, knowledge and beliefs (Hativa & Goodyear, 2002). One of the main things we know about research into approaches to teaching is that some ways of teaching do not seem to be related to successful student learning (Marton, Entwistle & Hounsell, 1997; Ramsden, 1993, 2002; Prosser, Trigwell & Taylor, 1994; Prosser & Trigwell, 1999; Biggs, 1999; Biggs & Tang, 2007). Broadly speaking, studies tend to identify student-focussed and teacher-focussed approaches to teaching. The former tend to be related to intentions that seek to help students to achieve conceptual development, while the latter tend to be related to intentions that are more closely related to transmission of information. One of the first things to note about approaches to teaching is that they are very different from concepts of teaching (Prosser & Trigwell, 1999). Approaches to teaching are about *doing*, about the strategies and intentions underpinning teachers' actions as they help students to develop their comprehension. Concepts of teaching are typically developed from the way teachers report *thinking* about something. Their structure is not divided into strategies and intentions, but is about the related ideas that make up the concept. For the purposes of discussing these ideas in this chapter, we will concentrate on studies reported in Trigwell, Prosser, and Taylor (1994) and Kember and Kwan (2000).

In Australia, Trigwell et al. (1994) followed early work into student conceptions of learning (for example Säljö, 1979; Marton et al., 1983) with an investigation into teacher conceptions of student learning and teacher conceptions of teaching. They identified qualitatively different categories of teacher conceptions of student learning across a sample of 24 university teachers. Relatively poorer conceptions focused on learning as accumulating information and acquiring concepts, while relatively better conceptions focused on conceptual development and change. In the same study, qualitatively different conceptions of teaching were identified, ranging from teaching as primarily being about transmission of concepts and teacher knowledge to teaching in order to help students develop and change their conceptions. Shortly after, a group of related studies looked at links between academics' educational conceptions and design involving ICT (for example, Bain & McNaught, 1996; Bain, McNaught, Carmel & Luekenhausen, 1998) which provided a way of describing qualitative differences amongst the educational beliefs of teachers and the designs they engaged in. Some years later in Hong Kong, another related study investigated approaches to teaching in higher education with 17 teachers from engineering, social work and allied health professions (Kember & Kwan, 2000). Conceptions of teaching were categorised as 'transmission of knowledge' or 'learning facilitation'. Approaches to teaching were broadly categorised as content-centred or learning centred. The analysis provided dimensions of the strategies involved: instructional strategies, focus towards the class or individual, type of assessment, accommodation for students' strengths and weaknesses, and the source of knowledge or experience. The researchers were able to place the lecturers' approaches to teaching on a continuum for each of these five dimensions. Each tended to be either more content centred or more student centred. Kember and Kwan also found consistent associations between conceptions of teaching and approaches to teaching.

Studies such as these suggest that the quality of teaching is related to how teachers approach and report thinking about their teaching. Metaphorically speaking, some experiences of teaching involve conceptions of students as empty vessels, into which the teacher pours knowledge. This contrasts strongly with other ways of experiencing teaching which view the challenge as helping students to become active engaged learners, eager to experiment with, and develop their own personalised understanding of, the key ideas of the topics under study (Prosser & Trigwell, 1999). Our core interest in this chapter is to see whether similar conceptions and approaches can be found in situations where e-learning and face-to-face learning are combined.

In following discussion we summarise research that has investigated teaching in such situations. We regard these studies as exploratory rather than exhaustive, and point towards an emerging set of ideas that warrant serious consideration. Although we are not very comfortable with the term 'blended learning' (cf. Oliver & Trigwell, 2005), this phrase has been used quite extensively in the studies we report and to avoid confusion and awkward circumlocutions we will use it here. In this chapter, the term is used to mean situations in which e-learning is playing a part in a broader set of learning activities, such as those associated with lectures, laboratories, tutorials, seminars, clinics and the like.

Variation in Teacher Conceptions of Blended Learning

In a number of methodologically-similar investigations carried out across campus-based universities in Australia and Great Britain over the last decade, teachers have been found to report qualitatively different ways of experiencing blended learning and teaching (for example Jones, Asenio & Goodyear, 2000; Roberts, 2003; Ellis et al., 2006; Gonzalez, forthcoming; Ellis et al., 2009). The experience of teaching across face-to-face and online contexts is not the same for all teachers.

The following extracts come from interviews in two of the studies looking at the teaching experience at universities in England and Australia (Ellis et al., 2006 and Ellis et al., 2009) They illustrate some key aspects of the variation of the experience of teaching.

Extract 1

Interviewer:	How do you think your students experience the way you've blended their classroom and online learning experiences?
Teacher 1:	The students go to class and they complete their tasks in the way they've always done them. They're also learning because I'm giving them lecture notes online before they come to class.
Interviewer:	What is it that's helping them to learn in this type of experience?
Teacher 1:	They're learning because they're using all the materials I can give them as early as possible, rather than just a text book and handouts in class.
Interviewer:	What are they doing with the materials?
Teacher 1:	They're printing them out, bringing them to class, writing notes on my notes while I'm talking, but writing less because I've already written down what I'm saying for them.

There are a few points to note about the discussion above in terms of what it tells us about the teacher's perspective on e-learning. It seems that the teacher's role in the experience is the thing that is focussed on. It is the teacher giving the students lecture notes, and it is the teacher talking to the students. It also seems that the teacher is using the online environment as a way of distributing lecture notes before lectures believing that an early distribution online somehow equates to learning. This seems to ignore the fact that a similar experience could be achieved through the university printing service, probably at a lesser cost. Understandably, this latter strategy would mean more pre-semester planning on the part of the teacher than publishing lecture notes online each week. Notwithstanding this benefit for the teacher, the ideas underpinning this type of concept of face-to-face and online learning are teacher-centred and not really related to active learning.

Extract 2

Interviewer: Do you have any ideas about how students are experiencing the combined classroom and online learning you are providing in their university course?

Teacher 2: I hope the students understand that one complements the other, adding a broader depth and motivating mix to their experience. Good students will be able to take more control of their learning over the activities, especially in the online activities where it is possible to enable them to work more independently.

Interviewer: Does that mean they are not able to be autonomous in class?

Teacher 2: No, not at all. We use lots of interaction in class in discussions that are related to their online activities. This allows them a good deal of control over how discussions are shaped. The way we talk about topics in class helps them to become more immersed in the topic so when they are learning more independently online, they can depart from a more contextualised understanding of what they are trying to achieve.

In contrast to the first discussion, the ideas underpinning this teacher's awareness of student learning seems to be more aware of the student perspective. A key focus is on the development of student autonomy, a goal which is supported by a combination of both the face-to-face and online contexts in which the teacher is playing a supporting, rather than emphasised, role. In this extract, there appears to be a synergistic relationship between the two contexts, each preparing the student to get to grips with the key issues of a topic with more understanding, almost as if the teacher can help the student to leverage off the opportunities provided by each context towards a better overall comprehension. Some parallels are to be found in how teachers conceive of teaching across face-to-face and online contexts.

Variation in Conceptions of Blended Teaching

Not surprisingly, there are some parallels between teacher conceptions of blended learning and teacher conceptions of blended teaching.

> Teacher 3: When I think about teaching, blending face-to-face and online experiences, it is about providing my teaching in a number of modes. You can provide the same course information in the lecture, or workshop and in online resources so that the students can engage with it. I like to have all my teaching notes online because if I have all my information there I know that that the students have a good basis. It's usually much better than the notes they can take. If they have this information from a number of different modes, they'll learn, it's more interesting.

The way that teacher 3 talks about the idea of teaching above is similar to teacher 1 in the section on teacher conceptions of blended learning. The conception is predominately about how the teacher is related to the online environment. The teacher seems to conceive of learning as getting the same information in a number of different modes. This does not seem to be the case for teacher 4.

> Teacher 4: It is quite a challenge linking the physical and virtual learning contexts of the students when they are combined in one course. You can do it if you focus on their learning outcomes. Teaching is then about helping them to develop their own ways of thinking that are likely to help them understand what they're trying to learn irrespective of which context they are in as they develop their comprehension. When technologies are involved, it's up to you to give them a way of integrating knowledge from different sources into a deeper understanding. You draw on all the resources you think will help students learn as they move between the tutorial room and online context towards the learning outcome.

This concept of teaching focuses on the student and their learning outcomes. It foregrounds the student's point of view – trying to achieve an outcome, involving a process that traverses between the face-to-face and online contexts. The motivation for including learning technologies is to help the student to develop their overall understanding, linked to the course outcome. In comparison to the previous conception of teaching, this extract shows a greater awareness of, and concern for, the students' learning and how they integrate knowledge in order to understand.

The qualitative distinction being made in the examples above is consistent with the results of some other interview-based studies. Gillian Roberts (2003) carried out in-depth interviews with 17 teachers from a university in Scotland. The interviews were about 'learning and teaching with the World Wide Web', but the interviews were set up in such a way that teachers with very different uses of ICT felt free to talk about what they did. Of the 17 interview transcripts, seven turned out to cover the full range of conceptions held. The interviewees' conceptions of teaching fell into two broad categories: (i) teacher-centred/subject-focussed conceptions of teaching and (ii) student-centred/learning-focussed conceptions of teaching. Examining these in more detail, Roberts identified three categories of conceptions of 'teaching with the WWW'. The first of these was essentially concerned with the World Wide Web as an information resource. Teachers holding this conception emphasised the value of online access to subject information. The second category of conception focused on the use of ICT to support individual, independent, self-paced learning. The third conception involved groupwork on analysis and decision-making tasks as well as group discussions (Roberts, 2003, pp. 145–148).

Similarly results, though telling a more detailed story, were found in recent postgraduate research studies by Carlos Gonzalez (Gonzalez, forthcoming; 2009). These studies carried out similar analyses to Roberts, using in-depth phenomenographic interviews with a range of university teachers in Australia. These teachers varied considerably in their experience of teaching and in the subjects taught. Gonzalez identified four conceptions of teaching: (i) transmitting the basic information of the discipline, (ii) transmitting the lecturers' understanding, (iii) developing student's understanding, (iv) changing students' understanding and/or promoting critical thinking. When discussing conceptions of teaching using ICT, the study also uncovered some qualitatively different categories. Those which were identified as fragmented conceptions saw e-learning primarily as a source of information provided by lecturers or as a medium for occasional online communication. In contrast, cohesive conceptions saw teaching using ICT as a way to enable students to apply and reflect about what is being discussed, or as a medium to support knowledge building.

In trying to discover the reasons why teachers report such qualitatively different experiences of blended teaching, underlying conceptions of learning technologies have been investigated as a related factor.

Variation in Teacher Conceptions of Learning Technologies

Variation in teacher conceptions of learning technologies may explain some of the variation in experiences of blended teaching (Ellis et al., 2009; Patron, Ellis & Barrett, forthcoming). In the context of this research, learning technologies are defined as any technologies that are used in course design and teaching in order to help students achieve their learning outcomes. Most of the contexts of the teachers reporting below are ones in which the e-learning aspect of the experience has been online learning.

The idea of *convenience* emerges as a salient way of characterising learning technologies.

> Teacher 5:   Learning technologies make things easier. If the students miss a lecture, they can catch up. They help the teacher to deliver stuff, maybe when students can't come at some times. You just have to schedule them into the semester to make sure the students use them. Because they're networked, then the technologies let you give the students lots and lots of resources.

The above conception of learning technologies is pragmatically orientated. Timetable clashes or absences can be alleviated through use of the technologies. There also seems be an emphasis on the *volume* of learning resources and a use of the technologies to make sure the students have access to as many resources as the lecturer can find.

> Teacher 6:   It seems to me that learning technologies are there to support the way students are developing their understanding of the topics they are studying. They should be aligned to the objectives of the course and they often can provide ways of learning about ideas, about different perspectives on topics and from specific resources which are difficult to provide to students otherwise. Learning technologies help to link learning between classes as the students work on tasks which begin in class, continue online and then are reviewed in the following class.

The conception of learning technologies outlined by teacher 6 does not emphasise logistical convenience or providing a large quantity of resources as the main purpose of the technologies. Instead it focuses on affordances for learning different perspectives and ideas and for providing specific resources related to course objectives. This conception also shows an awareness of close links between the face-to-face and online situations when activities are spread across both contexts. A similar idea was identified in a related study which revealed teacher conceptions of an e-learning tool used for capturing the student experience of a field trip (Patron et al., forthcoming). For teacher 7, the e-learning tool is a way of developing the comprehension and understanding of the students as they engage with the meaning of the field trip study.

> Teacher 7:   (using the tool) they would learn about geography, get

> information on diverse fields of knowledge, they would sharpen their senses in the cognitive process, they would learn about their real surroundings. A structure for new knowledge, learning about cases that are different from their own reality, mental structure to be able to understand different realities.

The main point to note here is that the more holistic conceptions described by teachers above do not separate a focus on the student and the development of their understanding when considering learning technologies in experiences of teaching. From the few studies completed to date, this seems to be a notable characteristic of experiences of blended teaching which explains some of the qualitatively different dimensions. Some of the less powerful, more fragmented, ideas associated with e-learning refer mainly to providing information or offering different modes of learning (as ends in themselves), avoiding timetable clashes and emphasising access to a vast array of resources. Some of the more powerful and cohesive ideas include helping students develop greater independence, the integration and alignment of blended learning activities with learning outcomes and the provision of different points of view on key ideas.

We began this section on teacher conceptions by noting the prior research into experiences of teaching in higher education. As a result of insights from those studies, we understand the importance of links between how teachers report thinking about their teaching and how they approach it. To understand how e-learning is situated within the experience of teaching, we need to better understand how teachers approach teaching and design when e-learning is involved.

Approaches to Blended Teaching

Rogers' (1995) distinction between 'early adopters', the 'late majority' and the 'laggards' has become an established way of thinking about technological innovation in teaching as in other sectors of work. Whether teachers embed learning technologies into their strategies relatively early or later than their colleagues, the underlying intention behind their use may vary significantly. Consider the approach described by teacher 8.

Teacher 8:   I use e-learning tools in the learning management system my university provides. They help me to tell students when they are supposed to be giving me something, or if I've forgotten to give them a handout in class, I can put it up online. Also, if a student has missed the class, I can refer them to the resources I've put up online without them having to come to my office. The main thing I have to do when I'm using those tools is make sure the students know how to use them so that they do not miss out on the instructions I give them.

In this approach, there is an emphasis by the teacher on managing student activity. In this case, this activity is primarily about handing in assignments or tasks on time, receiving handouts from the teacher and knowing how to use the online tools to complete these tasks. This way of using e-learning in an approach to teaching does not seem to have a holistic understanding of how it may be embedded in, or related to, strategies used to develop student understanding of the key topics and issues that they are studying. The approach is yet to develop a holistic way of integrating e-learning in relation to student learning outcomes of the course.

Some approaches to teaching involving e-learning, yet to be strongly related to student learning outcomes, are comparatively more prospective in nature than the approach described in the preceding extract. In these situations, the approach involves using an incremental and trialling strategy to see how the students respond and how the teacher experiences it.

> Teacher 9: Frankly, I'm not very confident with e-learning. I tend to just try things out bit by bit and see if it works. Like the other week I put up an Excel spreadsheet online with the formulas I wanted the students to use and become familiar with. It had examples and they were able to see what would happen to the quantities when they changed different amounts in the formula. It seemed to work okay. Next year I want to build an assessment task around it if I get a good response from the students about how they used it.

In contrast to the approach adopted by teacher 8, teacher 9 has a forward-looking, or prospective approach to using e-learning. There seems to be some awareness of how students might use it to develop their understanding of the relationship between formulas describing quantities, but the use of e-learning is yet to be more deeply embedded in the approach, such as integrating it explicitly into the learning outcomes or into the assessment framework.

The approach described by teacher 10 seems to be different yet again.

> Teacher 10: E-learning is just a natural part of the way I approach teaching. I hope the students do not see any artificial separation between the way they are learning and studying in class, online and at home. There are important elements in all three contexts that need to be related to each other if the students are going to get the main ideas

they need to understand what's going on. So in class they have a chance to interact with each other together on the topic and get a feeling for the overall picture, then they can reflect on it online, looking at it from different perspectives and seeing how we can do, and then they can follow up on both of these experiences when they're writing and reading about it at home. I try to help them experience these things as one, as if there is no real separation in the developing of their understanding across all the contexts.

This way of approaching teaching using e-learning has integrated its use at a conceptual level. There is an orientation to the underlying concept which not only starts from a student perspective, but has absorbed the variation in mode, subordinating it to the greater imperative of understanding. As a consequence, the approach seeks to remove boundaries in the experience between physical and virtual contexts, which has the benefit of linking more closely the learning the student is experiencing during and between classes.

Variation in quality of approach to blended teaching, as described in the preceding interview extracts, was also found in the research by Gonzalez (2009). That study identified qualitatively different approaches to teaching involving e-learning. The strategies underpinning the approaches to teaching were categorised into information-focussed, communication-focussed and collaboration-focussed categories. The latter two categories were the most learning-focussed approaches, in which teachers concentrated on developing student thinking and knowledge building. Combinations of these strategies and intentions resulted in two qualitatively different groupings of approaches to teaching using e-learning: those that were predominately information focussed, with an intention to provide course information, up-to-date materials and course announcements, and those that were student focussed, with an intention to engage students in knowledge building.

The complexity of integrating teaching strategies across face-to-face and e-learning contexts changes and shifts with each new wave of technological innovation. To try to conceive of some underlying principles that can accommodate changes in the technological base of approaches to teaching, it is worth considering teaching strategies involving e-learning in more detail.

Teaching Strategies Involving E-learning

The following passage is an extract from an interview with a science teacher at a campus-based, research-intensive university. The interview was transcribed and then the teacher and interviewer reviewed the transcript to unpack some of the ideas that had not been sufficiently elaborated. The experience described by the teacher has some characteristics in common with those of teachers interviewed in the studies mentioned above. These characteristics include: stages of experimenting with how e-learning can be integrated into an overall approach; how the teacher modifies the way they think about and approach teaching as they grow in confidence through many experiences, and how strategies employed as part of the approach become more embedded in the design.

The transcript is in two parts. The first part discusses a transition period lasting about five years, during which the teacher became more familiar with, and confident about, integrating e-learning into their teaching. The second part discusses how the teacher rethought the dimensions of the learning space and strategies used when lectures, practical tutorials and e-learning were involved.

Interview Transcript Part 1

Interviewer: How do you approach your teaching in a context where they are learning in class and online? Do your strategies change?

Teacher: They change, because the development of the strategies is organic. There's a time dimension here. I first started using online multiple choice questions – initially I used them just to help the students with the content. A big problem my students have is identifying rocks and in solving a geological map problem. So the first year I actually started to use that system I think I only got about a hundred questions up on the Web. And some of it was really low level multiple-choice of you know rock contains x, y and z, what do you call it? And now there're about four or five hundred questions and more complicated ideas and better images. So we can assess understanding that goes through the whole course.

Interviewer: In what other ways have your strategies changed?

Teacher: I have also developed a range of learning resources that the students can interact with. Those resources and the multiple choice questions have helped me to think differently about my teaching to what I was doing four or five years ago. Four or five years ago I would say to a class that if we haven't done it in the room, it will not be examined. If we haven't looked at a particular topic in a practical tutorial or in the lecture theatre, it's not examinable. Now I say to the students that the framework for what we're doing for the topic is provided by the prac, lecture theatre and the online activities, such as discussions and problem-solving. You need to have absorbed the ideas from the online resources. I don't expect you to have memorised every sentence or every word or every term, but I think I could reasonably expect you to understand the concepts behind that. We don't have time to cover everything in minute detail here. But remember, it's a problem-solving exercise. You need to know that stuff because I'm going to ask you a question and you're going to have to process it and do something with it. So it frees up the classroom a bit. Cause I've got this time problem.

Interviewer: What is the time problem?

Teacher: One of the consequences of this class getting bigger is that they don't get as much practice time as they did. So I've converted a number of pracs that they used to do in the lab to take-home exercises. The notes and the resources that they need to solve it are online and they can ask me questions in class if they're stuck. But I can put stuff in a place and say – send an email to everyone – saying the stuff you need for the next take-home exercise – the notes and theory, we've done them briefly in class. The really important stuff we've done in the lecture theatre as a small problem. The notes you need I think have got generations of students through this topic using the online resources. If you missed the class or if you don't quite understand it and want to go through it, it's on the course website.

Interviewer: Do you find yourself referring to the course website in class much?

Teacher: Yes. It all – and I don't it formally set up – I'm going to do this, this and this – it just, to a certain extent it just happens. We've done this, you need that. I'll rework an old manual or I'll rework an old exercise. There's an example, there's some theory, there's what you got to go and do. And we bounce backwards and forwards.

Interviewer: Between?

Teacher: Between the things.

Interviewer: What things?

Teacher: Well there's a task that is about a construction problem that runs for the whole semester which means they have to understand the content to come up with a final solution. And then there's stuff on the course website that is – there are resources or there are questions with worked answers or feedback that allows them to go backwards and forwards through the concepts in their own time.

| Interviewer: | For what purpose? |
| Teacher: | To get on top of what they need to do to solve the various parts of the problem. Either take-home exercises or the major project design work for the semester. |

In the first part of the transcript, the teacher describes some of the strategies used over the previous five years. These can be summarised as follows:

- incrementally trialling aspects of e-learning. In this case, the teacher started with multiple choice questions and then moved to integrating these with redesigned theoretical and practical resources;
- using e-learning to deal with learning challenges brought about large cohorts of students and insufficient time;
- designing tasks that are linked across different learning situations: lectures, practical tutorials and online activities;
- providing tasks with worked answers online to help students engage with key topics when they choose to do so.

A marked characteristic of these strategies is how the teacher seemed to build up both the resources and an understanding of how to link the resources together to support student learning over a number of iterations of teaching the course.

The experience relayed through the interview extract above provides some important ideas for those responsible for helping teachers become accustomed to using e-learning as part of their teaching approach. It seems likely that most teachers will benefit from having time and a chance to experiment with what e-learning strategies work well for their students. Teachers need a chance to make e-learning strategies a normal part of their toolkit for helping their students learn. It is reasonable to expect some period of transition between when a teacher first trials e-learning as part of an approach, to when it is a more integrated and embedded strategy. Chapter 8 discusses what meaningful design approaches might involve.

In the second part of the transcript, the teacher goes on to describe the tasks in the course and how they relate to the different learning contexts in which the students find themselves.

Interview Transcript Part 2

| Interviewer: | Can you talk a little bit about the major project design work and the take-home exercises? |
| Teacher: | Yes. What I find with students is I need to explain, we're going to learn within a three-dimensional space; in the lecture theatre, you're going to do exercises that you take home and work on, and there are some practice |

ones on the course website that you can use to come up to speed.

Interviewer: Can you explain how the students' learning is related to these learning spaces in terms of the assignment for the project and home exercises?

Teacher: When they do the assignment online, it comes in, get's marked, it's given back the next week in class. Then I go through the formal answer and the best way to answer it. And the common misconceptions that I identified in that class from the answers that they put in. So if they've made – if forty students out of a hundred and eighty have made the same mistake, they've misunderstood something or they weren't in class when we did that – which is quite common – then there are forty people that got this wrong. They did this which means that they don't understand 'x' and this is what you really do. Let's try it again. There's a quick one. So I'll just draw a sketch on the board or frame a small problem then to rectify that misconception that I've identified in marking. And I do mark the whole – the major bits of work I mark rough. I just put numbers on stuff generally. But then the class know that I'll go through the answer slowly and thoroughly in the lecture theatre. So partly because of the changes to the way we run the degrees or the knowledge explosion and partly because of the advent of the Web.

Interviewer: How does this relate to the learning spaces?

Teacher: What's happening now is that there's no real separation of tasks or separation of problem to pracs, online, home study or lecture theatre. Bits and pieces of each come in to the different places. So even in the prac room some of the stuff I might have done in the lecture might become part of the prac. So for ten minutes we're going to do this now – you need to know this – here's some pictures – you're going to look at these rocks – this is what they look like – this is how we do it – OK off you go. So the learning spaces are sort of blending or sort of oozing into each other.

Interviewer: What are the learning spaces?

Teacher There's the lecture theatre, the prac room and then there's online or paper-based exercises and so on. The tasks that we might do in those spaces complement each other because I have a point of view on teaching is that there's no point in me just standing up and sprouting a whole bunch of content.

In this part of the transcript, the teacher provides a very important perspective on the different learning spaces we are providing to students when we involve e-learning in the strategies used. For this teacher, it seems that it needs to be made explicit to the students that their learning experience is going to involve more than just the classroom, that some explanation is necessary to help the students conceptualise how the different spaces they find themselves in within the course are related. For the teacher, the different learning spaces work in a complementary fashion to each other, offering different strategies for the learning activities required to reach the intended learning outcomes. One of the main impressions the teacher gives in this transcript is that their design and teaching provide coherence, from a student perspective, concerning how the different spaces relate to each other. There is no artificial separation between the spaces, simply because they are physical or virtual, at university or at home. Rather their meaning is shaped by the learning task, which traverses across the different learning spaces as the students come to a better understanding of the issues and ideas involved.

Associations Between Conceptions of, and Approaches to, Blended Teaching

Before looking at the available evidence about how categories of conceptions of and approaches to teaching involving e-learning are related, it is worth emphasising that researchers in the field are only just coming to grips with the complexities of this area. More studies, involving larger samples of teachers, are required before we can talk with more confidence about the strength of associations between how teachers report thinking about their approach when e-learning is involved, and the intentions and strategies they adopt within such work. That said, there is an emerging understanding about associations which are worth further exploration.

Roberts's study (2003) found tentative evidence of logical associations between orientation to teaching and orientation to teaching using the Web. In other words, teachers with a transmission view of teaching tended to approach the use of the Web for activities which revolved around imparting information to students. Similarly, teachers with a view of teaching that centred on student learning tended to use the Web as a way of facilitating students' understanding and intellectual development.

The two studies with teachers from research-intensive universities came to similar conclusions (Ellis et al., 2006; Ellis et al., 2009). Teachers who reported concepts of blended learning and teaching which separated an awareness of the student and his or her understanding from the experience, tended to think of, and approach, the experience of teaching with an impoverished understanding of what e-learning could achieve through integration with the other aspects of the student experience. In contrast, teachers who reported conceptions of blended learning and teaching which started from a student perspective and focussed on the development of comprehension, tended to approach the use of e-learning as a meaningful part of a student experience which maximised its benefits through integrating it across learning activities involving other face-to-face aspects of the course.

Gonzalez' study (forthcoming) emphasised an important dimension of the associations between teacher conceptions of blended teaching. He emphasised the challenges involved in reconciling (simultaneously held) cohesive conceptions of teaching with fragmented conceptions of teaching using e-learning. He labelled these as dissonant conceptions of blended teaching, whose internal tension may provide a lever for academic development around these ideas to resolve the contradictions.

Concluding Comments

In previous chapters, the student experience of e-learning in higher education has been argued to be one which sits predominately in a broader ecology of learning, where the effectiveness of e-learning experiences are more clearly understood when they are viewed in relation to the other key aspects of the experience. We saw that if the students' experience of e-learning is not one which is understood as part of an integrated whole, then the quality of the experience is likely to suffer.

A consistent message has been argued in this chapter, albeit argued from the perspective of teachers. Not all teachers conceive of, nor approach, e-learning as part of an integrated whole. When teachers report concepts related to their experience of teaching which separates a student perspective and a focus on learning from their own, then their approaches to teaching tend to be impoverished, both in the intentions underpinning their actions and the strategies used.

In brief, the ideas in this chapter suggest that when teachers do not focus on the development of student understanding and have poor conceptions of learning technologies, they tend to use e-learning as a way of delivering information, bolting it on to course design in an unreflective way. Teachers who focus on the development of student understanding and have richer conceptions of learning technologies, not only integrate e-learning into their approach to teaching, but also stress the importance of the integration of physical and virtual space. Given that e-learning is being considered within a broader ecology, it is unsurprising that issues such as the integration of learning across physical and virtual spaces has been a topic emphasised in some of the interview extracts.

To support a meaningful use of e-learning in the university student experience, it seems that adjustments to the ecological balance are required. We need a clear focus on the development of student understanding when designing courses that embed learning technologies. Universities also need to address issues such as the alignment of campus infrastructure, its physical and virtual spaces, to the way teachers are designing courses. The sustainability of issues such as these, raised by the introduction of e-learning into the student experience at university, shape the ideas in the remaining chapters of the book.

7

An Ecology of Learning
Practical Theory for Leadership, Management and Educational Design

Introduction

This chapter marks a gear-shift in the argument. The focus of attention in the last four chapters has been on describing student and teacher experiences of e-learning, within a broader ecology of learning. While a concern for the student experience remains at the heart of our argument, our focus now shifts to the implications of the changing structure of that experience for curriculum design and for the design and planning of university campuses – especially their 'infrastructure for learning'. A common thread is the *uncertainty* that accompanies educational planning and management at the university level. This uncertainty has a number of sources. For one thing, educational planning and curriculum design are not *deterministic* activities. Students and others exercise autonomy in making sense of the challenges and opportunities they encounter. Moreover, universities exist in a rapidly changing world. They are adapting to technological innovations, changes in student demand, fiscal instability and global competition. Each of these involves uncertainty and risk. In Chapter 7, we offer a way of conceptualising the links between successful students' experiences of learning, teachers' experiences of design and university leaders' experiences of campus planning, all framed within the idea of 'an ecology of learning'.

In this ecological view of learning, leaders in all parts and at all levels of a university have a key role in enabling their university to achieve its mission. This mission, we contend, is fundamentally concerned with learning – learning by students, teachers, researchers and members of society. Universities *ought* to be excellent learning organisations, understood in the dual sense of *organisations for learning* and *organisations that learn*. This also ought to apply to the constituent parts of a university. For example, the university library needs to be configured as an organisation that understands good learning, so that it can align itself with the needs of learners (not just their manifest demands) but also so that it can improve over time and adjust to change. On this view, learning is seen as good in itself, but also as vital in dealing with change and uncertainty (cf. Alexander, Silverstein, Angel, Ishikawa & Abrams, 1975; Brown & Duguid, 1996; Baumard, 1999; Weick & Sutcliffe, 2007).

Managing and Uncertainty

We now want to consider what the idea of an ecology of learning means for universities, and what implications this has for how universities should strive to manage the uncertainty inherent in a rapidly changing international higher education sector.

Coherent planning, ongoing activity and quality enhancement within a university are made more difficult by uncertainty (Hunt et al., 2006). This uncertainty has two origins. There is uncertainty because of changes, sometimes dramatic and unpredictable changes, in the university's operating environment. There is uncertainty because of the nature of the enterprise itself. Academic enterprise often embraces the following qualities; it is:

- reflective – it may take time to decide how best to proceed;
- creative – it brings together phenomena in new and unusual combinations;
- innovative – it can take unusual twists and turns to reach its goals;
- collaborative – it is increasingly the result of partnerships between individuals and groups of stakeholders;
- critical – insofar as academics have the habit of subjecting new ideas to critical scrutiny;
- cyclical – especially when the rationale for a past decision is forgotten and what appears to be a new idea is (re)subjected to critical scrutiny.

These qualities can legitimately create circumstances that are not amenable to classic rationalistic forms of management and planning.

When we consider the uncertainty brought about by the international context in which universities are located, we can add that academic enterprise is shaped by rapid developments in:

- how we discover, share and retrieve knowledge;
- technologies that enable us to change how we discover, share and retrieve new knowledge;
- the changing size and shape of the international higher education sector;
- rapid fluctuations in international flows of students; global competition for talent and resources;
- changes and inconsistencies in government policy.

Taken together, the qualities of academic enterprise mentioned above and the context in which universities find themselves today, mean that it is not difficult to understand why individual universities face a high degree of uncertainty. The challenge for each institution is to find sensible ways of organising their activity, despite (and to help deal with) high levels of uncertainty.

The Idea of an Ecology of Learning

We suggest that focusing on the *ecology* of a university can enable useful strategies to be put in place to manage the uncertainties faced by individual universities and by the sector as a whole. Ecological thinking can help identify structures and processes that are geared to dealing with change. It also helps identify and work with key relationships between the component parts of a university. To understand how this is possible, we will look at the following four key characteristics of the ecology of a university:

- *Ecological balance.* We suggest that the best way of thinking about a university being in ecological balance is when it is permeated by successful learning. Learning is a common goal for students (who seek to understand the world in new ways), teachers (who seek to help students understand the world in new ways and who seek a better understanding of how to do this), researchers (who seek to discover new ways of seeing the world), leaders (who seek to understand, interpret and respond to rapid changes going on in the world), and society (which looks to universities to facilitate better understanding of phenomena). It is worth noting that some individuals in universities can occupy several of these roles simultaneously.
- *Ecological self-awareness* is required for an institution to maintain its balance. This is the principle by which participants in the ecology are aware of their place and function in relation to the rest of the environment. Awareness of place and function presupposes the existence of a mutually shared agreement on what constitutes balance.
- *Feedback loops* enable the participants in an institution to help maintain its ecological balance. Participants require a reliable stream of timely, valid, action-oriented information for them to be aware of how their roles are playing out within the whole ecology. Feedback loops can help participants to be self-regulating and to manage uncertainty in the environment.
- *Self correction* by the parts of the system can be achieved through alignment to the ecological balance identified by the university. This alignment is symbiotically dependent on the previous characteristics.

Ecological management involves a thorough understanding of these four characteristics and their inter-relationships.

Learning as the Point of Ecological Balance

To judge whether an ecology is in balance, one needs to be able to identify the salient aspects that keep it alive and functioning well. For a university, a number of foci could be argued to signify its balance: research, teaching, learning and service to society.

The purpose of universities has been the subject of discussion for many centuries. Universities have been thought of as 'institutions of teaching', 'institutions of research', or 'institutions of service' since the Middle Ages (Bowden & Marton, 2004). John Henry Newman (1858) is strongly associated with the idea of a university as a teaching institution.

> {ix} The view taken of a University in these Discourses is the following: – That it is a place of teaching universal knowledge. This implies that its object is, on the one hand, intellectual, not moral; and, on the other, that it is the diffusion and extension of knowledge rather than the advancement. If its object were scientific and philosophical discovery, I do not see why a University should have students; if religious training, I do not see how it can be the seat of literature and science.
>
> (Newman & Turner, 1996)

In 19th century Berlin, Wilhelm von Humboldt articulated the idea of a university of research, an idea upon which research-intensive universities such as Yale and Harvard today base their purpose. It was not a concept that promoted teaching over research, as Newman did, but rather a concept of a university in which teaching was underpinned by research, almost as if the value of the teaching was determined by its symbiotic relationship with research within the same institution. Key ideas in his vision were *lehrfreiheit*, which is often claimed as the basis of academic freedom, and *lernfreiheit*, the right of student to knowledge (Szczepanski, 1968).

In the last few decades, the role of universities in preparing graduates for the workplace has developed a more extensive research-base (for example, see Boud, 1999; Boud & Garrick, 1999; Caldwell & Carter, 1993). This perspective emphasises a practical role for universities to fulfil, so that employers and industries are seen as immediate beneficiaries of the work of universities through the provision of work-ready graduates.

Bowden and Marton (2004) argue for *learning* to be the governing principle for the organisation of universities. It is in the concept of learning that the other purposes find their strongest connections. Teaching, research and service can all be understood to yield and promote learning: learning for students in the case of teachers, learning for humanity in the case of researchers and learning for particular communities in the case of service.

Because of this, the university as an institution of learning seems to us to be the most useful way to articulate the balance of a university as an ecology. It is in learning that links with the other purposes of a university find a home. At a high conceptual level, this way of conceiving the purpose of a university brings about a parallel between the ecology of learning and the ecology of a university, since, in this argument, universities are conceived of primarily as institutions of learning.

Ecological Self-awareness

The idea behind *self-awareness* here is that participants in the university ecology of learning have a responsibility and need the ability to understand their role in relation to the whole. Drawing on the language we introduced in Chapter 2, we can say that this is a *non-dualistic* view of the role of participants, as it requires them to be simultaneously aware of the structure, purpose and key ideas of their own area as well as how the part (department, unit, etc.) in which they work is related to the structure and purpose of the whole university. It is also non-dualistic in the sense that we argue against a view of participants sitting 'outside' or 'above' the ecology, analysing its parts as if they were separate from their own. A separation of the two is likely to encourage a fragmented understanding of how the parts of a university interact. Rather, the strength of our conception lies in the way it emphasises the interrelatedness of the awareness of the part from *within* the whole.

Feedback Loops

A characteristic of an ecology required to develop self-awareness within a context of uncertainty is *timely and meaningful feedback*. Without ongoing feedback loops, managers of areas within the university, whatever their level, lose their sense of direction, are unable to tell whether their area is properly aligned with other areas of the university, and with the work of the university as a whole. Feedback which informs, and is informed by, the university at different levels, allows a type of self-awareness to develop that enables its parts to independently, intelligently and continually adjust their structure and purpose to fit the direction of the whole more effectively.

Self-correction

When parts of the ecology of a university seek to maintain balance, using feedback, there needs to be a point of reference and a way to align to that point. The point of reference chosen here is *learning* in its broadest possible sense for higher education. The concept of self-correction put forward here is based on 'constructive alignment' (Biggs & Tang, 2007).

Constructive alignment, at the level of the student's experience, involves aligning the intended learning outcomes of students in a course with the learning activities they are expected to engage in. Their performance is measured through summative assessment tasks that are designed to see to what extent the students have achieved the intended learning outcomes.

At the level of a university and its parts, this concept can be adapted by using evaluation of the student's experience of learning, the teacher's experience of teaching and a researcher's experience of researching, to inform how a university engages in planning for its future. In the same way that a teacher tries to increase the likelihood of a student reaching the desired outcomes of a course, a university may inform its decision-making and investment in its fabric and support systems with the experiences of its students, teachers and researchers to increase the likelihood that desired outcomes are met. Taken to a logical conclusion, the arguments here and in the ensuing chapters push for the mission statement of the university as a point of reference that articulates the ecological balance of the institution, and the framework of reference for capital investment of the university.

Ecological Management: Maintaining a Balance

One common way universities manage uncertainty in planning is through using a project management approach. This approach has its place in the management strategies of a university, but we argue that it needs to be part of a more holistic management approach that focuses on sustaining an ecology – a type of ecological management.

The basis of an approach to *ecological management* is the continuous oversight of the interplay amongst the characteristics of the ecology: maintaining the ecological balance of the university, encouraging stakeholders to develop and articulate self-awareness in relation to the university mission, putting in systems to develop and improve self-awareness through continuous feedback loops, overseeing the self-correction of the parts of the university in relation to its mission statement. If these characteristics form the basis of principles for managing the ecology, then they offer a way of sustaining the balance in the face of uncertainty.

These principles of the idea of 'an ecology of learning' are drawn on as a way to discuss university planning in a context of uncertainty brought about by rapid and challenging changes in ways of encountering and working with knowledge. They could be used to discuss any aspect of a university; here we discuss the areas of governing bodies, university executives, policy boards, faculties, services managed for all faculties (central shared services) and communication.

Leadership in the Ecology of a University

Leadership takes many forms in a university. It includes leadership in the governing body, the policy board, the executive, at the level of faculties, schools and in programme design and teaching, and in service provision. For learning to be led effectively in an ecology, it needs to have representation at all of these levels, or loss of balance and misalignment will occur.

Governing Bodies of Universities

At the level of the governing body (in some universities, this is called the senate or council), leadership is required to protect the place of learning in the *value system* of the institution. If learning is a key part of the value system of a university, one would expect, for example, student representation in the governing body. While necessary but not sufficient, this type of strategy is consistent with the idea of sustaining a balance on learning issues through feedback, straight from the horse's mouth so-to-speak. Student representation, or at least student input, is a legitimate strategy for all levels of leadership described here.

Student inclusion in the governing body of a university does not necessarily mean an ecological balance of learning will be adopted. For a start, *student* learning is only one (albeit the most important) of the areas of 'learning' inherent in a broad use of the term. An ecologically informed perspective at the level of the governing body will embrace changes in the landscape of higher education internationally with a view to planning how the university may need to adapt its value system to most effectively position itself and its mission. For example, if we consider changes in the use of e-learning for universities internationally over the last few years, a number of issues need to be addressed in order to maintain an ecological balance at the governing level:

- E-learning is a key part of the structure of a student experience of learning that is related to qualitatively different experiences. Consequently, it is a core part of the enterprise of learning and teaching as students and teachers strive towards a deeper understanding of phenomena. (For evidence of uptake of e-learning in higher education internationally, see the reference list at the end of this book and summary publications on aspects of e-learning internationally such as Hawkins and Rudy, 2004, 2007; Zastrocky et al., 2007).
- E-learning is part of a broader ecology of learning in modern universities; it requires integrated planning with key areas of a university (for example finance, policy, property, IT networks, libraries).
- To achieve outcomes from this planning, sustainable budgets need to be endorsed for the purposes of improving the learning experiences of students, enabling the learning and teaching goals of faculties and modernising the e-systems of universities to benefit from strategic planning in related areas, such as e-research or client relations management systems.

University Executives

Where governing bodies have an eye on the medium and longer term issues that confront a university, and may concern themselves with guarding the value system of a university, *strategic and operational* responsibility in the shorter term is usually the concern of a university executive.

For the main purpose of a university to be embedded in everyday academic enterprise, that is, for learning to be seen as a primary goal and outcome at the executive level, each of the executive members needs to be aware of how a concept of learning underpins their context in relation to the other portfolios in the executive. In addition, there should be an executive member with lead responsibility for the key learning systems in a university. To be effective, this person should report directly to the most senior member of the executive (Bates, 2004).

In recent years, many universities have established, as an executive post, an advocate for learning and teaching. This role is an essential part of the executive, focussed on developing institutional understanding and performance, and needs to have a responsibility that encompasses e-learning as part of the learning and teaching system. Without leadership at this level, a capacity to leverage benefits from changes to learning and teaching are unlikely to be realised. Not only will possible benefits be missed, but an unmanaged or uncoordinated approach to the effect of changes brought about by developments such as e-learning in a university is likely to lead to variable standards, unsustainable budgeting and wasted resources.

A key role for the executive member responsible for learning and teaching is educating the governing body of the university and the executive of the purpose of, benefits arising from, and resources required for, change. Without this, strategic planning, the professionalisation of teachers, the learning of students and the reputation of the university will suffer as internal uncertainty surrounding the sustainability and ongoing provision of systems that support learning is put in question.

Policy Boards

At the level of a policy board, such as an academic board responsible for the development of academic policy, leadership is required for a *policy-led framework* for the planning, maintenance and improvement of learning systems. Without a principled and informed framework in which to make decisions, leaders at all levels of the institution will find it very difficult to know how to align the operations of their area to a common framework and how to efficiently go about getting appropriate feedback to maintain their alignment.

Using e-learning as an example, an integrated policy development approach is appropriate, but hard to achieve. This is because e-learning policy guidance for key areas of oversight by policy boards (such as evaluation, assessment, learning and teaching activities, course development and resourcing) need to be embedded in a policy which encompasses the whole of each of these areas, not just the e-learning part.

Key purposes of policy development for e-learning include the identification of responsibilities for quality assurance, standards for support that students and teachers may rely on, and integration and alignment with the philosophy and policy framework for the learning and teaching system. These are serious outcomes that need to be achieved for an ecology of learning embracing e-learning to find its balance and develop self-awareness. Without a policy-led frame of reference in which to make decisions, managers of key parts of the university will not be able to make informed choices.

Faculties

At the level of faculties, deans and their representatives will benefit from aligning their faculty systems so that they represent the value systems of the university ecology promoting learning. Key instruments for faculties are learning and teaching plans which need to be more elaborate than in the past. For example, planning for learning spaces is more complex than in the past because of the subtleties of interaction between physical and virtual spaces and their integration with learning activities. Learning and teaching plans should address how space needs are related to learning goals. These plans can then act within feedback loops to the executive responsible for making decisions about investments in campus space.

It is common for faculties to be divided up into smaller parts such as schools or departments. These need to adopt the same principles of alignment to their faculty, as their faculty does to the university. It is often at this level that leadership for the core business of learning and teaching and research is most closely related to those involved in the learning, teaching and research. It is feedback from these participants, that is from those who will be most affected by decisions on university planning, that must be drawn upon by those responsible for campus planning, if the ecology of the university is to function effectively.

Centrally-managed Shared Services

Service provision within the university, such as provision of student services, libraries, IT networks and property, require leadership which is self-aware of the place of the services in an ecology promoting learning. Head librarians, chief information officers and directors of property and student services cannot afford to plan for the future in ways that are unrelated to each other, as knowledge and knowledge systems are dependent on interrelated spaces that span across all of these portfolios. The planning and everyday enterprise of these services need to be inculcated in the same academic framework that leaders in learning, teaching and research operate. It is only then that integrated planning has a chance of meeting the immediate and medium term requirements of learners, teachers and researchers.

Before moving on to the issue of communication, it is worth noting that imbalances in an ecology may occur if any of the key functions of the above areas of a university, that is oversight of values, strategy and resources, and policy development, become too dominant. For example, an executive may have operations tied up so tightly that it is difficult for a policy board to create debate sufficient to develop useful new policies; a governing body might impose a value system too tightly on an executive, hampering innovation necessary for effective leadership; or a policy board might put in a framework which is too inflexible for the executive or deans to operate in a responsive fashion in the face of uncertainty and change. Such imbalances might occur within a university at any stage of its operations, and require constant vigilance by stakeholders in all of these areas to strive for balance.

Communication

An effective communication system and strategy is a mandatory part of an approach to managing uncertainty in universities. Communication is not just about setting up committees and blogs or making sure people talk to each other. Good communication also involves developing a shared language, gathering evidence and intelligence and ensuring distribution of information in a timely manner to those within the institution who are best placed to act upon it for the benefit of the university. In an ecology, we expect constituents to align their internal operations in such a way that their relationship to the whole promotes the ecology's goal, which in the case of a university we argue is learning. Leaders of universities have a responsibility to provide the means for their constituents to seek and obtain appropriate information in a timely manner, and when appropriate, to provide such information directly.

If universities do not have the concepts and language to share knowledge about how new parts of an ecology of learning are demanding some realignment of existing parts of the ecology, a lack of familiarity with the ideas involved can cause communication failure. Using e-learning as an example, too often discussions can be dominated by technically impenetrable terms, the meaning of which can be opaque to those in less technical, more learning-oriented positions. Conversely, an oversimplification of the role of e-learning in the student experience of learning will mean that the understanding that can be enabled by knowledge recursively bound up within technical structures[1] will be lost, or put at risk.

A useful strategy for raising e-learning issues within the teaching and learning system of a university is to leverage off existing networks. Many campus-based universities have identified faculty representatives to assist the head of the faculty with key issues at a faculty level, for example, through the work of pro-deans for learning and teaching. Such a network can be used by senior executives responsible for learning and teaching at the university level as a working group to initiate, identify, plan for and evaluate, developments in the university's learning and teaching system to integrate e-learning. This support could include planning and educational design support, some production and trialling support, e-learning support for students and teachers during the teaching period, and advice on evaluation for e-learning within a more holistic approach to evaluation which encompasses the whole student experience. Ongoing discussion is required about support systems to help teachers integrate e-learning effectively (Latchem & Lockwood, 1998; Epper & Bates, 2001; Laurillard, 2002).

Communication in the ecology of a university is not only about the *how*, but also about the *what*. A frequent challenge for leaders is providing a starting point for discussions which have sufficient commonality amongst stakeholders to capture their attention. A problem for university leaders involved in campus planning is that the inherent uncertainty in the process can make it difficult to provide a framework in which discussions can be fruitfully directed to the identification of relevant outcomes. Using rich descriptions and analyses of what learners and teachers are actually doing with the e-learning resources, within the broader ecology of learning, (cf. Chapters 3–6) is a good way of linking decision-making with real experiences.

Design Knowledge for Leadership in an Ecology

Leaders may have one or more areas over which they are responsible. Conceiving of an interrelated structural awareness of related areas within the university is a key part of leadership in an ecology of learning. It allows links to be made between a student experience of learning, the way teachers approach and think about their teaching, the approach adopted by service providers and the way Deans and the university executives support academic enterprise through managing the university environment. For leaders to be effective in any area of the ecology of a university, they need to be aware of the key structural aspects of their own area in relation to key structural aspects of the institution as a whole. This structural awareness is a prerequisite for leaders to effectively design feedback and correction mechanisms (Boland & Collopy, 2004).

Concluding Comments

In an ecology where learning is the point of reference for balance, a key aspect of structural awareness is the nature of successful student experiences of learning. We saw in Chapters 4–6 that successful student experiences of learning in which e-learning is part of the means are those in which traversing back and forth across physical and virtual contexts is not fragmented either conceptually (the way students and teachers report thinking about the experience), or in approach (the way students and teachers describe the strategies and intent underpinning their learning and teaching). A structural awareness of these experiences of learning and teaching provides a point of reference for leaders to design and manage feedback and self-correction mechanisms that are appropriate for their area in an ecology. For the university executive and deans, it might be the appropriate provision of teaching spaces, both physical and virtual, sufficient for the volume and variety of learning and teaching in the degree programmes for which they have responsibility. For librarians, it might be the provision of informal learning spaces suitably networked with access to virtual spaces including digital and print resources. For directors of property and the chief information officer, it might be a ten year building plan that integrates physical and virtual infrastructure aligned to the structure of the university's teaching programmes (see e.g., JISC, 2006; Carrick, 2007). For course leaders, adjustments to approaches to educational design, assessment and other aspects of teaching are required if they are to support successfully integrated e-learning experiences.

The main point here is, without some understanding of the structure of key aspects of the ecology, leaders are unlikely to be able to design mechanisms that will enable them to align activity in their area to the balance sought by the institution. In the next chapter, we explore some of the implications of this perspective at the 'meso-level' of course teams and 'teaching-as-design'. After that, we look at implications at the macro-level of campus planning.

8

Teaching-as-Design and the Ecology of University Learning

Introduction

Teaching in modern universities is very difficult to sustain as a solo activity, conducted by a lone academic. Co-teaching is becoming more common. But even where teachers manage their own individual courses, the need to work in a team arises in a number of situations: for example, in activities such as clarifying assessment standards, planning programmes so that they are coherent to students or mapping graduate attributes across a curriculum.

The suspicion that teaching is hard to sustain as a solo activity is reinforced when learning technologies come into the picture. It is rare for an individual academic to have all the knowledge and experience needed to make the best choices among learning tasks, technologies and ways of organising students, and to make sure that these choices are aligned to best effect. We have a strong sense that the increasing complexities of designing for productive student learning – given the changing array of student needs, teaching methods and curriculum demands – will encourage more teachers to do more of their work in collaborative programme teams. In principle, such teams also offer better opportunities for specialist educational development and technology staff to contribute to the improvement of learning opportunities: their contributions are amplified by working with a group, and can crystallise more readily into the improved practices of a course team than into the work of the solo academic. The combined or extended team of academics and educational development and technology specialists can also embrace more complex approaches to educational design, and make use of appropriate design tools and methods – tools and methods that have not been taken up widely by solo academics, in part because of the time involved in mastering their use.

The purpose of this chapter is twofold: to explain the notion of 'teaching-as-design' and to show how the design work of teaching teams fits into the broader ecology of university learning. Among other things, teaching-as-design implies that teaching teams have a lot of work to do before the first student arrives on campus, and that regular evaluation, reflection and review are needed to close the loop between students' experiences of learning and the (re)design and ongoing enhancement of all aspects of educational provision. Many of the books that offer advice about educational design assume teachers are working on a 'greenfield' site – setting up a new course or programme. In actuality, most educational design work is aimed at improving existing provision. This presents a very different set of problems from those encountered when setting up something new. For example, enhancement of existing courses and patterns of learning and teaching can rarely tackle everything at once: at any one time, some aspects of curriculum, resources, etc., have to be treated as fixed constraints and the enhancement focus has to illuminate other areas on which to work. The other feature of educational design we need to mention at this point is that design work applies at several scale levels, but not everyone can deal with issues at every level. For example, some staff – usually working for a 'central' unit with university-wide responsibilities, will have a remit that includes such things as changing the university-wide learning management system, upgrading the ICT facilities in lecture rooms, or installing wireless access points. Programme-level teaching teams usually have to take these as givens – they are inherited constraints over which they have very little power (Conole & Jones, forthcoming). Conversely, staff in 'central' units, even at very senior management levels, have little or no power to influence the details of how a course is taught. Failure to achieve a reasonable degree of integration up and down the levels can create major problems in an institution, and the uncertainties and miscommunications that arise can be a serious threat to sustainable innovation.

The Idea of Teaching-as-Design

Teaching in higher education is a multi-faceted job. Individual beliefs and preferences, departmental and disciplinary traditions, student numbers, the affordances of the teaching spaces available and access to other resources all combine to shape the ways in which teachers teach. The classic image of university teaching evokes lecturing to a large group, or tutoring a small one. But teaching also includes course and curriculum planning; consulting employers, professional bodies and academic colleagues about course goals, standards and requirements; setting assessment tasks; identifying useful learning resources; preparing lists of recommended reading and links to useful websites; creating or updating course websites; allocating students to working groups; scheduling activities; briefing teaching assistants (where available) and updating lecture notes. Most or all of this goes on before the first student comes onto campus. Once semester begins, in addition to lecturing, running seminars and tutorials, supervising laboratory or other practical classes, providing ad hoc advice about course requirements and counselling students who have academic or personal problems, university teachers also spend a great deal of time marking assignments and providing feedback (though rarely in enough detail to keep students happy). At semester's end there may be an exam to invigilate, answers to mark, exam boards to attend and course evaluation data to scrutinise. A wise teacher will make notes about what went well and less well, what needs changing next time round, what should be kept and what scrapped.

Within this complex mix, the classic activities of lecturing and taking tutorials can be seen to make a significant, but far from exclusive, call on the teacher's time. And if we look at things from the students' point of view, these supposedly core teaching activities become even less salient. Of course, they are the main opportunities for students and teachers to meet, and they provide a good chance for students to get a better sense of what the teacher values (or says they value). But if we think about how the *students* spend their time, then the work that teachers put in to lectures and tutorials diminishes in significance. Especially in the arts and social sciences, students spend a great deal of time doing things other than attending lectures and talking in seminar or tutorial groups. They devote much more time to tackling the required reading and in preparing essays. Even in the sciences, where there may be much more timetabled face-to-face activity, the quality of what students do depends less on how well their teacher presents a lecture than on how well he or she has designed the activities in which the students are asked to engage. We are *not* saying that lectures are unimportant. Good lectures are very good ways of achieving some of the things that need to be achieved in higher education (Bligh, 2000; Schwartz & Bransford, 1998). The simple point is that students learn a very great deal outside the lecture room. As Tom Shuell pointed out, and as John Biggs has reminded us all, the thing that matters is *what the learner does* (Shuell, 1986, 1992; Biggs & Tang, 2007). The learner's mental activity is the thing that changes what they know: any changes in competence or understanding are dependent on what the learner does.

In thinking about educational outcomes and their improvement, it is therefore essential to take a view that focuses on learner activity. Everything else is at best secondary.

If the quality of students' learning activity is crucial, then much of what teachers do that makes a difference can be thought of as a kind of design work. For sure, significant amounts of teaching involve rapid interaction with students, improvisation, fast thinking and making decisions intuitively and on-the-fly. But much more of the work that teachers have to do actually provides them with opportunities to be more reflective and plan more carefully in their teaching. It is concerned with designing things such that the quality of students' learning activity is as good as it can be.

Focus on Learning: What Needs Designing?

This immediately raises the question of what needs designing and we are quick to say that it is not *learning* that needs to be designed. Indeed, one of our objections to the term 'learning design' (e.g. Koper & Tattersall, 2005) is that it suggests the impossible – that learning itself can be designed. (It *might* be reasonable to talk about learners designing their own learning. We would nevertheless want to say that one cannot design somebody else's learning, just as one cannot design somebody else's feelings or experience.)

Learning activity is key: what the learner does is what makes a difference to their learning outcomes. As Figure 8.1 points out, such outcomes can be of various kinds – often classified as cognitive, psychomotor and affective. (Cognitive outcomes are concerned with thinking and understanding; psychomotor outcomes with skilful movement and perception; affective outcomes with emotions, attitudes and predispositions.) Giving due recognition to other accounts of learning, we would also want to give space, among candidate learning outcomes, to such things as shifts in one's sense of identity, and the degree to which one has become part of a community or culture, adopting its values, perspectives and practices. These too are reflected in Figure 8.1.

Figure 8.1 also emphasises the activity to outcome connection. While different kinds of outcome are achieved in different ways, all are dependent on activity. That activity may be mental (e.g., quiet reflection, or practising vocabulary). It may be physical (e.g., using laboratory equipment, or carrying out a dissection). It will often be both. It may involve tools or other artefacts (e.g., in using a computer or reading a book).

Once the centrality of students' activity is recognised and accepted, the teacher's design attention can focus on that which *can* be designed. What is the strongest influence on what students actually do? Usually, it is the tasks which teachers set that have the strongest influence on students' activity. Of course, students rarely do exactly what they are told. Indeed, teachers often set tasks in such a way that some creative interpretation is necessary and so that students can adapt the task to create a better fit with their own needs and interests. In addition, there are likely to be numerous other influences on what students actually do and some of these will – from time to time – prove more powerful

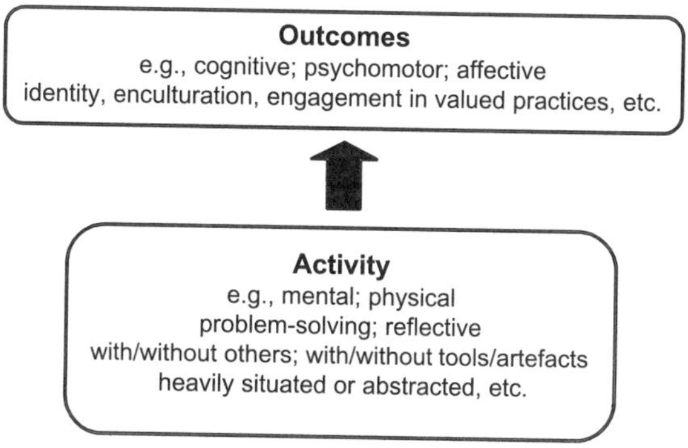

Figure 8.1 Learning outcomes depend on what the learner does.

than what the teacher has set. Nevertheless, a crucial resource for students' learning activity is the task set by the teacher.

Figure 8.2 represents the fact that learning tasks (as set by the teacher) are transformed by the student through their own interpretive and other work, such that it is the student's activity that mediates between the task as set and the educational outcomes achieved. Tasks as set have an *indirect* effect upon learning outcomes (Winne & Marx, 1982; Goodyear, 2000).

There are numerous potential influences on the processes of transform-ation that turn a task specification into an activity. For activities that last a significant time – hours or days rather than seconds or minutes – the processes that shape and reshape the actual activity can be quite complex, and change over time. As an example, think of a student setting out to tackle an assessment task that involves writing a 3,000 word essay. Imagine there is a deadline six weeks away, that the essay is worth 30% of the total marks for the course, and that the teacher has set a specific essay question. There will normally be an initial stage in which the student tries to make sense of the task specification – what the teacher means by the essay title, what qualities they will be looking for in the final essay, how much scope there is for personal interpretation, what kinds of reading will be needed, what kinds of evidence will need to be deployed? After that, as time goes by, the student will work on the essay: by reading, thinking, making notes, talking to peers, drafting and revising. The quality of this real-world activity will be influenced by a number of factors, including the other competing demands on the student's time, energy and attention. There will be some serendipity in the work, and some slippage and satisficing of goals as the deadline approaches. In short, much may happen to intervene between the task as the teacher set it and the learning outcomes that result from the student's activity. Many of these outcomes may best be thought of as *by-products* of the activity of producing the artefact – in this case an essay – that the task requires.

As we have seen in Chapters 4 and 5, students' conceptions of learning, and approaches to study, are heavily bound up in this task–activity nexus. Indeed, one can argue that an approach to study is a way of describing what is happen-ing when students translate tasks they are set into actual learning activity. When we interviewed them to find out about their approaches to study, what they described was their *intentions* – what they hoped to achieve by acting in particular ways – and their *strategies* – what they actually did. Both of these are retrospective, and somewhat abstracted and tidied up, *accounts* of their trans-lations of tasks into activities, but they nevertheless give us some compelling insights into the task–activity nexus.

Because of this, it must be acknowledged that the connections between tasks as set and learning outcomes are sometimes tenuous. Moreover, it is likely that only a subset of what the student has learnt will be visible to the teacher in the artefact submitted by the student. Does this make task design

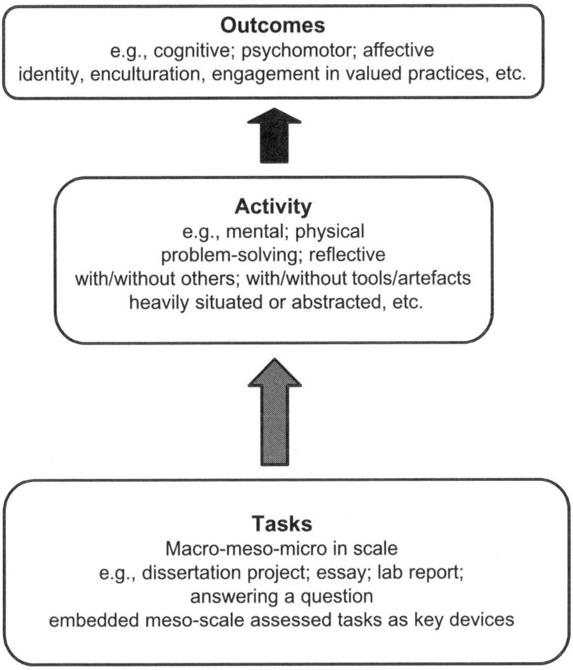

Figure 8.2 Tasks as set have an indirect effect on learning outcomes.

irrelevant? No, it does not. In some circumstances it may be appropriate for the teacher to design a task so that there is a much *tighter* link between task and activity (and thereby, though with less certainty, because the quality of activity will still be variable, to outcomes). Areas of safety-critical training may well require this kind of tight coupling. At the opposite extreme, teachers can sometimes be seen to hand over task design, largely or completely, to the student. Examples would be in programmes that use student-designed or negotiated assessment tasks as key learning activities (see e.g. Brook, Hunt & Hughes, 1994; Boud, Cohen & Sampson, 1999). But, we would argue, much of higher education practice, for good as well as bad reasons, sits between these extremes and necessarily involves situations in which there is some interpretative work, satisficing and slippage in the task–activity nexus (Goodyear & Ellis, 2008). This being so, task design remains a core responsibility for most teachers.

Figure 8.3 emphasises the point that tasks are not the only influence on student learning activity. As we explained in Chapter 2, learning activity is *situated*. The nature of the activity is influenced by the social and physical context in which it occurs. By pointing out that learning activity is socially situated, we mean that the web of relationships with other people influences the activity: what is done, how it is done and, to an extent, why it is done. We label the social context with the term 'people' in Figure 8.3. In some situations,

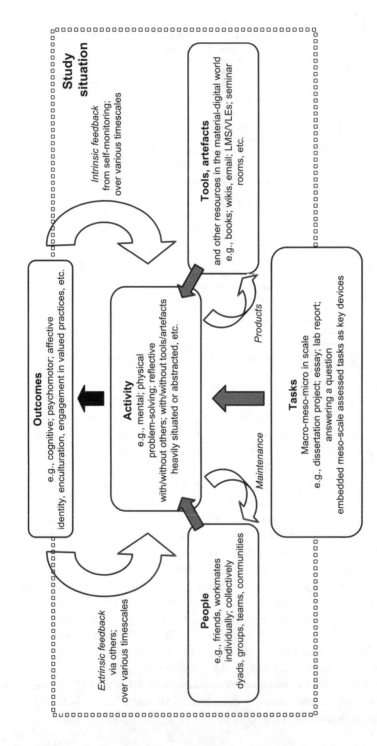

Figure 8.3 Key influences on learning activity and learning outcomes.

it may be that the strongest influence on the learner's activity comes from their relationship with just one other person: a close friend or colleague. In other situations, the influence may come from a small group – perhaps a workgroup to which the student has been assigned by the teacher. Bigger and more diffuse social groupings may also have influence. Examples would be where the student feels themself to be part of a learning community, or an apprentice member of a community of practice. In such cases, community norms, values, practices, language, history, etc., can influence the student, and how they approach their work, in ways that are sometimes powerful and sometimes quite subtle. Among the ways in which relations with others can influence the student's activity, we can think of things such as the manner in which work, effort and academic achievement are talked about, and the images of being a 'good' or 'savvy' student that emerge from such talk. Also, we can point to the ways in which divisions of labour allow some things to be done, while other experiences get closed off. The division of effort within a workgroup has strong implications for the nature of an individual student's activity, and what they gain from it.

In a similar fashion, we need also to think about the ways in which learning activity is *physically* situated. (For simplicity, we include the digital in the physical here.) What someone can do is often influenced quite powerfully by the tools and resources that come to hand (Säljö, 1995; Bowker, 2006), though the effects can sometimes be subtle and difficult to unravel (Salomon, 1993; Hutchins, 1995).

These social-cultural and physical-digital influences on the learner's activity need to be taken into account by the teacher as designer. A key point is that the teacher cannot design the social relationships within which the learner's activity is embedded. Neither can they design all the details of the learning place – the immediate, concrete, physical–digital environment in which a learner's activity is set. Students play a significant role in configuring their learning places. They make choices about the tools and resources they will use. They take responsibility for creating a 'defensible space for learning' – within which they can protect themselves from unwanted interruptions and can bring to hand the things they need. But they do this in an environment that they have not created themselves – whether we are thinking of studying on campus, at home, at work or while travelling. Students, teachers and others *co-configure* the learning place (cf. Nardi & O'Day, 1999; Crook & Barrowcliff, 2001). In a similar vein, teachers cannot prescribe friendships and workmates. Students exercise considerable freedom in choosing who to spend their time with, who they talk to about their work, and whose views they most value. Even in groupwork tasks, where the teacher has determined group membership, students still exercise some freedom in choosing how much or how little effort they will invest in group tasks, how far they will rely on their colleagues to get the job done, and the extent to which they will turn a group task into a number of parallel individual tasks. But they do this in a social milieu that has, in part, been created by the actions of teachers. Teachers and administrators create such things as classes and year groups. Many teachers are interested in creating the conditions within which a 'learning community' can prosper. They cannot create or design a community, but there is social engineering work they can do to make it more likely that community will evolve and thrive. In this sense, relations between activity and context exemplify Giddens's notion of *structuration*, which we introduced in Chapter 1. Students exhibit agency – a significant level of control over their activity – within a context that influences, but is also created by, aspects of their activity. In Figure 8.3, we have tried to represent this with the feedback loops labelled 'products' and 'maintenance'. The 'products' loop represents the fact that some student activity, either directly, or as a by-product, creates and assembles resources, tools and other artefacts that enrich the students' learning places (Wild, Modritscher & Sigdarson, 2008). The 'maintenance' loop represents those aspects of student activity that, directly or indirectly, have the effect of maintaining and improving their social/working relationships (with peers, teachers, members of their extended communities, etc.).

To sum up, Figure 8.3 alerts us to the following issues. First, learning outcomes depend on student activity. Tasks are resources for activity, not prescriptions of it. Activity is also strongly influenced by social and physical context. Teachers cannot design these in detail, but they do have a responsibility for setting in place some of the social and physical resources on which students will draw. Design is therefore an indirect process, through which teachers aim to influence but not control the students' activity.

Layers in Design

Figure 8.3 is a very abstract way of thinking about the problem-space of educational design. Lots of very different things are grouped together under the headings 'people' and 'tools, artefacts, etc.'. Building a shared understanding of teaching-as-design is easier if we now shift to looking at some of the complexities hidden away by Figure 8.3.

One recognised way of simplifying a complex problem is to break it down into smaller parts. There are lots of models of educational design that take a 'divide and conquer' approach. They take a big problem, such as the design of a whole course, and break it down into more manageable chunks (e.g. planning one lecture at a time). While this can be helpful in tackling problems that are difficult because they are *large*, it is not necessarily helpful in dealing with problems that are difficult because they are *complex* (e.g. ones in which there are many internal dependencies between the elements of the solution). For complex problems that involve lots of interdependent elements, a good strategy is to simplify by separating out the thing that has to be designed into several relatively self-sufficient functional elements or 'layers'. A

useful analogy would be to think about the design of a building and to visualise separate layers that provide different functions. For example, Stuart Brand
(1997, pp. 13) suggests that the design of any building can be decomposed into
six layers: site, structure, skin, services, space plan and stuff.

- site: the geographical setting and the legally defined building site,
  having boundaries and context;
- structure: the foundation and load-bearing elements of the building;
- skin: the exterior surfaces;
- services: the communications wiring, electrical wiring, plumbing,
  sprinkler system, heating, ventilating, air conditioning, and moving
  parts like lifts and escalators;
- space plan: the interior layout – where walls, ceilings, floors and
  doors go;
- stuff : Chairs, desks, phones, pictures, kitchen appliances, lamps, etc.:
  things that move around inside spaces.

An instance of this approach of simplifying through layering, in the educational design area, is Goodyear's four-layer 'pedagogical framework' (see e.g.,
Goodyear, 1999, 2005). This offers a way of thinking about tasks and intended
learning outcomes by identifying four loosely-coupled design layers.

Goodyear's notion of a 'pedagogical framework' emerged as part of an
attempt to compare and contrast the main educational features of a large
number of technology-based learning innovations funded by the European
Union's Socrates and Minerva programmes. It is a simple attempt to identify
and relate four main layers in the design and execution of these innovations
(Table 8.1).

The pedagogical framework offers a way of handling some of the complexity of task design, by suggesting that most of the issues involved in enacting a
pedagogical approach can be categorised as being concerned with one of the
four levels shown in Table 8.1. It helps structure the problem space of deciding
how teaching will be conducted. This can be particularly helpful when one
also acknowledges that the four levels need not be tightly-coupled. While there
are usually advantages to having coherence across levels, the relations are
not tight, deterministic ones. There is scope for some freedom of action,
improvisation, the introduction of variety, etc.

The pedagogical framework is principally concerned with the 'how' of teaching and learning, rather than with *what* is to be learnt. Decisions about what is
to be learnt map onto the specification of learning outcomes (Figure 8.3).
Considering scale and layering introduces the notion that intended learning
outcomes vary in scope, and can be seen as nested. There can be very broad
brush outcomes (e.g., 'acquire the ability to communicate effectively with a
range of personnel'), nested within which one can find more specific or

Table 8.1 Pedagogical Framework

Philosophy	Beliefs about the nature of knowledge and competence; about how learning occurs; about how people should and should not be treated, etc. Examples might include positivism, realism and interpretivism; constructivism and behaviourism.
High level pedagogy (HLP)	A broad educational approach, such as cognitive apprenticeship, collaborative knowledge-building, problem-based learning or programmed learning. An HLP does not contain direct prescriptions for action, but it foregrounds some kinds of possible action, and backgrounds others. An HLP is a way of turning a philosophical position into a space of commitments and possibilities.
Pedagogical strategy	A broad brush depiction of plans, e.g. about a sequence of tasks that will be proposed. Best seen as a way of communicating and negotiating within a programme team and with students. Best stripped of its commercial and militaristic resonances of outwitting a rival or enemy. A device for joint sense-making, which avoids the fine detail of pedagogical tactics. Examples would include collaboration scripts.
Pedagogical tactics	The detailed moves through which a strategy is enacted, or out of which a strategy emerges.

Source: Goodyear, 1999.

finer-grained outcomes (e.g., 'recognise the dangers inherent in writing satirical memos').

Gibbons and Rogers (2008) have also drawn on the layering approach as a way of separating out design issues that can be treated in bundles. Their approach uses seven layers: content, strategy, message, control, representation, media-logic and data management. These are defined in Table 8.2.

In our view, the layering used in Table 8.2 is particularly appropriate if one thinks about educational design as being focussed on the crafting of communication and messages.

Our own preference is for a focus on *situated activity*. Receiving and interpreting instructional messages is one kind of activity and although it is important, we do not see it as necessarily the best focus when thinking broadly about learning and educational design. From a broader perspective, we can use the concept of design layering to help decouple things which are best managed separately, and also to help identify who has responsibility for what. The layering idea can be applied to each of the three main design components we discussed with the help of Figure 8.3: tasks, 'people' and 'tools, artefacts, places'.

Table 8.2 Gibbons' Instructional Design Layers

Content layer	A design must specify the structures of the abstract subject-matter to be taught, must identify the units into which the subject-matter will be divided, and must describe how elements of subject-matter will be made available to instructional functions performed by other layers.
Strategy layer	A design must specify the physical organisation of the learning space, social organisations of participants, their roles and responsibilities, instructional goals, allocation of goals to timed event structures, and strategic patterns of interaction between the learner and the instructional experience.
Message layer	A design must specify the tactical language of message structures through which the instructional experience can communicate content-derived information to the learner.
Control layer	A design must specify the language of control structures through which the learner expresses messages and actions to the source of the learning experience.
Representation layer	A design must specify the representations that make message elements visible, hearable, and otherwise sensible: the media representation channels to be used, the rule for assigning message elements to media channels, the form and composition of the representation, the synchronisation of messages delivered through the multiple channels and the representations of content.
Media-logic layer	A design must specify the mechanism by which representations are caused to occur in their designed or computed sequence.
Data management layer	A design must specify data to be captured, archived, analysed, interpreted and reported.

Source: Adapted from Gibbons & Rogers, 2008.

One way of doing this is to see what comes into focus when we look at the main areas of educational design at different scale levels. For example, the area of task design changes some of its characteristics when viewed at different temporal scale levels (e.g. tasks that last a few minutes or a few hours; tasks that extend over a whole degree programme). The 'people' area also has different characteristics when viewed at different social scale levels. There are important differences between (a) putting students into pairs to tackle a task, and (b) arranging a programme so that it can support both full-time and part-time students. The design area that we have labelled 'tools, artefacts, etc.' can be seen as a nested hierarchy ranging from a whole university campus down to a mouse, pen, PDA or paper. (The interpenetration of the digital and material worlds upsets this neat hierarchy, but for now this simplification is not unhelpful.)

Different groupings of university staff have responsibilities for different scale levels or layers in these design areas. The solo teacher may well have a lot of autonomy to design short tasks (e.g. holding a buzz group in a lecture) but will usually just inherit, as a given, some of the constraints set by arrangements at larger scale levels (e.g. the length of a semester). Programme teams can work at micro and meso levels. For example, they will often have some say in the kinds of rooms to be used for face-to-face work with students. They typically have a high level of control over the intended outcomes of a programme, though within constraints set by the university's statements about generic graduate attributes, and/or requirements set by professional accrediting bodies. The macro level – the broadest layers of design activity – tend to be the preserve of university managers and staff who have a university-wide remit. We are thinking here of such things as decisions about which learning management system to use, about whether to increase the number of lecture rooms or flexible learning spaces, about whether to create a new programme or close down programmes that are under-recruiting, etc. In a well-functioning university, there will, of course, be a great deal of information flow and negotiation across layers and levels. Also, as we have noted above, none of the people working in a design role has complete control over any of the design areas. That said, it is still worth observing that different groups tend to orient their design activity to particular layers in the design space.

Also relevant to this point is that design activity at different levels tends to draw on different knowledge sources. For example, it is much easier to make good use of psychological research arising from detailed studies of short learning episodes if one is thinking about the design of short learning tasks than if one is considering broader issues of course design. Research on knowledge-sharing activities in communities of practice is easier to use if one is thinking about programme design rather than whether to use a buzz group in tomorrow's lecture.

Self-awareness, Feedback and Self-correction: Iterative Design and Sustainable Improvement

University teaching is a complex activity which a conscious design approach can help to simplify and improve. Thinking about how teaching-as-design fits into the broader ecology of learning is a good way of reminding ourselves that students' learning activity is at the heart of design consciousness – awareness of that central purpose of 'good learning' is key. As we saw in Chapter 6, it is not always the case that teachers adopt a carefully planned approach, or one that is centred on good ideas about student learning.

Another key aspect of this awareness (design consciousness) is that once a task is designed, it develops a life of its own. It becomes part of the students' experience as a learning activity and they may respond to it in more or less helpful ways for the development of their understanding. Effective designers will approach their work knowing that feedback from student learning can help with the incremental improvement of designed tasks.

Incremental revisions of designed tasks will vary depending on the level in the ecology: the micro, for example, might focus on the internal structure of the key aspects of the task; the meso, might be concerned with how teams of teachers, tutors and/or students are likely to interact with the task in light of faculty policies and culture; the macro might consider the interplay of university enterprise technologies and physical spaces to afford learning. Another key aspect of the development of self-awareness about task design is that designing is rarely undertaken on a *tabula rasa*, even when tasks are being designed for the first time (Laurillard, 2002). The ecology in which the design occurs will provide constraints of which the teacher must become aware.

Teachers rarely think that they get the design of a task right the first time. It is reasonable to assume that most designs will go through an iterative process of use, feedback, redesign and reuse. In an ecology of learning, this cycle tightens the links between design and teaching, reinforcing the idea of teaching-as-design.

We find it helpful to think about the traces of student activity as an artefact that can inform the incremental improvement of a design. The use of student feedback, obtained via course experience questionnaires, focus groups, etc., can be very valuable in thinking about the improvement of a course. But it is just one source of data. When students are making use of virtual environments, for example to hold discussions, share work or co-ordinate activity, they leave persisting traces. These may be simply the artefacts they have created – such as discussion logs – or they may also include various representations of group processes – such as graphs showing contributions over time. In short, the whole set of online traces left by students at the end of a course is a potentially valuable, complex artefact. It may sometimes be too complex to use in the time-pressed business of setting up a new virtual space for the course the next time it runs. But routinely to delete such artefacts is wasteful.

There are a number of alternatives. One is to design the virtual space for a course so that parts of it persist from year to year – allowing students to read, re-use and improve upon the work of previous years, while having their own fresh-minted space to operate within. Another is for the teacher to select what they see as most useful and repurpose it for next year, editing and annotating as they see fit.

Our main point is that the 'learning loop' of feedback and incremental redesign means that the quality of a design improves steadily over time. If everything has to be recreated from scratch, the teacher's time is dissipated over an excessive range of jobs: some of which do not need academic expertise and attention. If the teacher's time can be focussed on selective improvements, then quality increases. Having a sharp sense of 'good learning' makes it much easier to prioritise areas for improvement.

From an ecological perspective, feedback on design also needs to flow from other sources, not just from the students. For example, some aspects of a design may have unintended consequences for library staff, IT services or other teachers. In a well-functioning ecology, such information flows to where it is needed, on a timely basis.

Aggregation of feedback on task design across many courses can be particularly illuminating for staff who have faculty-wide or university-wide remits. Not least, being able to spot trends in technology choices, and in other decisions that have consequences for infrastructure, means that planning can stay ahead of the game, rather than merely reacting to crises. We examine some of these challenges more deeply in Chapters 9 and 10.

9
Leadership for Learning
Perspectives on Learning Spaces

Introduction

The ideas associated with an ecology of learning – balance, self-awareness, feedback, alignment and sustainability – can be used to help university leaders address a wide range of concerns and goals. Examples include leadership in relation to curriculum development, graduate attributes, quality assurance, quality enhancement, personnel and recruitment and external relations. We do not have space to address all of these issues, so to provide an illustration of the power of the concept of a learning ecology, we have chosen to focus on leadership in relation to learning spaces. We have chosen this topic for a number of reasons. The benefits of an integrated conception of physical and virtual campus design are not yet generally well-understood in universities. If universities get this wrong, then the costs involved are serious, not just in terms of capital expenditure, but also in relation to the effectiveness of the scholarly enterprise, which is dependent on integration of academic processes across the physical and virtual. Also, well-designed learning spaces have immediate benefits for students and teachers and knock-on benefits for university leaders charged with safeguarding the university's learning mission. Interest in this field has been growing quite rapidly in recent years. The research base is still quite small, but we present and discuss some of its key insights in this chapter.

Learning Spaces

A key argument pursued throughout the book so far has been that e-learning is part of a broader student learning experience in the majority of universities, and its role is best understood within the context of improving student understanding. In this chapter we focus on the first part of the argument, the association of e-learning with the broader student learning experience and the implications that follow.

As we showed in Chapters 4 and 5, when teachers introduce e-learning activities the structure of the students' learning experience can become more complex. This is not necessarily a good thing. Its significance is that at the level of learning activities, students are more likely to find themselves pursuing an idea back and forth across physical spaces (lectures, tutorials, laboratories, seminars, clinics, libraries, and the like) and virtual spaces (learning management systems, ePortfolios, Web 2.0 technologies, faculty databases providing learning materials, library catalogues, etc.). Depending on the design of activities, the success of learning arising from the activity may largely depend on how successfully a university has integrated these two sets of spaces *from a student perspective*. It is from this perspective that the issue of learning spaces in campus design needs to be considered.

A major challenge for university leaders responsible for learning spaces is how to deal with the uncertainty involved in their provision. Uncertainty and complexity are created by changes in student needs, qualitative and quantitative variations in disciplinary/faculty space requirements, the speed of change of learning technologies, and changing cost/benefit ratios. Chapter 9 considers these types of issues as a way of setting up the context for Chapter 10. Chapter 10 puts forward a case for a principled approach to campus planning using the ideas of an 'ecology of learning'.

Relating an Ecological View of Learning to Leadership

Chapter 7 identified some key aspects of an ecological view of learning. Viewing a university as an ecology of learning, we suggest effective leadership necessitates:

- maintaining an ecological balance – where the balance sought is an environment which promotes ongoing successful and meaningful learning, whether it be through teaching, which guides students' activity, or through research, (learning through the creation of new knowledge);
- ensuring that self-awareness develops throughout the university – which involves all parts of the university being aware of how their structure and purpose relate to learning and the mission of the university;
- maintaining feedback loops – such that timely, reliable, action-oriented information flows to where it is needed;
- facilitating continuous self-correction – enabling all parts of the university to adjust their activities through ongoing self-management in order to better align to the mission of the university, and to mesh more effectively with each other.

The successful oversight of these key aspects of an ecology of learning can be thought of as a type of ecological management by leaders, one which prioritises learning as the key purpose of universities. For leaders at all levels of a university, maintenance of these aspects is a legitimate role.

In this chapter, we use these principles as a way of discussing leadership in relation to campus planning. We suggest that it is possible to apply an ecological view of learning to any aspect of campus planning, especially where planning has to acknowledge uncertainty. For the purposes of this chapter and the next, we apply it to the core example of teaching and learning spaces. We do not have room to deal appropriately with research spaces, though we would argue that holistic planning of all such spaces – as spaces that support learning in its various guises – is highly desirable.[1]

Implications of an Ecological View of Learning for Learning Spaces

A poorly designed seminar room or a poorly designed learning management system can both undermine the quality of the learning experience, especially when they are intended to support a single learning activity but are experienced by students as incompatible. To inform approaches to planning for learning spaces, we need to understand more deeply how successful student learning occurs across physical and virtual spaces.

The research considered in Chapters 4–6 identified elaborations in the structure of the experience of learning, mostly occurring as students traversed back and forth amongst physical and virtual spaces within the same activity. The experiences reported by students involved strategies which were often qualitatively different in nature. A key concept in understanding the qualitatively different nature of student experiences of e-learning was *approach to learning*. The structure of an approach to learning when e-learning is part of the means is comparatively complex. If students are expected to use an increasingly diverse range of e-learning systems in their learning, then it needs to be acknowledged that they are being asked to develop a variety of strategies to traverse back and forth across physical and virtual spaces, as they move towards a deeper understanding of ideas.

The experiences of learning described by students in Chapters 4 and 5 suggest that teachers cannot assume that the mere provision of e-learning (as part of the learning opportunities offered to students) will lead either to understanding or to the development of appropriate learning strategies. If such developments were automatic then we would not have been able to identify some student experiences of learning that were oriented towards a surface approach. Similarly in Chapter 6, some experiences of teaching did not seem to make the most of e-learning, particularly when teachers reported thinking about, or approaching, teaching using strategies in which e-learning was not integrated into course design, but was 'bolted-on' as an afterthought. For teachers, there seems to be a significant professional and pedagogical area of development in which fresh thinking about approaches to design and teaching should be informed by knowledge of the structure of students' experiences of learning when e-learning is a significant part of the means used.

One of the main implications of our research into student and teacher experiences is this idea of the need for seamless integration of physical and virtual learning contexts. It follows that if the learning context does not promote an effective integration of learning back and forth across physical and virtual spaces, then the quality of student learning will be put at risk.

This conclusion is reinforced by comments from teachers in the interviews in Chapter 6. The interviews suggested qualitatively different experiences of teaching when the activities traversed physical and virtual contexts. The more successful teachers tended to remove boundaries and blockages between the face-to-face and online experiences so that 'students do not see any artificial separation between the way they are learning and studying in class, on-campus, online and at home' (Teacher 10). This type of integrated approach to teaching in contexts in which students are learning face-to-face and online was particularly evident in the longer interview extract with the science teacher.

> Teacher: What's happening now is that there's no real separation of tasks or separation of problem to pracs, online, home study or lecture theatre. Bits and pieces of each come in to the different places. So even in the prac room some of the stuff I might have done in the lecture might become part of the prac. So for ten minutes we're going to do this now – you need to know this – here's some pictures – you're going to look at these rocks – this is what they look like – this is how we do it – ok off you go. So the learning spaces are sort of blending or sort of oozing into each other. (See part 2 of the long interview extract in Chapter 6.)

This type of insight arising from empirical research is a useful source of knowledge for university leaders seeking to develop a way of nurturing effective student learning through shaping the university environment. For the purposes of the argument in this chapter, leadership practice which is informed by an ecological view of learning, should develop self-awareness by drawing on this type of knowledge.

Physical and Virtual Spaces

The implications of a seamless integration between the physical and virtual experiences of students (and teachers) are serious for the development of appropriate modern learning spaces in universities. It is important to have a sense of scale. It would not be uncommon for a publicly-funded, medium sized university in one of the richer countries of the world, with around 25,000 students, to have an annual property and IT capital budget – that is a budget for development as opposed to operational costs – of over US$100m. The estimated spend on campus facilities in the United States alone for 2007 was US$18 billion (Oblinger, 2006b). If the underlying principle for the investment of this capital is to improve the strategic positioning of the university with respect to its learning, teaching and research goals, then investment that leverages benefits by integrating physical and virtual spaces for student, teacher and researcher needs is a key challenge.

Elaborating Categories of Learning Spaces

The idea of the university as an ecology of learning resonates with some recent international developments in planning and researching learning spaces. As the learning benefits of integrating virtual and physical spaces are starting to be realised, investment in a variety of learning spaces is occurring in many higher education systems. One of the main challenges in planning for this investment is identifying an appropriate mix, which clearly reveals costs in relation to benefits.

Learning spaces include recreational areas such as lawns, foyers and cafés, provided with wireless connectivity to provide informal learning opportunities, small formal spaces such as seminar, laboratory or lecture rooms, whole buildings and whole campuses. The development of such learning spaces also varies in scale, scope and cost: from (no cost) temporary reconfigurations through to ten-year capital building programmes. The greater the complexity and cost, the more careful leaders have to be in ensuring that space planning is aligned with the key learning, teaching and research goals identified by the university. Today, university leaders find themselves in a context in which the conceptualisation of learning spaces must be intimately linked to learning and teaching outcomes. Depending on the maturity of institution, and the tenure of the leader, different opportunities for shaping the learning spaces of the university may present themselves. In few other areas do senior leaders find themselves with as much uncertainty and as much risk exposure because of the scale and longevity of the investment.

In the next few pages we review the different scales of learning spaces that present opportunities for campus development. The issue of scale is an important one as an ecological perspective on a wireless-enabled café reveals different challenges for a university leader compared with the challenges involved in renewing the internals of a building. Students can benefit from both being integrated with the learning experience, but the issues that have to be resolved for this to happen effectively are contextually dependent.

Conceptualising 'Learning Space'

Before discussing some of the research into learning spaces in terms of its implications for the ecology of a university, it is worth considering the conceptual complexity behind the term 'learning spaces'. One of the challenges when considering this term is delineating the boundaries of the space the term is meant to imply. If we throw 'time' into the mix, it can change our concept of a learning space from something which might be conceived of as a place where learning occurs, to a social construct which is dependent on the interaction of people (Goodyear, 2006). In the following discussion, the meaning of 'learning space' is related to the focus of the studies being reported.

Developing a Language to Talk about Virtual and Physical Spaces

The terms 'virtual learning space' and 'e-learning' are closely associated. Some writers use the terms almost interchangeably, though we think there is value in distinguishing between activity and the space/place (virtual, physical or both) in which that activity is set.

Many books have been written over the last couple of decades about the affordances of e-learning and of its associated learning spaces. Notable texts in the area include Anderson and Elloumi (2004), Andrews and Haythornthwaite (2007), Clark and Mayer (2002), Collis and Moonen (2001), Garrison and Anderson (2003), Lockwood and Gooley (2001), Naidu (2003), Palloff and Pratt, (1999, 2003) and Salmon (2001, 2002). Many other books have addressed the issue of improving the experience of learning on campus by integrating e-learning technologies with more traditional forms of support for learning (e.g. Bates, 2000; Bates & Poole, 2003; Epper & Bates, 2001; Jochems, van Merrienboer & Koper, 2004; Laurillard 2002). A key issue for university leaders of campus-based universities is that an investment in a virtual learning space needs to be conceived of in relation to the physical learning spaces and how an investment in both is justified in terms of the learning and teaching goals of the institution. This requires a fundamental rethink of our concepts and language of spaces, not just playing around the edges (Chism & Bickford, 2002). We argue that a useful point of departure for this rethink is acknowledging the elaborated structure of the student experience of learning: that more and more teachers are requiring students to take their ideas with them as they interact with people and resources in class and online. Consequently, when it comes to deciding a strategy for investing in learning spaces, physical and virtual infrastructure need to be considered together. It does not make sense to invest in either physical or virtual spaces without an explicit strategy for how this investment is integrated into the conceptualisation, investment and management of the other. Apart from the educational benefits, the opportunity cost of not managing to leverage space needs from virtual infrastructure will be billions of dollars each year, if the US estimates on campus facility spending are any indication (Oblinger, 2006b). To better integrate virtual spaces with the physical, we need to develop a way of talking about both in relation to each other and to the mission of a university.

Categories of physical learning spaces in universities are comparatively well understood. Physical spaces include for example, lecture theatres, seminar and tutorial rooms, clinics and laboratories, libraries, lawns, halls of residence, foyers and cafés. Some important learning spaces are not under the university's control: an off-campus study bedroom being one example. Field trips also transform spaces outside the university into (temporary) learning spaces.

Categories of virtual spaces are less well understood and subject to more change – in response to developments in technology and how disciplines and other communities are interacting and creating and sharing knowledge. As we mentioned earlier, whether one thinks of these things as tools or spaces is often a matter of perspective rather than something inherent in the tool/ space itself. For example, Facebook can be seen as both a network of semi-private spaces and a set of tools for furnishing and advertising changes in those spaces.

Typical categories of virtual learning spaces provided by universities at the beginning of the 21st century include learning management systems (such as Moodle, Blackboard, dotlrn), ePortfolios (such as Nuventive, PebblePad, Desire2Learn), a range of Web 2.0 technologies which facilitate open access and social interaction, sequential task design systems like LAMS (Dalziel, 2003), interactive Web-casting and communications software (such as Adobe Connect and Mediasite), private virtual spaces (such as email and disk space for the storage of digital objects). Students develop their own virtual social spaces, often outside the university context (such as when using social software like MySpace or Facebook).

The names in some of these categories, and the categories themselves, will doubtless change over the next decade. However, some shared understanding of the nature and affordances of various kinds of virtual learning space is necessary if university leaders are to make sensible decisions about integration and trade-offs between virtual and physical space.

For example, there is some debate about the extent to which universities should make provision for non-university virtual space to be linked to university-provided virtual space. There are decisions to be made about what the institution needs to provide and what can legitimately be left to students. What investment and management strategies are needed to make best use of combinations of students' personal technologies and university-provided spaces?

The general point is worth emphasising. When planning for learning spaces, universities need to plan for both physical and virtual spaces. To do this, they need a shared language that can represent the structure and affordances of physical and virtual spaces, as well as their integration and their connections with learning activities and intended learning outcomes. One of our goals in the remaining pages is to introduce language and ways of thinking about physical and virtual spaces for the purposes of campus planning.

Small-scale Learning Spaces

By small-scale spaces we mean spaces that are smaller than an entire building. Planning and design approaches for small scale spaces typically involve a room or suite of similar rooms in relation to which some consideration has to be given to the integration of physical and virtual space in order to provide better support for learning.

The information students discern in the physical environment of a learning space is conditioned by a number of designed characteristics of that space. A worryingly high number of learning spaces have poor acoustics, poor lighting and/or poor temperature control. Each of these can inhibit learning (Weinstein, 1981; Gee, 2006; Graetz, 2006). Relatively early research also looked at the aesthetics of small scale learning spaces, making connections between design features and requirements for learning (Justin, 1965; Knirk, 1987).

Technology configuration issues highlighted in this early research focussed on acoustics, the affordances and requirements of front and rear projection, the use of television, and achieving synergies between the architectural design of spaces such as lecture theatres and the use of technologies within those spaces (Haft, 1972).

Some psychological research has investigated links between the physical environment and learners (e.g. Weinstein, 1981). Weinstein's study noted that the relationship between the environment and learning is moderated by social, psychological and instructional variables. Barriers to learning in the physical environment can often be attributed to poor architectural design approaches (Chism, 2002). For example, arranging computers in rows has thwarted the best attempts of teachers to stimulate group work and more team-based approaches (Brett & Nagra, 2005). Studies into instructional variables are often restricted to a specific discipline with particular learning space requirements such as Engineering (Berggren, Brodeur & Crawley, 2003), or salient characteristics of a pedagogy such as large enrolment, interactive, IT-rich experiences (Beichner & Saul, 2003), or an approach to an entire undergraduate curriculum (PKAL, 2007).

In order to combine thinking about physical and virtual spaces, Bennett (2007b) offers some key questions to consider during the design process for learning spaces.

- What is it about the learning that will happen in this space that compels us to build a bricks and mortar learning space, rather than rely on a virtual one?
- How might this space be designed to encourage students to spend more time studying and studying more productively?
- For what position on the spectrum from isolated study to collaborative study should this learning space be designed?

- How will claims to authority over knowledge be managed by the design of this space? What will this space affirm about the nature of knowledge?
- Should this space be designed to encourage student/teacher exchanges outside the classroom?
- How might this space enrich educational experiences?

These types of questions can be used to open up a dialogue within a university about developing a shared understanding of strategic reasons for investing in a complementary way in physical and virtual spaces.

Buildings as Learning Spaces

The ability of university leaders to shape learning spaces is often related to the stage in which institutional capital planning is occurring. Since campus master-planning can take years to realise, the best intentions of a leader to shape the master-plan for the immediate good of students, teachers and researchers may be delayed simply because of the time it takes to realise building plans for learning spaces. A useful strategy is to assess at which stage of development the planning for learning spaces across the university is occurring, and to make the most of that. For example, whole buildings may be at an early stage of construction or an internal fit-out may be required in an existing building.

An ecological perspective on buildings as learning spaces could adopt a variety of frames of reference in order to motivate the design; for example, it could use the goals of the university (Long, 2006), an approach to learning and teaching (Holtham, 2006) or pedagogical principles (Lynch, 2006). Good examples of the redesign of whole buildings for the purpose of learning can be found in many university libraries.

Libraries

It is not hard to argue for a library to be conceived of as a learning space, although to do so means the fundamental concept of libraries in many institutions necessarily changes from being a place where things are kept, to being a place where learners go to learn individually or in groups, getting access to learning resources either from library shelves or virtually. Some researchers argue that the concept of libraries is not moving sufficiently quickly to keep up with changes in the integration of virtual and physical sources of information (Bennett, 2006). The library reconceived as first and foremost a place of informal learning moves its role closer to the centre of an ecology of learning. This is a fundamentally different idea from the concept of a place in which information is stored for users.

Libraries have been one of the first areas of universities to actively embrace the integration of physical and virtual learning spaces in architectural design. Library experiences for most users in universities are already shaped by an integration of physical and virtual contexts. A significant debate, captured through a Delphi study in America (Ludwig & Starr, 2004), assembled specialists in health sciences libraries who provided commentary on the strategic direction of library services. Key outcomes from the study pointed towards an increasing speciality of libraries being hubs and managers of information rather than repositories, connected virtually, providing specialised services to different disciplines and providers of spaces for group learning. Students and staff of these disciplines seek to access the growing variety of sources of knowledge and information effectively, both from within the library – physically when working with peers in groups – and externally through the library when researching from home or work. A re-design or re-purposing of library spaces has occurred in many countries (for example Gordon, 2003; Jamiseon, 2004; Forrest, Hinchcliffe, Arp & Woodard, 2005; Lippincott, 2006; Lombardi & Wall, 2006; Michael-Barber, 2006). It is becoming more common as universities seek to align investment in their buildings to the learning/teaching/researching goals of the university.

Common approaches to repurposing library space include the development of information commons and integrating smaller configurations for learning into existing library spaces (Gordon, 2003; Forrest, Hinchcliffe, Arp & Woodard, 2005; Lippincott, 2006). Information commons have gained some traction as the benefits of integrating information technology, staff and library resources together provides significant benefits to students and researchers. While libraries have a good record of offering new developments in information technology to users, information commons are often characterised by the provision of a wider selection of software and a richer saturation of computers and access to virtual resources and communication networks. This occurs because learning commons have the potential to co-locate a variety of services for students and teachers, including library resources, IT systems and support and learning spaces for small and large groups. Co-location reduces the overall costs of provision. For example, library IT support can be extended to include support for IT in the learning spaces without setting up another separate unit of IT support for the latter.

Another approach to library redesign is to reconceive the whole physical environment of a library from a perspective of learning, rather than hiving off one section as a commons. In this approach, any space in the library has the potential to be reconceived from the perspective of supporting a learning situation: ranging from private reflection to large group work on projects. This type of approach often raises questions that go straight to the heart of the issue about the purpose of libraries.

How can the library balance its traditional role as an acquirer and preserver of substantial collections with its emerging role as a user-centred, service-rich space for research, collaboration, and creativity and remain agile enough to respond quickly to the changing work patterns of its patrons?

(Lombardi & Wall, 2006)

It is not uncommon for these types of questions to drive the discussions underpinning the redesign of libraries, but they are often accompanied by more pragmatic discussions about how to realise change. Care must be taken so that practical strategies – such as those designed to increase the amount of space to be repurposed, increasing e-resources, moving low use books and other print resources to an off-site repository and increasing the use of compact storage solutions – do not become ends in themselves and displace the library from its central role in the ecology of learning.

No matter which approach is adopted to the repurposing of library space for learning, international trends to date suggest that the changes are usually accompanied by an increase in the amount of space for informal learning and collaboration. This approach to the redesign of libraries puts their conceptualisation closer to the centre of an ecology of learning and meets what has been referred to as the 'sleeping giant' of academic demand: collaborative learning space (Foote, 2004). The frequency of group-work and inquiry-based learning has substantially increased in higher education over the last few decades. One only needs to look at the proliferation of approaches to curriculum design such as problem based learning for evidence (Norman & Schmidt, 1992, 2000; Boud & Feletti, 2001). Given the complexity of what students are expected to do in groups outside class, it is no longer sustainable for teachers to send them off in the vague hope that they might find the space they need somewhere in the university to learn successfully. A planned and integrated approach to students' unsupervised learning activities is called for if universities are concerned about the quality of their overall experience of learning.

The Campus as a Learning Space

In planning for campus development which seeks to reduce unmet physical space needs by making better use of virtual space, universities do not need to seek to change their profile as providers of a campus-based experience (Wedge & Kearns, 2005). On the contrary, it is in the interest of many universities to reinforce their uniqueness in the international education sector through the quality of the campus-based life they offer. However, this does not reduce the need for serious strategic planning of, and investment in, integrating physical and virtual spaces for learning. There have been a number of studies into campus master-planning which seek fundamental integration of the physical and virtual spaces of a university (for example De Noriega & Gonzales, 2004; Fisher, 1999; Guckert, 2002; Webster, 1999). If a shared understanding amongst all the stakeholders of the university of the rationale and cost/benefits underlying the approach is not in place, then the success of the planning will be undermined and successful outcomes put in jeopardy.

It is useful here to reflect on the meaning of the term 'university campus'. As a result of rapid developments in knowledge and technology, the external and internal boundaries of what constitutes a 'campus' have become blurred. The physical aspects of a university's campus remain comparatively more bounded for the purposes of planning, while the virtual aspects are comparatively less bounded. The interplay between the two is a significant contributor to the uncertainty inherent in planning for the development of university campuses. We use the term 'university campus' to refer to both its physical and virtual dimensions.

Rationales for Investing in Learning Spaces

The discussion on research into learning spaces in the preceding paragraphs shows there have been a number of drivers behind it: uncertainty inherent in planning for the future, campus master-planning, small scale learning space design, identifying the value of stakeholder input, the influence of e-learning and virtual spaces on the design of physical spaces and seeking to justify expenditure on space. Finding the best possible evidence to justify capital investment in academic spaces is one of the main roles of many university leaders.

Cost/Benefit Arguments

Universities seek a long life and good returns from their investment in learning spaces. Historically, most planning attention with respect to learning spaces has been focused on bricks and mortar, with supporting technologies usually representing a small portion of projects. Uncertainty in forward planning for teaching spaces increased towards the end of the 20th century, with group-based and problem-based learning becoming more common as whole disciplines adopted these types of approaches. The uncertainty often arose because demands on quantity of space required to support these approaches to learning are typically greater than is the case with traditional lecture/tutorial/laboratory models and the extent to which universities should support the model with space became a cost/benefit issue.

With the influence of e-learning on the structure of student and teacher experiences, the amount of uncertainty has been magnified (Bourlova & Bullen, 2005; Cohen & Nicol, 2007). Some implications for planning of learning spaces from this association are clear. For example, libraries do not need to increase their shelf space for journals. Most journals have adopted an e-publication model which facilitates access and integration of such resources into existing collections and learning experiences through virtual space without the need for more shelf space. Other implications are not as clear, and this is where a need for sustainable planning principles arises.

There has been some attempt to apply cost/benefit models to the evaluation of investment in virtual spaces for learning (see for example, Cohen & Nicol, 2007; Nicol & Cohen, 2003; Bacsich et al., 1999). This research has identified a number of challenges for campus planners who seek to quantify direct benefits from investment:

- Universities do not typically quantify costs for teaching and learning at small enough units (such as courses) to assess these in relation to income (such as student fees).
- E-learning for campus-based universities is part of a broader ecology, used to a different extent in different courses, making it very difficult to identify the real cost of e-learning at meaningful units of measurement (such as courses).
- It is difficult to measure, and consequently argue for, investment in virtual learning spaces if metrics such as correlations between levels of such investment and the development of student understanding are expected.

To overcome these types of difficulties, models for assessing the benefits of investment in e-learning that have been put forward (Nicol & Cohen, 2003a, 2003b), encourage university managers to assess the benefits at a higher level than courses, usually in reference to other indicators that may be meaningful to the institution such as realising a university's strategy in the relevant area.

Leveraging Learning and Teaching Infrastructure for Research

It is outside the scope of this book to treat the topic of leveraging learning and teaching infrastructure for research activities in depth. Yet, it would be incomplete to discuss learning spaces in the ecology of learning without referring to the benefits of leveraging learning and teaching space off investment in research infrastructure and vice versa, especially in universities seeking to develop a research culture not only for research itself (Shavelson, 2002), but to underpin research-led or research-enriched teaching (Jenkins, Breen, Lindsay & Brew, 2003).

The area of e-research (Anderson & Kanuka, 2003) is one which offers an indication of possible future trends in development in spaces for learning and teaching in universities. In university cultures where research-led experiences are encouraged, emerging aspects of e-research may influence the learning and teaching agenda.

- E-research makes the boundaries and collaborations of research partnerships more permeable. The virtual spaces that are required to enable e-research, such as the interrogation, synthesis and communication of digital data, can be drawn on by teachers in their curriculum design. This type of approach not only has the benefit of inculcating students into the ways and means of research, but it also can benefit the research agenda of a university by promoting a culture of research more widely.

- E-research is changing the nature of data collection (JISC, 2008). 'Naturally occurring' data sets are being drawn on from existing digital sources for research purposes. Useful learning tasks can be included in research design that help both students to learn the rigour of research work, and the sample size of data drawn on by researchers.
- Legitimate learning tasks for students can be designed to investigate first cut analyses of large data sets. The sharing of large data sets over virtual spaces will accelerate scholarship.

Another area of overlap is in information management. Examples of this currently existing internationally are university libraries which have a mandate to support both student learning and researcher/teachers. However, the demands for interoperability between enterprise software applications, those in learning, teaching, research and libraries as well as student records, finance and human resources, are not easily met and require large budgets to meet user needs in a seamless fashion. The decision by a university to invest in enterprise information management systems that overlap learning, teaching and research needs to be accompanied by an analysis of the interoperability between the software systems in each area. This is an area of rapid change for universities, one accompanied by a large amount of uncertainty about what the future holds.

Within the area of information management, topics such as communication and presentation technologies for research (Feuer, Towne & Shavelson, 2002; Ginsparg, 2000), collaborative work spaces and large data transfer, are all areas in which an integrated concept of virtual and physical spaces can benefit learners and researchers, especially in relation to the support models that both groups require for an efficient use of the spaces (Abowd & Mynatt, 2000). Investment in spaces and associated support models, with an eye to meeting the needs of all these groups, will improve cost/return ratios by eliminating duplication of services to separate groups or roles.

The earlier section in this chapter, 'Relating an Ecological View of Learning to Leadership', offered some rationales for investing in learning spaces for university leaders. These are just the beginning of a process that university leaders need to engage in if they are to successfully involve the university community in the process. A closely linked stage is the development of specifications for learning spaces.

Challenges for the Development of Specifications of Learning Spaces

What is the best way to go about identifying the specifications for learning spaces at a university? Given what we know about the nature of student learning and the associations we might find with virtual and physical learning spaces, it is too simplistic an argument to restrict specifications to perceived or imaginary attributes of spaces to the learning outcomes of students.

Specifications for learning spaces across university campuses should go beyond recommendations of the type often found in building projects, such as rules of thumb of square metres per student or work station. To support experiences of learning, and to gather the support of the university community necessary for their sustainability, their specifications need to be guided by an awareness of multiple perspectives of legitimate stakeholders on the process, a goal not easy to achieve (Bickford, 2002). In other words, a more holistic, university-wide understanding of the expectations of learning spaces from leaders at all levels of the university is required.

The following evaluation questions for learning spaces helps unpack the term 'university leaders' which we have been using throughout the chapter. In this context, leaders are senior managers who head up key areas across the university, and have responsibility for aligning their area to the mission of the university. While we have given examples of leaders by describing the perspectives below, other perspectives could legitimately exist depending on the structure of the university in question.

Legitimate Perspectives of University Leaders on Learning Spaces

Since a sustained enterprise-level approach to the development of learning spaces represents a significant intellectual and financial commitment by the community of a university, there are a number of legitimate stakeholder perspectives on learning spaces that should be taken into account.

With so many legitimate perspectives, the scope of evaluation issues for learning spaces is complex. From the ecological perspective adopted in this book, clearly the point of balance expected from learning spaces is for students to be supported in achieving their learning outcomes. However, given the mix of responsibilities that overlap in the provision of learning spaces across a university (pedagogical, managerial, financial), no single evaluation approach is likely to capture all perspectives successfully.

The following are some of the key evaluation issues, framed as questions, which should be considered in relation to one another, not atomistically. This is by no means an exhaustive list. Furthermore, some of the questions could legitimately be found under more than one of the following headings, but for the purposes of efficiency, have been listed only once.

Students

- To what extent does the learning space help me understand what I need to learn?
- How much confidence does the space inspire for collaboration and creativity?

- How attractive is it to go and learn in the space?
- How much support for my learning does the space provide?

Teachers/Researchers

- To what extent does the learning space help me to help students understand what they need to learn?
- How much confidence does the space inspire for collaboration and innovation?
- How much support for my teaching does the space provide?
- To what extent does the space either decrease or increase my workload?
- To what extent does the space help me to integrate my research into the student experience?

Provosts/Rectors/Vice-Chancellors

- To what extent do the learning spaces align with the university's mission?
- To what extent do the learning spaces embody the university's academic values?
- To what extent do the learning spaces contribute to the university's strategic position locally, nationally and internationally?

Deputy Provosts/Rectors/Vice-Chancellors (learning and teaching, including heads of academic development units)

- To what extent do the learning spaces meet the goals of the university learning and teaching plan?
- To what extent do the learning spaces help students and teachers to meet their learning outcomes?
- To what extent do the learning spaces meet the curriculum demands of the faculties?

Chief Financial Officers

- What are the capital and operational costs of maintaining the learning spaces in relation to the benefits identified by the other stakeholders?
- To what extent does the cost of maintaining the learning spaces support the strategic position of the university?

Directors of Property

- To what extent is the learning space inventory meeting the learning, teaching and research demands of faculties?
- To what extent does the portfolio of learning spaces meet national or

international benchmarks for the quality of the fabric for university spaces?

- How desirable is the projected capital building plan and operational costs for the portfolio of learning spaces in relation to Gross Floor Average for similar categories of spaces in comparator institutions?

Chief Information Officers

- To what extent does the information technology (IT) and its support model in the learning spaces meet the academic demands of students, teachers and researchers?
- To what extent does the IT and its support model in the learning spaces add value to the physical spaces?
- To what extent does the IT and its support model meet national or international benchmarks and best practice?
- How does the projected capital plan and operational costs for the IT services in learning spaces compare with plans and costs for similar IT services in other universities?

Librarians

- To what extent do the learning spaces integrated into the library meet the academic demands of students, teachers and researchers?
- To what extent do the library services integrated into learning spaces outside the library meet the academic demands of students, teachers and researchers?
- To what extent can academic enterprise be better supported by new combinations of library services, IT, learning spaces and appropriate support models?

Registrars/Directors of Student Services

- To what extent are informal learning spaces used to increase opportunities for learning?
- To what extent do learning spaces make allowances for diversity in the student population?
- To what extent can informal learning spaces legitimately increase the amount of recreational space for students?

Architects

- How well do the architectural principles embodied in existing spaces align with the university community's conceptions of 'good learning'?
- To what extent can the university articulate the type of specifications required for the future development of learning spaces, both physical and virtual?

- To what extent do learning spaces add to the functionality, capacity and aesthetics of the university campus?

Concluding Comments

Gathering legitimate stakeholder perspectives on learning and learning spaces is just the start of a hard intellectual process. A robust, sustainable approach to campus planning also needs principles to help manage the uncertainty associated with rapid changes in technology and in the knowledge practices of people within and outside the university. This is the problem we address in Chapter 10.

10

Relating the Idea of an Ecology of Learning to Campus Planning

Introduction

In Chapter 10 we adopt the perspective of university leaders responsible for developing a learning spaces strategy for whole-of-campus planning. Using the four key aspects of the idea of an ecology of learning (focus on learning, the development of self-awareness, maintaining feedback processes and self-correction), we consider a principled approach to planning for both physical and virtual spaces.

Developing a Principled Approach to Managing Uncertainty

University leaders do not wish to make mistakes. Looking around the world at innovative learning space developments, it is not hard to identify examples where university leaders have, in the last five years or so, invested in some kind of flagship prototype for small scale learning spaces only to find that they are locked into a technology which has already been superseded. Where there is a tight integration between the virtual and physical functionalities of the learning space, decoupling may prove uneconomic. It sometimes turns out to be more effective and cheaper to provide a learning functionality virtually, such as by grouping students into different configurations using an e-learning discussion tool, rather than to redesign a tutorial room physically in which furniture configurations mimic the grouping configurations used in a learning activity. However, this type of leveraging of virtual space presupposes that the e-learning systems are already part of the fabric of university spaces and that teachers and students know how to make the most of them for their learning. For campus-based universities, this is far from being universally true, although some have developed an integrated approach to planning and development that encompasses physical and virtual spaces with varying degrees of success and cost/risk minimisation (for example De Noriega & Gonzales, 2004; Guckert, 2002; Webster, 1999).

What universities seek is a frame of reference which is likely to be longer-lasting for investment, one that will traverse the peaks and troughs of technological booms and busts, embodying a more measured and enduring vision that can extract learning benefits from virtual spaces through integrating them with physical spaces but which also avoids locking the physical and the virtual together.

A practical and sustainable principle for investment in virtual spaces is what many universities are seeking – one which stands in contrast to flagship-type approaches to learning space development. The latter sometimes fall into the dangerous territory of attributing agency for the learning development of students predominately to space, as well as locking the design of spaces into superseded understanding. As the research reported in the earlier chapters shows, it is how, what and why students and teachers approach and conceive of the learning experience that offers some way into identifying why qualitatively different experiences of learning occur. Space influences activity through its affordances for learning. It does not determine activity or outcomes.

The danger of attributing agency to technologies in experiences of learning at university is worth reflecting on. With the periodic adoption of new technologies into the practices of higher education, the structure of learning activities can change, as students and teachers pick up on the educational affordances of the new technologies. For example, they can search large databases of knowledge in ways which would be unmanageable without the technology, both in terms of the time required and the geographical distances they can overcome within a single session. Networked technologies similarly enable discussions to take place among geographically distributed student groups and to extend over longer time periods. However, the inclusion of technologies in the experience does not ensure the students will learn. A poor concept of, and approach to, learning will not result in the development of student understanding, irrespective of the use of technology. One of the key points in the discussion in Chapters 4 and 5 was that the quality of learning arising from experiences involving e-learning was closely linked to what students say they think they are learning, what strategies are adopted when using the technologies, and the intent underlying their use. If we accept these points when considering campus planning, then a rationale for investing in appropriate spaces is to *enable* students and teachers to engage in the kinds of activities that align with 'good learning' and with key kinds of intended learning outcomes. It does not make sense to try to justify the large investments required by trying to find evidence of a direct link between the development of student understanding and the existence of space with particular qualities. Other important influences are always at work in the ecology of learning, including how and why students and teachers approach learning in particular ways. The mere existence of a space does nothing to explain why two students in the same space experience qualitatively different learning.

The Mission of the University as the Driver

If we accept the idea of the university as an ecology of learning, then the rationale that most clearly moves investment of learning spaces to the heart of the ecology is the adoption of a learning-centric university mission as the driver for investment.

There has been some evidence of using mission statements as a driver for the conceptualisation of libraries (Bennett, 2007a). In that study, students and teachers were surveyed about their perceptions of learning spaces and about how they interacted with the spaces. To achieve a more enduring vision for the university, the responses of the student and teachers were interpreted in terms of the mission of the university, rather than in terms of what it would take to immediately satisfy student wishes. The frame of reference, therefore, is grounded in the nature of academic enterprise in the future: a combination of what students want, teachers think and leaders are willing to provide. This approach can avoid unbalancing the ecology by prioritising any single group's perspective.

While this may seem a subtle point, its implications in terms of the approach to planning campus spaces are serious. University leaders responsible for planning spaces will improve their ability to plan if they draw on any source of data which starts to illuminate how students, teachers and researchers traverse back and forth between the virtual and physical spaces as they pursue learning outcomes in the context of the university's mission. Information required for this type of approach includes:

- the mission statement of the university;
- surveys of students, teachers, researchers, deans and heads of schools, faculty managers, librarians and support services, about the spaces needed to meet the university's mission (Bennett, 2007a; Christensen Hughes, 2002; Walton, 2006);
- research into the nature of student and teacher experiences of learning and teaching, particularly where the activities concerned have particular implications for combinations of physical and virtual space;
- research into the nature of teacher/researcher experiences of using research-based approaches to teaching;
- campus maps of physical and virtual spaces in relation to each other and how these relate to student and teacher usage;
- data indicating the size and shape of e-learning in relation to the whole curricula of the university;
- quantities and categories of different learning, teaching and research spaces;
- data indicating associations between physical and virtual traffic related to learning on campus;

- estimates of the maintenance and support costs of learning, teaching and research spaces, both physical and virtual;
- data indicating associations between faculty learning, teaching and research needs, and scale and the gross floor average required to service these goals;
- evidence indicating the size and scale of library services required to service faculty learning, teaching and research goals;
- evidence indicating the shape and scale of IT spaces required to meet faculty learning, teaching and research goals;
- evidence of institutional experiences of similar projects already completed and the financial implications of those;
- strategies for sustainable financial reinvestment in learning spaces.

There are sure to be other categories of useful data. It is not an exhaustive list that is important, rather the underlying approach suggested by such a list. While drawing on as much data as possible to illuminate how students, teachers and researchers are pursuing their goals, leaders of the capital investment plan must continually return to evidence about the nature of experiences of learning, teaching and research within the ecology as the point of orientation for shaping the investment process. This will help to reduce the likelihood that the investment will create facilities which do not really meet the *needs* of stakeholders (Bennett, 2007b).

Seeking as much evidence-based knowledge about how students, teachers and researchers learn, teach and research across physical and virtual spaces is a fundamental strategy for reducing uncertainty. Doing this once and without a framework of reference, however, is unlikely to provide a sustainable vision that endures beyond the next cycle of technological and knowledge innovation. What is needed is a self-renewing and self-sustaining approach to planning that will allow all the stakeholders to engage in meaningful decision-making, in relation to each other and in ways that further the university's mission. The following sections describe the principles of planning that could usefully underpin a sustainable and self-renewing approach to visioning for the future campus. Where illuminative, some aspects of planning at the University of Sydney are used to provide examples in this chapter.

Principles of Planning for Campus-based Universities

Adopting an ecological view of learning, principles of planning that seek to maintain the ecological balance of a university can be summarised as;

- identifying the ecological balance of the university;
- developing self-awareness of the state of the ecology of the university;
- overseeing illuminative feedback loops on the operations of the ecology of the university;

- ensuring that there are sufficient self-correcting mechanisms in the ecology;
- maintaining the balance of the ecology of the university through responsible management.

While these principles could be applied to any aspect of the ecology, planning for learning spaces is used as a focus for the following discussion.

Identifying the Ecological Balance of the University

As a principle for planning, ecological balance is equivalent to the point of being, the reason for existing, the purpose of the university. To provide a principled frame of reference for planning for the future campus, it is necessary to identify its ecological balance. This requires drawing on the mission statement of the university, its strategic learning, teaching and research plans, its policy framework and all the supporting documentation that reveals the underlying values and purpose of the university. It is within this framework that the planning should unfold. Such a process may produce a review of the alignment between key aspects of the ecology; the mission statement, strategy, ideals and values. However, in order to maintain an ecological balance in a context of uncertainty, this should be enabled by the set of feedback loops that routinely keeps a university and its constituent elements informed, rather than by some artificial process that is somehow managed 'outside' or 'above' the ecology.

When applied to learning spaces, identifying the point of ecological balance goes to the heart of the theory of the university as an ecology of learning. In this approach, it is possible and useful to conceptualise all space categories at the university in relation to a mission of learning. As the next section will discuss, developing self-awareness of the structure of a learning space inventory within an ecology requires a definition of the measurement by which a balance is determined.

Self-awareness

To allow an ecology to maintain its balance, participants need points of reference. For those considering planning for learning spaces, self-awareness of the institution's space inventory in relation to some measurement indicating an appropriate provision of space is required. The choice of what constitutes this measurement is a matter of some debate and goes to the heart of a theory of the university as an ecology.

Common approaches to developing a space inventory involve tabulating categories of space in relation to each other using gross floor average (GFA) and useable floor average (UFA) as measurements. This then allows rules of thumb to be developed for square metres for different types of space. High level examples of this include space allocated to teaching, research and administration. Institutions tend to drill down from this level, many to the level of being discipline-specific (for example biological science laboratories, seminar rooms for arts, computer laboratories for the information sciences). This type of approach presupposes some rationale for determining an acceptable level of GFA in the first place.

The identification of total GFA could be primarily based on a strategic comparison, that is, comparing GFA averages amongst universities of similar size and type. The Space Management Project in the UK suggests a ratio based on guided learning hours, which because of a lack of sector-wide data availability had to be reduced to being broadly the same as teaching contact hours (SMG, 2006a). An alternative approach, one informed by a theory of the university as an ecology, would be measured in terms of learning activity. This is not a new concept. Professor Diana Laurillard, on a visit to the University of Sydney in 2001 discussed the Open University's approach to course design, which used student learning hours as the point of reference for the design (Laurillard, 2002). In an ecology where learning is enabled by e-learning, we need to move beyond a definition of learning hours being more or less equivalent to teaching contact hours. Clearly it is not. With the widespread adoption of teaching approaches that require informal, out-of-class collaboration amongst students, universities have a responsibility and pressing need to support the quality of informal learning on campus and at home in similar ways to how they support formal learning. If we do not find sustainable ways of supporting the informal learning experiences of students related to their university studies, then the quality of the learning experience will be put at risk.

If we accept measuring learning activity as the point of departure for estimating learning spaces provision, then how do we measure it when students, teachers and researchers traverse back and forth between physical and virtual spaces in pursuing their goals? This is an area of much uncertainty which requires strategies to be developed as part of ongoing academic enterprise management. We need better self-awareness.

Awareness of the Structure of Learning Space Inventory

Many universities are hampered by a lack of space. For some metropolitan universities, this is realised by being landlocked through a lack of affordable space adjacent to existing land, and for others this is a result of a lack of forward planning and/or investment in building programmes.

Virtual learning spaces have a role to play in helping universities to leverage investment in technological infrastructure to improve the choice and quantity of their learning space inventory. Figure 10.1 shows one way of representing a learning space inventory in the ecology of a university.

Figure 10.1 is meant to represent the structure of possible learning spaces available to universities, including physical and virtual spaces. All categories

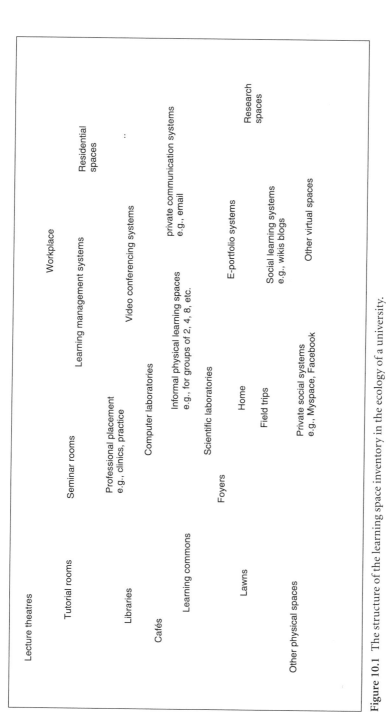

Figure 10.1 The structure of the learning space inventory in the ecology of a university.

have been put in the same box to indicate that almost any combination of spaces could be used by universities for the purposes of achieving their goals.

For many universities at present, this type of structure of learning space inventory is not the standard by which forward campus planning is determined (SMG, 2006, 2006b). While exceptions may be found, even the way the structure is represented in Figure 10.1 can indicate how non-typical combinations of spaces may have the capacity to improve a university's ability to meet its mission. The premise underlying Figure 10.1 is that worthwhile university learning experiences can occur in individual categories or in combinations of these categories. Given this, while still helpful, common rule of thumb estimates of GFA and UFA for physical learning spaces miss a significant part of the picture. Universities need to develop ways of indicating the size and shape of virtual activity that support their learning, teaching and research enterprise. Without developing some insight into how virtual spaces are supporting academic enterprise, uncertainty is being caused by:

- an awareness that space needs are different now, combined with an uncertainty about how to move to a new balance;
- differences between predicted and actual use of space by learners, teachers and researchers, exacerbated by the failure to consider virtual space use in relation to physical space use;
- changes in experiences of learning, teaching and research causing changes to demand in different categories of space;
- lack of awareness of the extent to which the existing spaces fall short of requirements for current and immediate future practices of learning, teaching and research;
- lack of ways of measuring how the integration of virtual space with physical space improves the overall functionality of spaces.

In the next section we discuss some emerging ways of understanding how the interplay between virtual and physical spaces is shaping aspects of the academic enterprise.

Awareness of the Relational Structure of Physical and Virtual Spaces

One way to develop self-awareness of the structure of spaces for learning and teaching is to review different layers of physical and virtual systems. When linking physical and virtual spaces, or talking about this intersection amongst stakeholders from different areas in the university, it is not uncommon for a lack of shared ideas and concepts to undermine the quality of discussion and decision-making. This is one aspect of what we mean by developing a shared language for talking about this area. Many of the ideas below are presented to try to help tease out concepts which will provide a basis for discussing and planning learning spaces. We begin with an overview of both physical and virtual spaces, and then discuss ideas related to different 'layers'.

A project at the University of Sydney looked at different layers of physical and virtual space at the city campus from an ecological perspective. Figures 10.2 to 10.11 show the different layers.

The maps in Figures 10.2 to 10.11 are one way of representing the structure of physical and virtual spaces for learning and teaching at the university: starting with the more physical systems, teaching spaces and ending with the more virtual systems, course websites.

- Figure 10.2 is an unannotated map providing an overview of university facilities on the Broadway and Darlington campuses, including some proposed buildings.
- Figure 10.3 divides centrally-managed teaching spaces into those with more than 70 seats (lecture theatres), and those with less than 70 seats (mostly seminar and tutorial rooms).
- Figure 10.4 divides faculty-managed teaching spaces into those with more than 50 seats, and those with less than 50 seats. There is no principled reason for the different cut offs between size of spaces in maps 2 and 3. Rather it reflects the way information has been stored in databases about these facilities.
- Figure 10.5 identifies location and size of laboratories and ancillary rooms across the Darlington and Camperdown campuses. Ancillary rooms are used in relation to laboratories as preparation areas, instrument rooms and workshops. These are generally owned by schools, being set up and managed by disciplinary areas.
- Figure 10.6 identifies library buildings and collections after their consolidation plans over the next few years.
- Figure 10.7 identifies AV/ICT facilities in centrally-managed teaching spaces. Broadly speaking, there is a large room AV/ICT standard operating in all of the lecture theatres (mostly >70 seats, with a few around the 50 seat mark).
- Figure 10.8 identifies video-conferencing facilities. This is divided into centrally managed spaces (of which there are two), and small room spaces and roll-about facilities owned by faculties.
- Figure 10.9 identifies wireless coverage. Additional information being collated for this aspect of the learning environment includes signal strength, capacity and main users by area.
- Figure 10.10 identifies a category of learning spaces that is one of the most difficult to define. One distinction being drawn for budget and management reasons is the difference between *teaching spaces* which are formally booked by teachers as part of the students' weekly schedule, and spaces in which students congregate to learn outside

Darlington Campus

Camperdown Campus

Figure 10.2 Unannotated map showing a global view of the city campuses (Darlington and Camperdown). Includes proposed buildings.

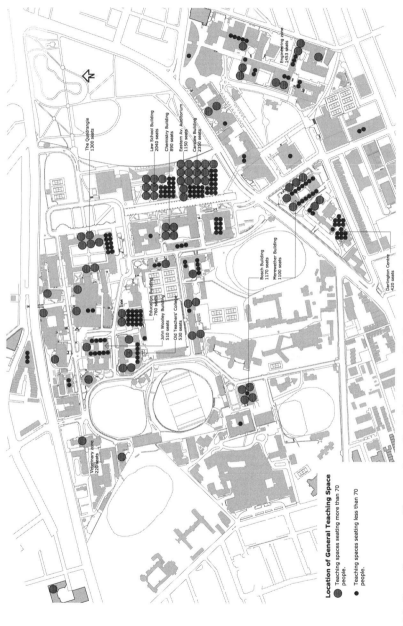

Location of General Teaching Space

● Teaching spaces seating more than 70 people.

· Teaching spaces seating less than 70 people.

The Quadrangle
1300 seats

Law School Building
2040 seats

Chemistry Building
890 seats

Eastern Av. Auditorium
1150 seats

Carslaw Building
2350 seats

Engineering zone
1453 seats

Education Building
760 seats

John Woolley Building
510 seats

Old Teachers' College
530 seats

Bosch Building
1170 seats

Merewether Building
1100 seats

Darlington Centre
420 seats

Veterinary zone
220 seats

N

Figure 10.3 Centrally-managed large and small teaching spaces: Darlington and Camperdown campuses.

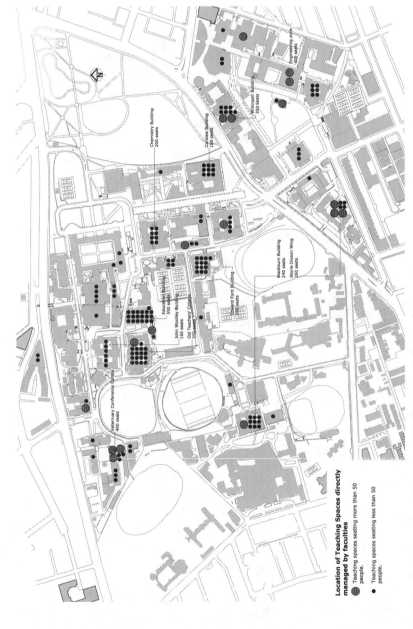

Location of Teaching Spaces directly managed by faculties

● Teaching spaces seating more than 50 people.

• Teaching spaces seating less than 50 people.

Chemistry Building
200 seats

Carslaw Building
180 seats

Wilkinson Building
350 seats

Engineering zone
400 seats

Education Building
550 seats

John Woolley Building
160 seats

Old Teachers' College
350 seats

Edward Ford Building
200 seats

Blackburn Building
240 seats

Storie Dixson Wing
260 seats

Veterinary Conference Centre
400 seats

Figure 10.4 Faculty-managed teaching spaces: Darlington and Camperdown campuses.

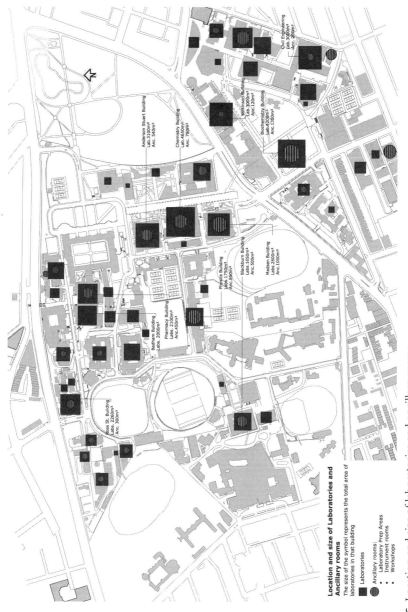

Anderson Stuart Building
Lab. 3100m²
Anc. 540m²

Chemistry Building
Lab. 4650m²
Anc. 780m²

Wilkinson Building
Lab. 3000m²
Anc. 120m²

Biochemistry Building
Lab. 4200m²
Anc. 1300m²

Civil Engineering
Lab. 3000m²
Anc. 200m²

Physics Building
Labs. 1750m²
Anc. 890m²

Blackburn Building
Labs. 1650m²
Anc. 500m²

Madsen Building
Labs. 2600m²
Anc. 1000m²

Pharmacy Building
Labs. 2100m²
Anc. 450m²

Badham Building
Labs. 2000m²

Ross St. Building
Labs. 2260m²
Anc. 300m²

Figure 10.5   Location and size of laboratories and ancillary rooms.

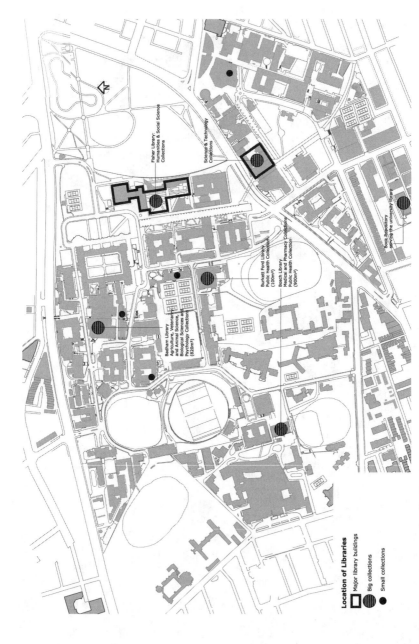

Location of Libraries

Major library buildings

Big collections

Small collections

Fisher Library:
Humanities & Social Science
Collections

Science & Technology
Collections

Burkett Ford Library
Public Health Collection

Bosch Library
Medical and Pharmacy Collections
Public Health Collection
(900m²)

Badham Library
Agriculture, Veterinary
and Animal Science,
Biological Sciences and
Psychology Collection
(820m²)

Book Repository
serving the university library

Figure 10.6 Library spaces and collections.

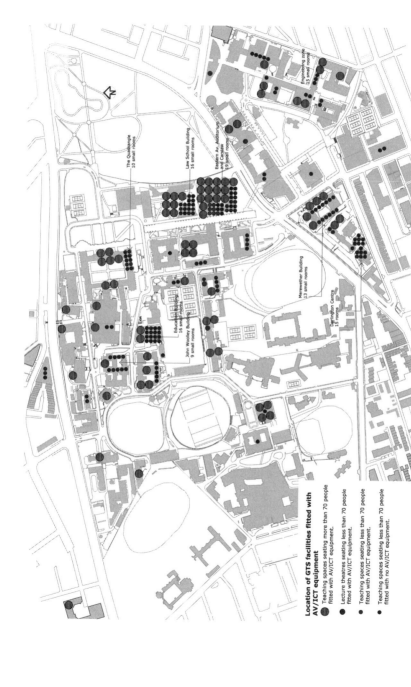

Location of GTS facilities fitted with AV/ICT equipment

- Teaching spaces seating more than 70 people fitted with AV/ICT equipment.
- Lecture theatres seating less than 70 people fitted with AV/ICT equipment.
- Teaching spaces seating less than 70 people fitted with AV/ICT equipment.
- Teaching spaces seating less than 70 people fitted with no AV/ICT equipment.

The Quadrangle
10 small rooms

Law School Building
16 small rooms

Eastern Av. Auditorium
and Carslaw
9 small rooms

Merewether Building
13 small rooms

Education Building
16 small rooms

John Woolley Building
9 small rooms

Darlington Centre
15 rooms

Engineering zone
15 small rooms

Figure 10.7 Audio-visual and information and communication technology (AV/ICT) facilities in centrally-managed teaching spaces.

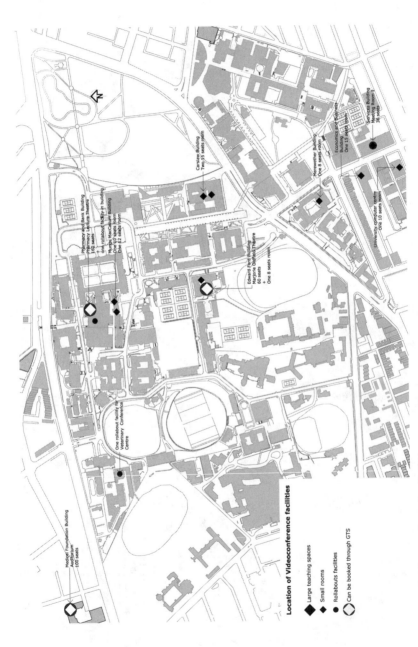

Location of Videoconference facilities

◆ Large teaching spaces
♦ Small rooms
● Rollabouts facilities
◇ Can be booked through GTS

Carslaw Building
Two 55 seats room

Merewether Building
One 8 seats room

Economics and Business
Building
One 15 seats room

Services Building
Meeting Room 1
36 seats

Pharmacy and Bank Building
Pharmacy Lecture Theatre
160 seats

One rollabout facility in building

Margie MacCallum Building
One 10 seats room
One 42 seats room

University computer entry
One 10 seats room

Edward Ford Building
Margorie Oldfield Theatre
60 seats
+
One 8 seats room

One rollabout facility near
Veterinary Conference
Centre

Medical Foundation Building
Auditorium
100 seats

Figure 10.8 Central video-conferencing facilities.

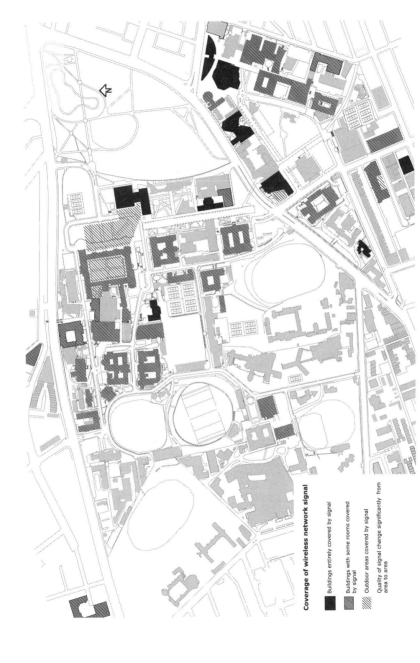

Coverage of wireless network signal

■ Buildings entirely covered by signal

▨ Buildings with some rooms covered by signal

▦ Outdoor areas covered by signal

▨ Quality of signal change significantly from area to area

Figure 10.9 Wireless coverage.

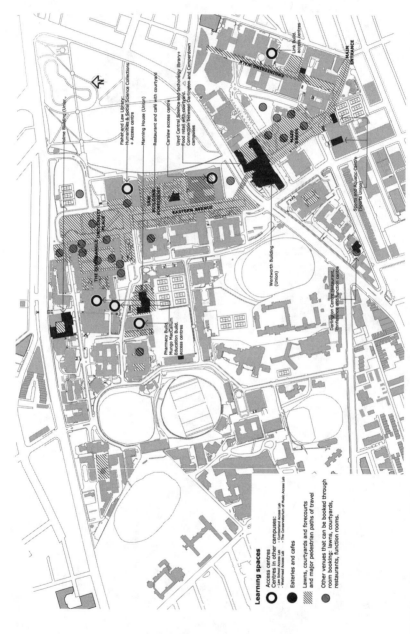

Figure 10.10 Learning spaces: cafés, lawns/forecourts, computer access centres.

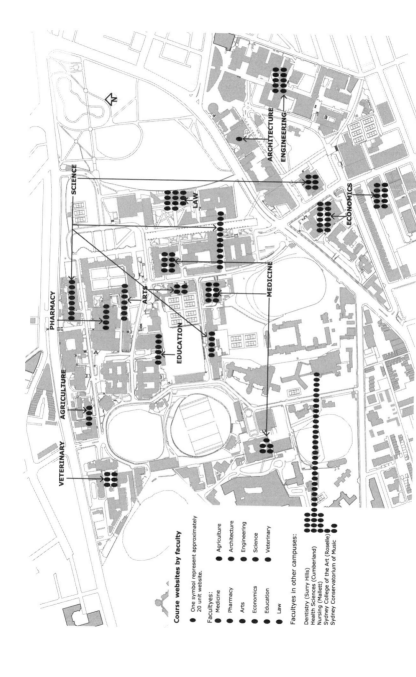

Course websites by faculty

● One symbol represent approximately 20 unit website.

Facultyes:
● Medicine ● Agriculture
● Pharmacy ● Architecture
● Arts ● Engineering
● Economics ● Science
● Education ● Veterinary
● Law

Facultyes in other campuses:
Dentistry (Surry Hills)
Health Sciences (Cumberland)
Nursing (Mallett)
Sydney College of the Art (Roselle)
Sydney Conservatorium of Music

VETERINARY

AGRICULTURE

PHARMACY

SCIENCE

ARTS

LAW

EDUCATION

MEDICINE

ARCHITECTURE

ENGINEERING

ECONOMICS

N

Figure 10.11 Course websites on enterprise Learning Management Systems by faculty.

class, labelled *learning spaces*. Additional information about which aspects of the physical environment are most popular for students out of class would be beneficial to their management and support for users.

– Figure 10.11 identifies course websites by faculty. The purpose of this map is not to geographically locate the websites, as they can be accessed from anywhere. The purpose is rather to identify relative sizes of the students' virtual learning environment on enterprise learning management systems. Each coloured dot on Figure 10.11 represents approximately 20 course websites. Precise figures and growth of this part of course profiles are shown in the following section. Over the last four years, this has been one of the most rapidly growing parts of the learning environment.

The point of representing the structure of the learning and teaching systems in this way is not to reveal the infrastructure at the city campus of the University of Sydney at a particular point in time. Rather it is to suggest one way for universities and their constituents to start to think about physical and virtual spaces in a relational manner. Usually, different areas in the university are responsible for different layers of spaces. A shared relational framework is needed so that:

- feedback loops can be set up about how both categories of space are growing and relating to each;
- university leaders, at various levels, plan and invest in parts of these layers which indicate a self-awareness of their role in the whole;
- that gaps in the academic spaces can start to be identified so that a better alignment between what exists and what is needed can be achieved through planning.

Most of the representations of spaces in Figures 10.2 to 10.11 are relatively easy to understand. However this is not necessarily the case with the last figure, showing the faculty distribution of course websites. For a university to be able to plan for leveraging its space requirements from virtual spaces, a deeper understanding of what is shown in Figure 10.11 is necessary.

Awareness of the Relationship Between Course Profile and Virtual Space

One of the most visible areas of growth in demand for learning spaces in campus-based universities is the extent to which teachers have integrated e-learning into course design (Hawkins & Rudy, 2004, 2007; Zatroscky et al., 2006). This section looks at a growing e-learning profile in the curricula of the University of Sydney as an example of how to measure the size and shape of e-learning growth to develop self-awareness about demand for virtual space.

Table 10.1 shows growth of e-learning at the University of Sydney from 2002–2007.

The University of Sydney is a campus-based, research intensive university. Its goal in introducing e-learning is to develop student understanding and enable faculty learning and teaching goals. In order for the university to be able to become aware of faculty demand for virtual space, it has needed to find ways of measuring the size and shape of e-learning in the curricula of the faculties.

Different approaches have been used to assess the size and shape of e-learning in universities. In 2002, the Open University in the United Kingdom used a grading of 'web-intensive, web-focussed and web-enhanced' for online courses (Ellis & Moore, 2006). Around the same time, some Australian universities used a government-led approach to grading courses in three modes. Mode A, were subjects where Web support was provided but students were not required to use it in order to pass the subject. Mode B, were subjects that required students to use the Web support in order to pass the subject; and Mode C, were fully online subjects.

At the University of Sydney, after internal discussion, benchmarking with British universities and modification of some of the ideas from the government-led initiative, the following hierarchy is currently used to assess the size and shape of e-learning.

Table 10.2 can be understood as a type of quality assurance hierarchy. From a student perspective, both categories in A are optional in the sense that a student is not dependent on using the website in order to pass the course. The hierarchy can also be used as a way of starting to develop a strategy for workload associated with different categories of websites. Given the relative greater importance from a student perspective of the websites in the B categories, it would not make much sense to spend more time in developing those in A relative to B. Consequently, faculties or schools can use the categories as a guide for developing workload recommendations for teachers who wish to start integrating e-learning into their course design.

The categories in Table 10.2 are provided to faculties as a way of developing a sense of the size and shape of e-learning across their award programme. The statistics are not intended to indicate dimensions of quality.

The point of these descriptions is not to suggest they are the only way to map the shape of e-learning across award programmes, or the best way. Rather they are the way that the community at one university is starting to grapple with understanding e-learning in a broader ecology of learning. The benefits of the approach for beginning to manage e-learning across 16 faculties and for over 45,000 students are emerging. Tables 10.3 and 10.4 below give some indication of this.

The combined purpose of Tables 10.3 to 10.4 is to give some information to faculty managers and university leaders about the size and shape of e-learning at the university. Table 10.3 is at the level of the university. It shows e-learning

Table 10.1 Growth of E-learning at the University of Sydney from 2002–2007

Course websites on three enterprise LMSs at the University of Sydney	2002 Year total	2003 Semester 1	2003 Semester 2	2004 Semester 1	2004 Semester 2	2005 Semester 1	2005 Semester 2	2006 Semester 1	2006 Semester 2	2007 Semester 1	2007 Semester 2
Faculty 1	–	–	–	32	32	32	32	38	35	32	32
Faculty 2	70	70	49	117	112	210	242	318	308	277	214
Faculty 3	56	15	55	51	108	162	190	179	196	194	118
Faculty 4	46	29	19	37	26	38	39	44	31	39	122
Faculty 5	14	22	21	26	31	55	53	50	50	31	44
Faculty 6	58	46	39	73	51	82	79	104	99	153	280
Faculty 7	5	–	–	208	198	220	208	220	206	252	218
Faculty 8	18	24	11	32	35	31	29	49	64	43	173
Faculty 9	12	70	80	83	90	119	126	112	107	61	88
Faculty 10	4	2	1	3	–	–	4	6	3	1	10
Faculty 11	1	1	1	–	–	–	3	8	22	53	29
Faculty 12	19	12	8	15	12	12	10	12	9	4	13
Faculty 13	1	–	–	–	–	2	17	41	31	30	61
Faculty 14	163	145	130	151	242	232	244	305	280	195	339
Faculty 15	95	67	65	62	65	100	100	–	–	–	–
Faculty 16	39	21	24	22	21	30	39	49	147	123	187
Faculty 17	30	56	28	43	65	56	59	57	59	109	57
Total course websites	631	1,110		2,065		2,745		3,239		3,582	

Table 10.2 Categories of Description of Course Websites at the University of Sydney

Category of course website	Description
A1 – informational	The course website provides information resources only (e.g., course outline, readings, links to other related websites).
A2 – supplemental	A1 + the course website provides activities requiring active student participation but these are not part of the assessment framework for the course.
B1 – blended (assessment)	A1+ The course website provides activities requiring active student participation and these are assessed as part of the students' performance.
B2 – blended (replacement)	A1+ The course website provides activities requiring active student participation and these have replaced some of the face-to-face class time of students.
B3 – blended (replacement and assessment)	A1 + The course website provides activities requiring active student participation and these are assessed and have replaced some of the face-to-face class time of students.
C1 – fully flexible	The course website supports a course which can be completed almost completely off campus (for example, the course might require a residential weekend).

coverage across all faculties for one semester. Table 10.4 is at the level of one faculty. It shows e-learning coverage in one semester.

Table 10.3 provides some indication of faculty demand for virtual space. In just one semester,

- 1,102 courses are complementing the face-to-face experience with what course designers consider to be essential information.
- 469 courses are requiring students to engage in some form of active e-learning (reviews of these courses indicate that much of this interaction tends to revolve around learning through discussions and learning through inquiry).
- 290 courses have their e-learning resources embedded in the assessment framework students are required to complete.
- 17 courses have reduced the amount of face-to-face time and replaced it with e-learning activities.
- 73 courses have embedded the e-learning resources in the assessment framework and have replaced face-to-face time with e-learning.
- 121 courses can be completed by students mostly away from campus.

If we take just one of these faculty level summaries and look at it at the

Table 10.3 Example of E-learning Coverage by Faculty in one Semester, University of Sydney

Faculty of registration	Approx no. of enrolments	No. of courses studied	Course websites**	% course websites**	E-learning coverage statistics											
					A1		A2		B1		B2		B3		C1	
					No.	%	No.	%	No.	%	No.	%	No.	%	No.	%
Faculty A	600	146	61	41.8%	41	67.2%	9	14.8%	5	8.2%			6	9.8%		
Faculty B	1,120	152	13	8.6%	6	46.2%	3	23.1%	1	7.7%	1	0.4%	8	2.9%	3	23.1%
Faculty C	6,100	1024	280	27.3%	160	57.1%	67	23.9%	39	13.9%					5	1.8%
Faculty D	450	54	5	9.3%	2	40.0%	2	40.0%	1	20.0%						
Faculty E	7,200	625	175	28.0%	108	61.7%	37	21.1%	21	12.0%			6	3.4%	3	1.7%
Faculty F	2,300	441	173	39.2%	95	54.9%	38	22.0%	25	14.5%			10	5.8%	5	2.9%
Faculty G	2,500	463	187	40.4%	99	52.9%	45	24.1%	20	10.7%			7	3.7%	16	8.6%
Faculty H	4,900	565	214	37.9%	60	28.0%	48	22.4%	52	24.3%	7	3.3%	10	4.7%	37	17.3%
Faculty I	1,700	120	88	73.3%	77	87.5%	11	12.5%								
Faculty J	1,800	185	86	46.5%	7	8.1%	37	43.0%	5	5.8%	5	5.8%	3	3.5%	29	33.7%
Faculty K	600	171	122	71.3%	76	62.3%	25	20.5%	13	10.7%	1	0.8%	5	4.1%	2	1.6%
Faculty L	1,100	55	44	80.0%	20	45.5%	5	11.4%	17	38.6%			2	4.5%		
Faculty M	4,400	833	339	40.7%	183	54.0%	91	26.8%	49	14.5%			9	2.7%	7	2.1%
Faculty N	600	110	10	9.1%	6	60.0%	1	10.0%	3	30.0%						
Faculty O	640	410	29	7.1%	18	62.1%	5	17.2%	5	17.2%			1	3.4%		
Faculty P	846	90	77	89.5%	26	45.6%	7	12.3%	11	19.3%	2	3.5%	1	1.8%	10	17.5%
Faculty Q	400	511	189	37.0%	118	62.4%	38	20.1%	23	12.2%	1	0.5%	5	2.6%	4	2.1%
Total *** coursework coverage	3,766	5,953*	2,092**	34.8%	1102	53.2%	469	22.6%	290	14.0%	17	1.0%	73	3.5%	121	5.8%

* The same course may be studied in more than one degree; ** Course websites on the University LMS. One website may serve more than one course. *** The breakdown of percentages in the 'Total' row are in relation to each other, not means of the columns

level of awards, associations between learning spaces and award design start to emerge.

Table 10.4 shows that in a relatively small faculty, all postgraduate courses in the degree programmes had a course website, and that mostly these were category C1. In the undergraduate courses, 47 of the 60 courses on offer had a course website; just under half of these websites were informational (45.6%) and about a fifth were integrated with student assessment (19.3%). These statistics are fairly straightforward to collect and calculate for a small faculty, but can become quite complex when larger student numbers and courses are involved.

From a dean's perspective, developing an awareness of award degree design in terms of the above structure raises strategic questions which help to align the design of award degrees and the space required to support them. For example;

- What functionalities and support models in the *physical* learning spaces are supporting the students' learning?
- Do the students have sufficient access to technologies in these spaces (audio visual and information and communication technologies (AV/ICT)) to help them to complete the learning tasks set in their courses?
- Do the teachers have access to the AV/ICT resources necessary to teach the courses?
- Is there remote and/or hands-on-help for students and teachers from support staff if something goes wrong in the class spaces?
- How does the configuration of seating add to the purpose of the learning space under consideration?
- How does the design of informal spaces on campus add to the student learning experience in those courses? Is there enough capacity in the precinct of the faculty for students to access informal learning spaces?
- Do the more infrastructure-intensive rooms (laboratories, etc.) have a sufficient standard of infrastructure installed?
- What functionalities and support models in the *virtual* learning spaces are supporting the students' learning?
- Do students have appropriate technological functionalities in their virtual learning spaces, enabling them to complete the learning tasks set in their courses?
- Do they have enough support while in the virtual spaces for their learning?
- Do teachers have sufficient support to help them orientate the technological functionalities in the virtual spaces to the learning outcomes of their courses?

Table 10.4 E-learning Coverage in one Faculty during one Semester at the University of Sydney

Semester totals		Approx no. of enrolments	No. of courses studied	Course websites**	% course websites**	E-learning coverage statistics											
Level of study	Degree					A1		A2		B1		B2		B3		C1	
						No.	%	No.	%	No.	%	No.	%	No.	%	No.	%
Postgraduate (Cwk)	GradCert	20	5	5	100.0%											5	100.0%
	GradDip	30	7	7	100.0%											7	100.0%
	Masters	29	16	16	100.0%			1								16	100.0%
	NonDegree	4	2	2	100.0%											2	100.0%
	Total Postgraduate (Cwk)*	83	30	30	100.0%	0	0.0%	1	9.1%	0	0.0%	0	0.0%	0	0.0%	10	90.9%
Undergraduate	Bachelor Degree 1	177	32	22	68.8%	14	63.6%	5	22.7%	3	13.6%						
	Bachelor Degree 2	586	28	25	89.3%	12	48.0%	2	8.0%	8	32.0%	2	8.0%	1	4.0%		
	Total Undergraduate*	763	60	47	78.3%	26	55.3%	7	14.9%	11	23.4%	2	4.3%	1	2.1%		
Total Coursework*		846	90	77	89.5%	26	45.6%	7	12.3%	11	19.3%	2	3.5%	1	1.8%	10	17.5%

* The same course may be studied in more than one degree; ** Course websites on the University LMS. One website may serve more than one course

- Do the virtual learning spaces have sufficient capacity for all students and teachers to engage with the learning tasks?
- Are the virtual learning spaces integrated with virtual research spaces in order to encourage research-led experiences of learning?
- Are the virtual learning spaces sufficiently integrated with the physical learning spaces so that the experience is a coherent one from the perspective of students and teachers?

These types of questions are posed at the level of award design in a small faculty. If we multiply these questions across 16 other faculties and aggregate upwards, we start to get a feeling for the scale and complexity of the university-wide demand for learning spaces, both physical and virtual.

- Is the quality of the university's virtual spaces sufficient for the learning and teaching goals of faculties?
- To what extent do the virtual spaces complement and integrate with the physical spaces?
- To what extent do the physical learning and teaching spaces on campus allow learners and teachers to traverse back and forth between the physical and virtual spaces as they pursue their learning outcomes?
- Do students and teachers in all faculties have sufficient access to their learning materials, both on campus and off campus?
- How can physical and virtual spaces be coherently conceptualised to create learning spaces which are better aligned to the mission of the university?
- How can concepts of learning spaces be related to, and informed by, student and teacher experiences of learning?
- What are the implications for support models that help students and teachers as they traverse physical and virtual spaces?

For universities seeking to leverage virtual space to extend the capacity of their physical spaces, an understanding of answers to these questions is strategically essential and is a necessary stage of planning in order to develop real self-awareness.

Feedback Loops about Learning Spaces

Universities need to decide which feedback loops are necessary to sustain in order to maintain their ecological balance. For physical learning spaces, national agencies make some recommendations about what type of feedback is useful (SMG, 2006a, 2006b; TEFMA, 2006; JISC, 2006; SFC, 2006).

International Benchmarks

The United Kingdom Space Management Group (SMG), including the Higher Education Funding Council for England (HEFCE), the Scottish Funding Council (SFC), the Higher Education Funding Council for Wales (HEFCW), and the British Government Department for Employment and Learning, commissioned a series of studies into how space is managed in tertiary institutions internationally. One study investigated the approach adopted by the Learning Skills Council in the United Kingdom in comparison to approaches to managing space in North America, Australasia, Hong Kong and Germany (SMG, 2006a).

The Learning Skills Council approach to determining university space needs involves; (a) advice on how to predict space needs and (b) benchmarks in the form of formulae which can provide some indication of the space required given the volume of teaching activity they engage in (SMG, 2006a). Prior to 1997, the Learning Skills Council (LSC) used the number of full time enrolled (FTE) students as the point from which a balance of space was estimated on the basis that the more students a university had, the more space was required. This approach was replaced by another in 1997 as variation in what full-time enrolment actually meant undermined its value as the best indicator for space needs on campus. Since then, the LSC has used 'guided learning hours' as the indicator by which rules of thumb for space are identified. Modelling by the LSC suggested that the more guided learning hours were delivered, the larger the space required.

To cope with variation in how universities collected data about space management, the SMG reports of 2006 used hours of teaching as equivalent to hours of guided learning.

In Australia, the Tertiary Education Facilities Management Association (TEFMA) publishes high-level ratios, benchmarks and other guidelines (SMG, 2006). Its unit of measurement to calculate space requirement is per equivalent full time student unit (EFTSU). Benchmarks for percentage occupation of GFA by high-level categories of parts of universities are shown in Table 10.5.

In North America, a range of approaches to measuring space requirements is adopted across the states and provinces. The study investigating the LSC approach identified that many states/provinces follow a methodology which is formulae-based, using space planning standards, space utilisation standards, and space programming/design standards. The example they gave required the following elements: an assumption of the size of the student station in the classroom ($1.67m^2$), weekly availability of room hours (say 35 hours), student occupancy ratio (on average 65% of the weekly room hours), weekly student clock hours. These elements can be combined in a formula:

Table 10.5 TEFMA Breakdown of Different High-level University Categories by Space Type

Group/category	% of total campus space	UFA/total campus EFTSU (m²)
Academic	43–57	4.5–6
Administrative	9–12	1–1.2
Commercial	2.8–4.2	0.3–0.4
General teaching	12	1.2
Library	10	1
Student services	4–8	0.4–0.8
Other	8	0.8

Source: SMG, 2006a. Reproduced with permission.

$$\frac{18 \text{ ASF (student workstation size)}}{35 \text{ (weekly room hours)} \times 65\% \text{ (space factor)}} = 0.79 \text{ ASF}$$
(student occupancy ratio)

For a university teaching 200,000 hours a week, the formula provides the space allocation summarised in Table 10.6.

It is clear that there is some international debate about fundamental units by which space requirement is calculated. In England it is guided learning hours, which in planning if not educational practice is taken to be the same as teaching hours. In Australia it is EFTSUs. In America and Canada, it depends on a formula based on teaching hours and rules of thumb for class usage, and space assigned per student. The report into managing space for the UK Space Management Group pre-empts the issue by concluding that sector-wide changes in learning and teaching methodologies may require a rethink about conceptions underlying the fundamental unit used to measure space requirement (SMG, 2006a).

Table 10.6 North American Example of Sample Space Standards

Type of space (example)	Space standard in net assignable square feet per workstation, square metre equivalent given in brackets	
Seminar room	20	(1.86)
Lecture theatre	12	(1.12)
Class laboratory	70–120	(6.5–11.15)
Computer laboratory	35	(3.25)
Office (director)	160	(14.86)
Office (faculty staff)	135	(12.54)
Office (staff)	110	(10.22)
Office (clerical workstation)	75	(6.97)
Office (post doctorates)	6	(6.32)
Office (doctoral students)	44	(4.1)

Source: SMG, 2006a. Reproduced with permission.

A Need for Common Language for Virtual Spaces in Universities

It is perhaps too premature to identify what sustainable data collection by each institution across the international higher education sector might look like if we were taking into account the impact of virtual space provision on the total space required. However, using the idea of an ecology of learning, it makes philosophical, strategic and economic sense to do better than we are doing.

It is also too simplistic to reduce the debate to saying that e-learning will reduce campus-based life because award degrees will shift towards distant experiences of learning. The evidence to date is that e-learning is part of a broader ecology, not a replacement for a face-to-face experience when considered across the sector as a whole.

It is clear that valuable learning and strategic benefits to campus-based universities can be obtained by developing a pedagogy that leverages the total amount of learning space by combining physical and virtual space in ways that will support student understanding and the attainment of their learning outcomes. An indiscriminate provision of virtual space will not achieve this. The research discussed in Chapters 4, 5 and 6 indicates that simply bolting on e-learning does not help students to learn. Rather it needs to be carefully integrated in terms of the learning objectives and outcomes of the course.

Clearly then, universities need to start addressing how to get feedback loops about combined physical and virtual space requirements necessary to meet their learning, teaching and research goals. Universities need to develop a way of talking about physical and virtual spaces and their intersection. The examples of layers of physical and virtual spaces and their affordances are one way of beginning this dialogue, as are the e-learning coverage statistics across faculties and award degrees. Yet we need more.

At Massachusetts Institute of Technology in the United States, a project has been put in place to provide information about the volume of virtual traffic in relation to the physical layout of the campus (see http://senseable.mit.edu/ispots/).

Software engineers using 3D animation software and campus managers responsible for putting in wireless points have collaborated in the iSpots project. Figure 10.12 shows graphically the type of information available to university planners. The grey objects in the figure represent the buildings on campus. The mountain-like peaks superimposed on top of the buildings represent the volume of virtual traffic captured by the wireless points located in the respective buildings. The data is also provided to planners in numerical form. Figure 10.12 shows very quickly which areas of the campus have the most virtual traffic, and offers some evidence for campus planners to decide how to support learners and teachers with location-based support services and physical spaces in those areas. This type of strategy is a useful and innovative

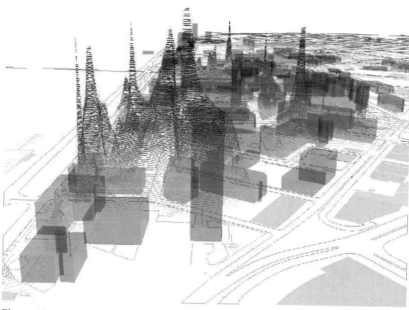

Figure 10.12 3D image from the iSpots project MIT.

Source: http://Senseable.mit.edu/ispots/

approach to gathering and sharing the empirical evidence needed to make sensible decisions about where to invest in virtual infrastructure.

One of the main outcomes from this discussion should be the need for a more standardised and transparent way of talking about and measuring learning and teaching activities in physical and virtual spaces.

Self-correcting Mechanisms and Learning Spaces

One way of building up evidence and concepts and using these to develop a language is through self-correcting mechanisms in the ecology of universities. Table 10.7 offers examples of common, high-level self-correcting mechanisms used by universities and self-correcting foci related to e-learning and virtual spaces. E-learning and virtual spaces have been emphasised in the final column. They are related to descriptions in the first few columns because of the recognition of how e-learning is changing the structure of the student experience, and the need for virtual spaces to be integrated into the ecology of a university in order to leverage the most benefit for its mission and the development of student understanding.

Table 10.7 is in three columns. The first two columns identify the purpose of some mechanisms used by universities to assess their direction and operations

Table 10.7 Self-correcting Mechanisms in Relation to E-learning and Virtual Spaces

Self-correcting mechanisms	Purpose	Examples of self-correction foci on e-learning and virtual spaces
Mission statement	Setting the philosophical direction and aspirations for the university, articulating its values, providing an overarching statement to encompass all legitimate activities.	– How might conceptualisation of combinations of physical and virtual spaces help the university to realise its mission? – What supporting role does e-learning play in helping the university to realise its mission?
University strategic plans/learning, teaching, research plans	Providing a clear strategic framework in which to make sense of the academic goals of the institution	– Which of the university's learning and teaching goals draws on the affordances of e-learning as a means to reach them? – What is the relationship between integrated physical and virtual research space and the university's strategic plan?
Faculty learning and teaching plans	Identifying the learning and teaching goals of faculties in relation to the university strategic plan	– What combinations of physical and virtual spaces do faculties require for their teaching and research goals? – What leverage can an appropriate use of e-learning provide to faculty demand for physical space?
Student evaluations	Identifying the student perspective on learning experiences	– What integration of e-learning experiences within the learning experience do students require to meet their learning outcomes? – How do students relate and rate these experiences in the context of their degrees? – What expectations of learning spaces for their courses do students hold?
Cyclical course review and redesign	Assessing the learning, teaching and resourcing needs for students and teachers to meet their outcomes	– What e-learning capacity do lecturers require to meet their approaches to designing curricula? – What demands on informal physical learning spaces are approaches to teaching putting on physical space?
Policy development	Providing a principled, value-led framework in which constituents can operate	– To what extent is the quality of academic enterprise in virtual spaces supported in policy? – How do university policies manage risk involved in academic enterprise that traverses back and forth between physical and virtual space? – To what extent do learning and teaching policies deal with risks involved in combining physical and virtual spaces in the experience of learning?

Policy/Academic Board visits to faculties	To assess the performance of faculties in relation to the policies of the University	– To what extent are faculties following the policy framework in how they manage their learning, teaching and research? – How should academic activity revealed through Academic Board visits inform ongoing policy development?
University-wide space audits, e.g. learning space inventory	To assess the status of spaces in relation to the ecological balance of the university	– What shared conceptions of categories of learning spaces exist across the university? – What proportional allocation of space across the categories of learning spaces best meets the mission of the university? – How can developments in combinations of physical and virtual spaces better meet the mission of the university?
University-wide financial audits of business units	To assess the financial performance of business units in relation to university standards	– What are the cost benefit evaluations of investment in physical and virtual space by key business units in relation to the ecology of the university? – How can a reconceptualisation of the integration of physical and virtual space enable the university to achieve its mission in a more cost-effective manner?
National-body audit visits to universities	To assess the performance of universities in relation to national standards	– What are the self-stated mission, values and strategic objectives of the university? – To what extent do university policies provide an appropriate framework for those aspirations? – How well is the university performing in relation to its self-stated objectives? – What quality assurance mechanisms are in place that manage academic enterprise that traverses between physical and virtual spaces in pursuit of the self-stated objectives?
International alliances and benchmarking	To identify best practice and standards in key aspects of university enterprise through discussion and comparison with similar institutions, or with institutions who have similar processes and objectives in particular areas of strategic importance	– How are other universities internationally conceptualising the integration of physical and virtual space to achieve their mission? – How are they managing physical and virtual spaces in a complementary fashion for competitive advantage? – How are universities similar in nature integrating e-learning in the student experience to enable faculties to achieve their learning and teaching goals?

in order to improve their performance. This is not meant to encompass all possible mechanisms, but to flesh out the range and types of activities that can enable self-correction arising out of reflection. Column 3 identifies evaluative questions about e-learning and virtual spaces that could legitimately be part of these mechanisms.

The purpose of providing these evaluation questions is to indicate the direction in which universities need to go if they are to:

- develop a shared way of thinking and talking about the intersection of virtual and physical spaces in an ecology;
- realise the benefits of e-learning and virtual spaces for the learning and teaching goals of faculties;
- leverage benefits for the mission of a university from e-learning and virtual spaces.

This type of approach and the associated development of a shared understanding across the higher education sector will help to reduce uncertainty in planning and improve the outcomes and value received from educational investment in infrastructure.

Concluding Comments: Future Visions of Campus-based Universities

Adopting an ecological perspective on universities in which the main mission is learning, one can argue that the key questions for university leaders concerned with the well-being of their institution are the following, which are interchangeable;

- How well are we meeting the mission of the university?
- To what extent is the ecology of the university in balance?

The challenge in answering these questions is that the university as a whole is a part of a broader ecology of society which is also subject to continual change. As a consequence, answers to these two questions are unlikely to be the same across different time periods. To manage a university in a way which can help mitigate the uncertainty inherent in academic enterprise, a type of *ecological management* is useful, one which can be described by drawing on the principles of an ecology of learning used to structure the arguments throughout this book:

- What is the ecological balance of the university at any given time? To what extent are the activities in the university oriented towards promoting learning in the broadest sense of the term?
- How self-aware is the university? The university community needs to be ready to reconsider its conception of what makes up legitimate

parts of the ecology of a university. Learning spaces is but one example.

- What feedback loops does the university need to maintain in order to make informed decisions? University leaders need to exercise constant oversight of the effectiveness of feedback loops if strategic information and knowledge is to be available for decision-making in an ongoing manner.
- What foci of self-correcting mechanisms are appropriate in order to maintain the ecological balance? The structure, scope and purpose of self-correcting mechanisms themselves need to be reviewed continuously to ensure that they are providing knowledge which is helping the university to maintain its balance, its values and strategic direction.

If university leaders include strategies to answer these questions in their approach to management, they will help to reduce the uncertainty that can accompany serious tasks such as campus planning for learning spaces.

11
Concluding Comments
The Ecological Perspective, Balance and Change

In this final chapter, we provide a summary of the position that we have come to adopt as a consequence of:

a. reflecting on research into students' experiences of university learning, with and without technology, and
b. adopting an ecological perspective on the problem of supporting worthwhile innovation, and the continuing enhancement of learning and teaching, in a sustainable fashion.

Our position can be understood in the following way.

It is possible to paint a picture of a time when learning and teaching in higher education could be viewed as essentially unproblematic. From time to time and place to place, there would have been a recognition that some specific things needed improvement, but there was not – within this arcadian landscape – a deep-rooted or widely sensed disquiet about the fundamentals of educational practice. Rather, there was a consensus that good teaching was concerned with the clear and effective transmission of valued knowledge to highly motivated, able students. In turn, good students would define themselves as well-tuned receivers, able to record and replay the knowledge they picked up. Students and teachers co-created and sustained a situation in which teacher-centred or subject-centred teaching approaches were in the ascendancy.

Over time, it became difficult to sustain a shared belief that this state of affairs was defensible. Higher education opened its doors to greater numbers of students; the variety of their needs increased; the criticisms of employers (and governments) gained strength and edge, and groups with expertise in higher education pedagogy began to proliferate and gain influence. Commentators note a shift to conceptions of good teaching and learning that stress the importance of students engaging actively in processes of personal sense-making and knowledge-construction, and of teachers adopting a more student-centred approach, in which information about students' pre-existing knowledge, needs and preferences guides teaching decisions. In short, a (more or less conscious) conspiracy to persist with transmissive educational practices turns out to be unsustainable, because of the mismatch with the changing demands of the world of work, exacerbated by pressures on the time and resources required to cope with diversifying student needs.

In actuality, current beliefs and practices in most universities represent a melange of the teacher-centred and student-centred. Within this mix, we can find teachers offering students opportunities to manage their own learning, negotiate assessment requirements, take on authentic, intellectually challenging tasks, make choices about who to work with, what tools and resources to use, what records of achievement to lodge in their e-portfolios, etc. We can also find plenty of examples of subject-centred and teacher-centred conceptions and approaches. In response, we can find students taking surface and achieving approaches to the richest and the leanest of educational opportunities. The evidence we presented in Chapters 4, 5 and 6 suggests that it is still common for teachers to be taking teacher and/or content centred approaches to teaching, and for students to be taking surface and/or strategic approaches to learning. Where teachers *are* striving to help their students work in more productive ways, it seems that they, and the well-intentioned colleagues who support them, have to work against the grain and commit levels of personal energy to the task that are unsustainable in the longer term.

If the ecology in which the student experience is occurring is not imbued with a strong and defensible sense of 'good learning', it is likely that teacher-centred experiences of teaching and surface experiences of learning will reoccur. A sense of good learning cannot come from any single, dominant source; rather, it is a set of tensely adjusted beliefs and constructs emerging from the experiences and values of students, teachers, employers, community groups, experts in pedagogy and researchers in the learning sciences. We presented a sketch of 'good learning' in Chapters 1 and 2. Here, we make the point that such depictions are rooted in history – change over time – but periods of provisional stability make it possible for them to imbue a university with a shared sense of purpose. Work needs to be done by university leaders to turn this possibility into actuality. The responsibility to continue to focus on what constitutes effective successful learning is an unceasing challenge. It is the first point of departure for considering what is at the heart of education and needs constant vigilance, particularly in a context of uncertainty.

Rapid social, economic and technological change create uncertainties for everyone working in a university. This uncertainty can distract from a focus on good learning. Managing the risks associated with these uncertainties is a core task for a university's leaders, at all levels. Poor pedagogical and technological choices can damage student learning and it can take a long while to repair both the causes and the consequences of such damage. The chance of making poor choices is increased by the uncertainties surrounding each new wave of technology, each new set of demands for better-prepared graduates, each new curriculum reform. It takes time for researchers and innovators to make sense of new pedagogies and the affordances of each new technology. It takes more time to produce useful sources of guidance and to disseminate them effectively. But it is rarely possible to put innovation 'on hold' while experts or enthusiasts try to sort out optimal strategies. Instead, university leaders must work *with* the ecology of learning that a good university needs to be. This means promoting the healthy functioning of the ecology, but also relying on it to adjust to new challenges. As we argued in Chapter 7, the ecology of learning needs to be imbued with a sense of 'good learning'. All organisational units within a university need to understand what this means. They need to understand their roles in relation to enhancing the student learning experience and in relation to what other organisational units are doing (the quality of 'self-awareness').

To reduce uncertainty and develop self-awareness in the ecology of a university, a key area of activity is the meso-level, the natural province of programme teams and the point at which 'bottom up' and 'top down' processes, information flows and fields of influence come to meet. This is the level at which university policies are translated into locally sensible action. Attention to the meso-level, by university leaders, helps mitigate the uncertainties and other damage associated with misalignment. In Chapter 8 we examined some of the advantages of conceptualising teaching work, at the meso-level, as a design-like activity. We argued that 'teaching-as-design' is more open than other paradigms of teaching to iterative improvement through the cyclical use of research-based evidence, feedback from evaluation and experience, and the contributions of colleagues with expertise in areas such as educational development and educational technology. The meso-level is also the point at which local experience, experimentation, etc., can be captured and – at least in principle – made available to the wider university.

To reduce uncertainty at the macro-level of a university, where leadership involves decisions that affect all areas of a university, uncertainty can be mitigated using the principles outlined as key to a well functioning ecology. Using the example of learning spaces, we have focussed on how planning for investment in them is creating a particularly difficult set of challenges for the leaders of campus-based universities. The arrival of e-learning – of flexible access to digital tools and resources – questioned the meaning of 'campus-based'. For many university leaders, the key intellectual problems now revolve around extracting pedagogical value from investments in physical and virtual infrastructure and managing the risks associated with unpredictable changes in what new combinations of the physical and virtual can do. By developing an approach to planning university infrastructure that is structured around a focus on learning, self-awareness, feedback and self-correction of all parts of the ecology, the uncertainty involved can be mitigated.

Teaching and leadership in today's universities can be difficult and demanding. Scarcity of resources intensifies work pressures, and in time-pressed jobs it is all too easy for good people to give up or burn out. Radical changes outside and within each university will continue to create uncertainty and risks: there is no point in hoping for a return to a stable state.

Dealing with these realities becomes more feasible if one adopts a conception of teaching and leadership as work set within an ecology of learning. Such an ecology needs to be imbued with a shared sense of 'good learning' – all parts of the university need to be aware of their role in relation to this central learning purpose. Once this awareness is established, intelligent use of feedback allows adaptation to changing circumstances, with sustainable levels of effort. In short, a dynamic world needs fluid, intelligent structures – ecology shows the way.

Notes

Chapter 7

1 It is worth reflecting on the issues of recursion, knowledge and technology. An example of knowledge recursively bound up within its technical structure is a library database on research. Adopting the perspective of a student looking for useful research, the knowledge is at first bound up with knowing how to access the database, either the URL and/or the password. Once access is established, the knowledge in the database may be bound up with knowing the syntax required to complete successful searches. Once a search has identified useful sources, access to those sources may be bound up with the file type in which the useful source is housed . . . and on it can go. This example is a reasonably common and simple one. Many of us may have been thwarted at the last step in the process because the computer from where the search began did not have a software program compatible with the file we finally identified. There are more complicated examples involving databases which require the user to import data from one application into another before they can finally access the target knowledge. The key point to understand from this example is the interplay between knowledge and technology as users work their way towards identifying an object which is bound recursively within the techno-logical framework in which the search is being conducted.

Chapter 9

1 Spatial arrangements can make students more or less aware of the research activity that takes place in their university. We, and others, believe it benefits student learning and research work if each understands the other (for example Brew, 2006).

References

Abowd, G. D., & Mynatt, E. D. (2000). Charting past present and future use in ubiquitous computing. *ACM Transactions on Computer-Human Interaction, 7,* 29–58.

Agostinho, S., Oliver, R., Harper, B., Hedberg, J., & Wills, S. (2002). A tool to evaluate the potential for an ICT-based learning design to foster 'high quality learning'. In A. Williamson, C. Gunn, A. Young & T. Clear (Eds.), *Winds of change in the sea of learning. Proceedings 19th ASCILITE Conference* (pp. 29–38). Auckland: UNITEC Institute of Technology.

Alexander, C., Silverstein, M., Angel, S., Ishikawa, S., & Abrams, D. (1975). *The Oregon experiment.* New York: Oxford University Press.

Alihan, M. (1939). *Social ecology.* New York: Columbia University Press.

Anderson, T., & Elloumi, F. (2004). The theory and practice of on-line learning. Athabasca University. Available at: www.cde.athabascau.ca/on-line_book

Anderson, T., & Kanuka, H. (2003). *E-Research: methods, strategies and issues.* Athabasca University. Available at: http://dusitweb.dusit.ac.th/new_ver12/document/e_Research.pdf

Andrews, R., & Haythornthwaite, C. (Eds.). (2007). *The Sage handbook of e-learning research.* London: Sage.

Asgarali Patel, J. M., & Rajendran, K. (2007). E-Culture and personality dimensions of university students. *Journal of the Indian Academy of Applied Psychology, 33,* 129–132.

Bacsich, P., Ash, C., Boniwell, K., Kaplan, L., Mardell, J., & Caven-Atack, A. (1999). *The costs of networked learning.* Sheffield: Sheffield Hallam University.

Bain, J., & McNaught, C. (1996). Academics' educational conceptions and the design and impact of computer software in higher education. In C. McBeath & R. Atkinson (Eds.), *Proceedings of the Third International Interactive Multimedia Symposium* (pp. 56–59). Perth, Western Australia: Promaco Conventions. Available at: http://www.aset.org.au/confs/iims/1996/ad/bain.html

Bain, J., McNaught, C., Carmel, M., & Luekenhausen, G. (1998). Describing computer-facilitated learning environments in higher education. *Learning Environments Research, 1,* 163–180.

Barab, S., & Plucker, J. (2002). Smart people or smart contexts? Cognition, ability and talent development in an age of situated approaches to knowing and learning. *Educational Psychologist, 37,* 165–182.

Barnett, R. (1997). *Higher education: a critical business.* Buckingham: Open University Press.

Barnett, R. (2000a). Supercomplexity and the curriculum. *Studies in Higher Education, 25,* 255–265.

Barnett, R. (2000b). *Realizing the university in an age of supercomplexity.* Buckingham: Open University Press.

Barnett, R. (Ed.). (2005). *Reshaping the university: New relationships between research, scholarship and teaching.* Buckingham: SRHE/Open University Press.

Barnett, R. (2007). *A will to learn: being a student in an age of uncertainty.* Maidenhead: SRHE/Open University Press.

Barr, S. (1968). *Notes on dialogue.* St. John's College: Annapolis, MD. Available at: http://www.stjohnscollege.edu/asp/main.aspx?page=6712.

Barrie, S. (2007). A conceptual framework for the teaching and learning of generic graduate attributes. *Studies in Higher Education, 32,* 439–458.

Barron, T. (2000). A smarter Frankenstein: the merging of E-Learning and knowledge management, ASTD learning circuits: Available at: http://www.learningcircuits.com/aug2000/barron.html (Accessed Nov 11 2000).

Baskin, C. (2001). The Titanic, Volkswagens and collaborative group work: remaking old favourites with new learning technologies. *Australian Journal of Educational Technology, 17,* 265–278.

Bates, A. W. (2000). *Managing technological change: Strategies for college and university leaders.* San Francisco: Jossey-Bass.

Bates, A. W. (2004). Why universities must change: The challenge of e-learning. Presentation at Open University distinguished scholar program. Available at: www.tonybates.ca/pdf/Why_universities_must_change.pdf

Bates, A. W., & Poole, G. (2003). *Effective teaching with technology in higher education: Foundations for success*. San Francisco: Jossey-Bass.

Bateson, G. (1973). *Steps to an ecology of mind*. London: Fontana.

Baumard, P. (1999). *Tacit knowledge in organizations*. London: Sage.

Beetham, H., & Sharpe, R. (Eds.). (2007). *Rethinking pedagogy for a digital age*. London: Routledge.

Beichner, R. J., & Saul, J. M. (2003). *Introduction to the SCALE-UP (student-centered activities for large enrolment undergraduate programs) Project*. Available at: http://www.ncsu.edu/per/Articles/Varenna_SCALEUP_Paper.pdf

Bennett, S. (2006). The choice for learning. *Journal of Academic Librarianship, 32*, 3–13.

Bennett, S. (2007a). Designing for uncertainty: three approaches. *Journal of Academic Librarianship, 33*, 165–179.

Bennett, S. (2007b). First questions for designing higher education learning spaces. *Journal of Academic Librarianship, 33*, 14–26.

Bereiter, C. (2002). *Education and mind in the knowledge age*. Mahwah, NJ: Lawrence Erlbaum Associates.

Bereiter, C., & Scardamalia, M. (2003). Learning to work creatively with knowledge. In E. de Corte, L. Verschaffel, N. Entwistle & J. van Merrienboer (Eds.), *Powerful learning environments: Unravelling basic components and dimensions* (pp. 55–68). Oxford: Pergamon/Elsevier.

Berggren, K., Brodeur, D., Crawley, E. F., Ingemarsson, I., Litant, W. T. G., Malmqvist, J., & Östlund, S. (2003). CDIO: An international initiative for reforming engineering education. *World Transactions on Engineering and Technology Education UICEE, 2*, 49–52.

Bickford, D. J. (2002). Navigating the white waters of collaborative work in shaping learning environments. *New Directions for Teaching and Learning, 92*, 43–52.

Biggs, J. (1987). *The study process questionnaire (SPQ): Manual*. Hawthorn, Victoria: Australian Council for Educational Research.

Biggs, J. (1999). What the student does: teaching for enhanced learning. *Higher Education Research and Development, 18*, 57–75.

Biggs, J. (2003). *Teaching for quality learning at university: What the student does* (2nd ed.). Buckingham: Open University Press.

Biggs, J. B. (2005). *Aligning teaching for constructing learning*. Higher Education Academy Discussion Paper. Available at: http://www.heacademy.ac.uk/embedded_object.asp?id=21686&filename=Biggs.

Biggs, J., Kember, D., & Leung, D. Y. P. (2001). The revised two-factor study process questionnaire: R-SPQ-2F. *British Journal of Educational Psychology, 71*, 133–149.

Biggs, J., & Tang, C. (2007). *Teaching for quality learning at university: What the student does* (3rd ed.). Buckingham: Open University Press.

Blackler, F. (1995). Knowledge, knowledge work and organizations: an overview and interpretation. *Organization Studies, 16*, 1021–1046.

Bligh, D. (2000). *What's the use of lectures?* (6th ed.). San Francisco: Jossey Bass.

Bliuc, A., Goodyear, P., & Ellis, R. A. (2007). Research focus and methodological choices in studies into students' experiences of blended learning in higher education. *The Internet and Higher Education, 15*, 231–244.

Bolland, R., & Collopy, F. (2004). Design matters for management. In R. Boland & F. Collopy (Eds.), *Managing as designing* (pp. 3–18). Stanford: Stanford University Press.

Boot, R., & Hodgson, V. (1987). Open learning: meaning and experience. In V. Hodgson, S. Mann, & R. Snell (Eds.), *Beyond distance teaching: Towards open learning* (pp. 5–15), Buckingham: Open University Press.

Boud, D. (1999). Situating academic development in professional work: using peer learning, *International Journal for Academic Development, 4*, 3–10.

Boud, D., Cohen, R., & Sampson, J. (1999). Peer learning and assessment. *Assessment and Evaluation in Higher Education, 24*, 413–426.

Boud, D., & Feletti, G. (2001). *The challenge of problem-based learning* (2nd ed.). London: Kogan Page.

Boud, D., & Garrick, J. (1999). *Understanding learning at work*. London: Routledge

Bourlova, T., & Bullen, M. (2005). The impact of e-learning on the use of campus instructional space. In *Advances in Web-Based Learning – Icwl 2005: Vol. 3583, Lecture Notes in Computer Science* (pp. 397–405). Berlin/Heidelberg: Springer-Verlag.

Bowden, J., & Marton, F. (1998). *The university of learning: Beyond quality and competence in higher education*. London: Kogan Page.

Bowden, J., & Marton, F. (2004). *The university of learning*. London: Routledge Falmer.

Bowker, G. (2006). *Memory practices in the sciences*. Cambridge, MA: MIT Press.

Brand, S. (1997). *How buildings learn: What happens after they're built*. London: Phoenix Illustrated.

Bransford, J., Brown, A., & Cocking, R. (Eds.). (2000). *How people learn: Brain, mind, experience and school*. Washington, DC: National Academy Press.

Brett, P., & Nagra, J. (2005). An investigation into student's use of a computer-based social learning space: lessons for facilitating collaborative approaches to learning. *British Journal of Educational Technology, 36*, 281–292.

Brew, A. (2006). *Research and teaching: Beyond the divide*. Basingstoke: Palgrave Macmillan.

Brew, A., & Sachs, J. (2007). *Transforming a university: The scholarship of learning and teaching in practice*. Sydney: Sydney University Press.

Bronfenbrenner, U. (1979). *The ecology of human development: Experiments by nature and design*. Cambridge, MA: Harvard University Press.

Brook, I., Hunt, J., & Hughes, P. (1994). Constraints on student-centred learning practices. In G. Gibbs (Ed.), *Improving student learning: Theory and practice*. Oxford: Oxford Centre for Staff Development.

Brown, J., Collins, A., & Duguid, P. (1989). Situated cognition and the culture of learning. *Educational Researcher, 18*, 32–42.

Brown, J. S., & Duguid, P. (1996). Toward a unified view of working, learning and innovation. In M. Cohen & L. Sproul (Eds.), *Organisational learning* (pp. 58–82). New York: Sage.

Brown, P., Hesketh, A., & Williams, S. (2003). Employability in a knowledge-driven economy. *Journal of Education and Work, 16*, 107–126.

Bump, J. (1990). Radical changes in class discussion using networked computers. *Computers and the Humanities, 24*, 44–65.

Burnett, C. (2003). Learning to chat: tutor participation in synchronous on-line chat. *Teaching in Higher Education, 8*, 247–261.

Caldwell, B., & Carter, E. M. A. (1993). *The return of the mentor: Strategies for workplace learning*. London: Routledge.

Carrick Institute for Learning & Teaching in Higher Education. (2007). *Places and spaces for learning*. Sydney: Carrick Institute for Learning & Teaching in Higher Education. Available at: http://www.altc.edu.au/carrick/go/home/pid/469

Chism, N. V. N. (2002). A tale of two classrooms. *New Directions for Teaching and Learning, 92*, 5–12.

Chism, N. V. N., & Bickford D. J. (2002). Improving the environment for learning: an expanded agenda. *New Directions for Teaching and Learning, 92*, 91–97.

Clark, J. (2001). Stimulating collaboration and discussion learning environments. *Internet and Higher Education, 4*, 119–124.

Clark, R. (1983). Reconsidering research on learning from media. *Review of Educational Research, 53*, 445–459.

Clark, R. (1994). Media will never influence learning. *Educational Technology Research and Development, 42*, 21–29.

Clark, R., & Mayer, R. (2002). *E-learning and the science of instruction*. New York: Pfeiffer.

Cohen, M., & Nicol, D. (2007). Managing investment in teaching and learning technologies. *Perspectives: Policy and Practice in Higher Education, 11*, 25–28.

Collins, A., & Ferguson, W. (1993). Epistemic forms and epistemic games: structures and strategies to guide inquiry. *Educational Psychologist, 28*, 25–42.

Collis, B., & Moonen, J. (2001). *Flexible learning in a digital world: Experiences and expectations*. London: Kogan Page.

Conger, S. B. (2005). If there is no significant difference, why should we care? *The Journal of Educators* On-line, 2. Available at: http://www.thejeo.com/Basu%20Conger%20Final.pdf

Conole, G., & Dyke, M. (2004). What are the affordances of information and communication technologies? *ALT-J, 12*, 113–124.

Conole, G., & Jones, C. (forthcoming). Sharing practice, problems and solutions for institutional change: comparing different forms of representation. In P. Goodyear & S. Retalis (Eds.), *Technology-enhanced learning: Design patterns and pattern languages*. Rotterdam: Sense Publishers.

Conole, G., de Laat, M., Dillon, T., & Darby, J. (2006). *Student experiences of technologies: LXP final report*. Bristol: JISC.

Craik, F., & Lockhart, R. (1972). Levels of processing: a framework for memory research. *Journal of Verbal Learning and Verbal Behavior, 11*, 671–684.

Crawford, K., Gordon S., Nicholas, J., & Prosser, M. (1994). Conceptions of mathematics and how it is learned: the perspectives of students entering university. *Learning and Instruction,* 4, 331–345.

Crawford, K., Gordon S., Nicholas, J., & Prosser, M. (1998). Qualitatively different experiences of learning mathematics at university. *Learning and Instruction,* 8, 455–468.

Creanor, L., Trinder, K., Gowan, D., & Howells, C. (2006). *LEX: The learner experience of e-learning, Final report.* Bristol: JISC.

Crook, C., & Barrowcliff, D. (2001). Ubiquitous computing on campus: patterns of engagement by university students. *International Journal of Human-Computer Interaction,* 13, 245–258.

Crook, C., & Light, P. (1999). Information technology and the culture of student learning. In J. Bliss, R. Säljö, & P. Light (Eds.), *Learning sites: Social and technological resources for learning* (pp. 183–193). Oxford: Pergamon.

Crook, C., & Light, P. (2002). Virtualisation and the cultural practice of study. In S. Woolgar (Ed.), *Virtual society? – technology, cyberbole, reality* (pp. 153–175). Oxford: Oxford University Press.

Dalziel, J. (2003). Implementing learning design: the learning activity management system. In G. Crisp, D. Thiele, I. Scholten, S. Barker, & J. Baron (Eds.), *Interact, integrate, impact: Proceedings of the 20th Annual Conference of the Australasian Society for Computers in Learning in Tertiary Education.* Adelaide, 7–10 December 2003.

Daniel, J. S. (1998). *Mega-universities and knowledge media: Technology strategies for higher education.* London: Kogan Page.

De Noriega, D. C., & Gonzales, G. (2004). Swords to plowshares: California State University, Monterey Bay. *Change,* 36, 32–42.

Dennan, V. P. (2005). From message posting to learning dialogues: factors affecting learner participation in asynchronous discussion. *Distance Education,* 26, 1, 127–148.

Dochy F., Segers M., & Sluijsmans D. (1999). The use of self, peer and co-assessment in higher education: a review. *Studies Higher Education,* 24, 331–350.

Dogan, M., & Rokkan, S. (Eds.). (1969). *Social ecology.* Cambridge, MA: MIT Press.

Duncan, O. (1964). Social organization and the eco-system. In R. Faris (Ed.), *Handbook of modern sociology* (pp. 37–82). Chicago: Rand McNally.

Ellis, R. A., & Calvo, R. A. (2004). Learning through discussions in blended environments. *Educational Media International,* 40, 263–274.

Ellis, R. A., & Calvo, R. A. (2006). Discontinuities in university student experiences of learning through discussions. *British Journal of Educational Technology,* 37, 55–68.

Ellis, R. A., Calvo, R. A., Levy, D., & Tan, K. (2004). Learning through discussions. *Higher Education Research and Development,* 23, 73–93.

Ellis, R. A., Goodyear, P., Brillant, M., & Prosser, M. (2008a) Student experiences of problem-based learning in pharmacy: conceptions of learning, approaches to learning and the integration of face-to-face and on-line activities. *Advances in Health Sciences Education,* 13, 675–692.

Ellis, R. A., Goodyear, P., Calvo, R., & Prosser, M. (2008b). Engineering students' experiences of learning through discussions in face-to-face and on-line contexts. *Learning and Instruction,* 18, 267–282.

Ellis, R. A., Goodyear, P., O'Hara, A., & Prosser, M. (2007). The university student experience of face-to-face and on-line discussions: coherence, reflection and meaning. *Association for Learning Technology Journal,* 15, 83–97.

Ellis, R. A., Goodyear, P., Prosser, M., & O'Hara, A. (2006). How and what university students learn through on-line and face-to-face discussions: conceptions, intentions and approaches, *Journal of Computer Assisted Learning,* 22, 244–256.

Ellis, R. A., Hughes, J., Weyers, M., & Riding, P. (2009). University teacher approaches to design and teaching and concepts of learning technologies. *Teaching and Teacher Education,* 25, 109–117.

Ellis, R. A., Marcus, G., & Taylor, R. (2005). Learning through inquiry: Student difficulties with on-line case-based material. *Journal of Computer Assisted Learning,* 21, 239–252.

Ellis, R. A., & Moore, R. (2006). Learning through benchmarking: Developing a relational, prospective approach to benchmarking ICT in learning and teaching. *Higher Education,* 51, 351–371.

Ellis, R. A, Steed, A., & Applebee, A. (2006). Teacher conceptions of blended learning, blended teaching and associations with approaches to design. *Australasian Journal of Educational Technology,* 22, 312–335.

Entwistle, N. J., & Ramsden, P. (1983). *Understanding student learning.* London: Croom Helm.

Entwistle, N., Tait, H., & McCune, V. (2000). Patterns of response to an approach to studying inventory across contrasting groups and contexts. *European Journal of the Psychology of Education, 15*, 33–48.

Epper, R., & Bates, A. W. (Eds.). (2001). *Teaching faculty how to use technology: Best practices from leading institutions.* Westport, CT: American Council on Education: Oryx.

Fauske, J., & Wade, S. E. (2003–2004). Research to practice on-line: conditions that foster democracy, community, and critical thinking in computer-mediated discussions. *Journal of Research on Technology in Education, 36*, 137–153.

Ferrell, G., Kelly, J., MacMahon, C., Probert, S., Quentin-Baxter, M., & Riachi, R. (2007). *CAMEL Tangible benefits of e-learning project: Final report.* Bristol, UK: JISC.

Feuer, M. J., Towne, L., & Shavelson, R. J. (2000). Scientific culture and educational research. *Educational Researcher, 31*, 4–14.

Fisher, K. (1999). A critical pedagogy of space. *Critical Pedagogy Networker, 12*, 1–7.

Fleming, P., Harley, B., & Sewell, G. (2004). A little knowledge is a dangerous thing: getting below the surface of the growth of 'knowledge work' in Australia. *Work, Employment & Society, 18*, 725–747.

Florida, R. (1999). The role of the university: leveraging talent, not technology. *Issues in Science & Technology, 20*, 67–73.

Florida, R. (2003). *The rise of the creative class.* New York: Basic Books.

Foote, S. M. (2004). Changes in library design: an architect's perspective. *Libraries and the Academy, 4*, 41–42.

Forrest, C., Hinchliffe, L. J., Arp, L., & Woodard, B. S. (2005). Beyond classroom construction and design. *Reference & User Services Quarterly, 44*, 296–300.

Fusilier, M., & Durlabhji, S. (2008). Predictors of student Internet use: data from three developing countries. *Learning, Media and Technology, 33*, 59–69.

Gale, T. (2002). Degrees of difficulty: an ecological account of learning in Australian higher education. *Studies in Higher Education, 27*, 65–78.

Garrison, D. R., & Anderson, T. (2003). *E-learning in the 21st century: A framework for research and practice.* New York: Routledge.

Geake, J. (2008). Neuromythologies in education. *Educational Research, 50*, 123–133.

Gee, L. (2006). Human-centered design guidelines. In D. Oblinger, (Ed.), *Learning spaces.* Washington, DC, Boulder, CO: Educause.

Geer, R. (2001). The necessity of considering cultural influences in on-line collaborative learning. Paper presented at the World Conference on Educational Multimedia, Hypermedia and Telecommunications, Chesapeake, VA.

Gibbons, A., & Rogers, P. (2008). The architecture of instructional theory. In C. Reigeluth & A. Carr-Chellman (Eds.), *Instructional design theories and models: Vol. 3.* Mahwah, NJ: Lawrence Erlbaum Associates.

Gibson, J. (1986). *The ecological approach to visual perception.* Hillsdale, NJ: Lawrence Erlbaum Associates.

Gibson, K., & Ingold, T. (Eds.) (1995). *Tools, language and cognition in human evolution.* Cambridge: Cambridge University Press.

Giddens, A. (1984). *The constitution of society: Outline of the theory of structuration.* Berkeley: University of California Press.

Ginns, P., & Ellis, R. A. (forthcoming). Evaluating the quality of e-learning at the degree level in the student experience of blended learning. *British Journal of Educational Technology.* Available online 24-7-08.

Ginns, P., Prosser, M., & Barrie, S. (2007). Students' perceptions of teaching quality in higher education: The perspective of currently enrolled students. *Studies in Higher Education, 32*, 603–615.

Ginsparg, P. (2000). Creating a global knowledge network. *BMC News and Views, 1*, 1–3.

Gonzalez, C. (2009). University teachers' experiences of teaching in blended learning environments. Unpublished PhD thesis, University of Sydney.

Gonzalez, C. (forthcoming). Conceptions of, and approaches to, teaching on-line: a study of lecturers teaching postgraduate distance courses. *Higher Education.* Available online 22-5-08.

Goodyear, P. (1995). Situated action and distributed knowledge: a JITOL perspective on electronic performance support systems. *Educational and Training Technology International, 32*, 45–55.

Goodyear, P. (1997). Instructional design environments: methods and tools for the design of complex instructional systems. In S. Dijkstra, N. Seel, F. Schott & R. Tennyson (Eds.), *Instructional design: International perspectives* (pp. 83–111). Mahwah, NJ: Lawrence Erlbaum Associates.

Goodyear, P. (1999). Pedagogical frameworks and action research in open and distance learning. *European Journal of Open and Distance Learning.* Lancaster University CSALT, Working Paper. Available at: http://domino.lancs.ac.uk/edres/csaltdocs.nsf.

Goodyear, P. (2000). Environments for lifelong learning: ergonomics, architecture and educational design. In J. M. Spector & T. Anderson (Eds.), *Integrated and holistic perspectives on learning, instruction & technology: Understanding complexity* (pp. 1–18). Dordrecht: Kluwer Academic Publishers.

Goodyear, P. (2001). Learning and digital environments: lessons from European research. In M. O'Fathaigh (Ed.), *Education and the information age: Current progress and future strategies* (pp. 1–25). Cork: Bradshaw Books.

Goodyear, P. (2002). Psychological foundations for networked learning. In C. Steeples & C. Jones (Eds.), *Networked learning: Perspectives and issues* (pp. 49–75). London: Springer Verlag.

Goodyear, P. (2005). Educational design and networked learning: Patterns, pattern languages and design practice. *Australasian Journal of Educational Technology, 21*, 82–101.

Goodyear, P. (2006). Technology and the articulation of vocational and academic interests: Reflections on time, space and e-learning. *Studies in Continuing Education, 28*, 83–98.

Goodyear, P. (2008). Flexible learning and the architecture of learning places. In M. Spector, D. Merrill, J. van Merrienboer & M. Driscoll (Eds.), *Handbook of Research on Educational Communications and Technology* (3rd ed., pp. 251–257). New York: Routledge.

Goodyear, P., & Ellis, R. (2007). The development of epistemic fluency: learning to think for a living. In A. Brew & J. Sachs (Eds.), *Transforming a university: The scholarship of teaching and learning in practice* (pp. 57–68). Sydney: Sydney University Press.

Goodyear, P., & Ellis, R. (2008). University students' approaches to learning: rethinking the place of technology. *Distance Education, 29*, 141–152.

Goodyear, P., & JISC Networked Learning Project Team. (2000). *Effective networked learning in higher education.* Lancaster: CSALT.

Goodyear, P., & Retalis, S. (Eds.). (forthcoming 2009). *Technology-enhanced learning: Design patterns and pattern languages.* Rotterdam: Sense Publishers.

Goodyear, P., & Steeples, C. (1992). IT-based open learning: tasks and tools. *Journal of Computer Assisted Learning, 8*, 163–176.

Goodyear, P., & Zenios, M. (2007). Discussion, collaborative knowledge work and epistemic fluency. *British Journal of Educational Studies, 55*, 351–368.

Gordon, H. (2003). Function changes form: evolution of the Sunshine Coast University Library. *Australian Academic and Research Libraries 34*, 169–176.

Graetz, K. A. (2006). The psychology of learning environments. In D. Oblinger (Ed.), *Learning spaces.* Washington, DC, Boulder, CO: Educause.

Greeno, J. (1994). Gibson's affordances. *Psychological Review, 101*, 336–342.

Greeno, J. (2006). Theoretical and practical advances through research on learning. In P. B. Elmore, G. Camilli, & J. Green (Eds.), *Complementary methods for research in education.* Washington, DC: American Educational Research Association.

Greeno, J., Collins, A., & Resnick, L. B. (1996). Cognition and learning. In R. Calfee & D. Berliner (Eds.), *Handbook of educational psychology.* New York: Macmillan.

Guri-Rosenblit, S. (1999). *Distance and campus universities: Tensions and interactions.* Oxford: Pergamon.

Gustafson, K. (2002). Instructional design tools: a critique and projections for the future. *Educational Technology Research and Development, 50*, 59–66.

Haft, J. S. (1972). Flexible teaching-learning spaces. *SO – Journal of Medical Education, 47*, 339–342.

Hager, P., & Holland, S. (Eds.). (2006). *Graduate attributes, learning and employability.* Dordrecht: Springer.

Hannafin, K., & Hannafin, M. (1996). The ecology of distance learning environments. *Training Research Journal, 1*, 49–70.

Hativa, N., & Goodyear, P. (Eds.). (2002). *Teacher thinking, beliefs and knowledge in higher education.* Dordrecht: Kluwer Academic Publishers.

Hawkins, B., & Rudy, J. A. (2004). *EDUCAUSE Core Data Service 2003 Summary Report.* Available at: http://connect.educause.edu/library/abstract/EDUCAUSECoreDataServ/43038

Hawkins, B., & Rudy, J. A. (2007). *EDUCAUSE core data service: fiscal year 2006 summary report.* Available at: http://connect.educause.edu/library/abstract/EDUCAUSECoreDataServ/45236

Hawley, A. (1950). *Human ecology: A theory of community structures.* New York: Ronald Press.

Hedberg, J. (2004). Designing multimedia: seven discourses. *Cambridge Journal of Education, 34,* 241–256.

Hendry, G. D., Lyon, P. M., Prosser, M., & Sze, D. (2006). Conceptions of problem-based learning: the perspectives of students entering a problem-based medical program. *Medical Teacher, 28,* 573–575.

Herring, S. (2004). Slouching toward the ordinary: current trends in computer-mediated communication. *New Media and Society, 6,* 26–36.

Herrington, J., & Oliver, R. (2000). An instructional design framework for authentic learning environments. *Educational Technology Research and Development, 48,* 23–48.

Holtham, C. (2006). Sir John Cass Business School: City of London. In D. Oblinger, (Ed.), *Learning spaces.* Washington, DC, Boulder, CO: Educause.

Hounsell, D. (1984). Essay planning and essay writing. *Higher Education Research and Development, 3,* 13–31.

Hounsell, D. (1997). Understanding teaching and teaching for understanding. In F. Marton, D. Hounsell, & N. Entwistle (Eds.), *The experience of learning: Implications for teaching and studying in higher education* (pp. 238–258). Edinburgh: Scottish Academic Press.

Howard-Jones, P. (2007). *Neuroscience and education: Issues and opportunities.* London: ESRC Teaching & Learning Research Programme (TLRP).

Hunt, L., Bromage, A., & Tomkinson, B. (Eds.). (2006). *The realities of change in higher education: Interventions to promote learning and teaching,* London, Routledge.

Hutchins, E. (1995). *Cognition in the wild.* Cambridge, MA: MIT Press.

Ingold, T. (2000). *The perception of the environment: Essays in livelihood, dwelling and skill.* Abingdon: Routledge.

Ipsos MORI. (2007). *Student expectations.* Bristol: JISC.

Ipsos MORI. (2008). *Great expectations of ICT: How higher education institutions are measuring up.* Bristol: JISC.

Jamieson, P., Dane, J., & O'Brien, M. (2004). *Building learning communities: Constructing appropriate teaching and learning spaces.* Paper presented at the Effective Teaching and Learning Conference, Griffith University, Brisbane, in November.

Jenkins, A., Breen, R., Lindsay, R., & Brew, A. (2003). *Reshaping teaching in higher education: Linking teaching with research.* London: Kogan Page.

Jeong, A. C. (2003). The sequential analysis of group interaction and critical thinking in on-line threaded discussions. *The American Journal of Distance Education, 17,* 25–43.

Jochems, W., van Merrienboer, J., & Koper, R. (Eds.). (2004). *Integrated E-learning: Pedagogy, technology, and organization.* London: Routledge Falmer.

Johansson, B., Marton, F., & Svensson, L. (1985). An approach to describing learning as change between qualitatively different conceptions. In A. L. Pines & L. H. T. West (Eds.), *Cognitive structure and conceptual change* (pp. 233–258). New York: Academic Press.

Joint Information Systems Committee [JISC]. (2006). *Designing spaces for effective learning: A guide to 21st century learning space design.* Bristol: JISC. Available at: http://www.jisc.ac.uk/uploaded_documents/JISClearningspaces.pdf

Joint Information Systems Committee [JISC]. (2008). *Research in the social biomedical sciences.* Bristol: JISC. Available at: http://www.jisc.ac.uk/media/documents/publications/bpsocialsciencev1web.pdf

Jonassen, D., & Reeves, T. (1996). Learning with technology: using computers as cognitive tools. In D. Jonassen (Ed.), *Handbook of research for educational communications and technology* (pp. 693–719). New York: Macmillan.

Jones, C., Asensio, M., & Goodyear, P. (2000). Networked learning in higher education: practitioners' perspectives. *Journal of the Association for Learning Technology, 8,* 18–28.

Jones, M., & Winne, P. (Eds.). (1992). *Adaptive learning environments: Foundations and frontiers.* Berlin: Springer Verlag.

Justin, J. K. (1965). *Lecture hall and learning design: A survey of variables, parameters, criteria and interrelationships for audio-visual presentation systems and audience reception.* New York: Society of Motion Picture and Television Engineers, Inc.

Kalantzis, M., & Cope, B. (2008). *New learning: Elements of a science of education*. Cambridge: Cambridge University Press.

Kaptelinin, V., & Nardi, B. (2006). *Acting with technology: Activity theory and interaction design*. Cambridge, MA: The MIT Press.

Kember, D., & Kwan, K. P. (2000). Lecturers' approaches to teaching and their relationship to conceptions of good teaching. *Instructional Science, 28*, 469–490.

Kennedy, G., Dalgarno, B., Bennett, S., Judd, T., Gray, K., & Chang, R. (2008b). Immigrants and natives: investigating differences between staff and students' use of technology. In *Hello! Where are you in the landscape of educational technology?* Proceedings ascilite Melbourne 2008. Available at: http://www.ascilite.org.au/conferences/melbourne08/procs/kennedy.pdf

Kennedy, G., Dalgarno, B., Gray, K., Judd, T., Waycott, J., Bennett, S., Maton, K., Krause, K. L., Bishop, A., Chang, R., & Churchward, A. (2007). The net generation are not big users of Web 2.0 technologies: preliminary findings. Paper presented at ASCILITE 2007 conference Providing choices for learners and learning, Singapore.

Kennedy, G., Judd, T., Churchward, A., Gray, K., & Krause, K. (2008a). First year students' experiences with technology: are they really digital natives? *Australasian Journal of Educational Technology, 24*, 108–122.

Kenway, J., Bullen, E., Fahey, J., & Robb, S. (2006). *Haunting the knowledge economy*. International Library of Sociology. London: Routledge.

Kim, S., & Sonnenwald, D. H. (2002). Investigating the relationship between learning style preferences and teaching collaboration skills and technology: an exploratory study. *Proceedings of the ASIST Annual Meeting*, 64–73.

Kirkwood, A., & Price, L. (2005). Learners and learning in the twenty-first century: what do we know about students' attitudes towards, and experiences of, information and communication technologies that will help us design courses? *Studies in Higher Education, 30*, 257–274.

Knight, P., & Trowler, P. R. (2001). *Departmental leadership in higher education*. Philadelphia: Open University Press.

Knight, P., & Yorke, M. (2004). *Learning, curriculum and employability in higher education*. London: Routledge Falmer.

Knirk, F. G. (1987). *Instructional facilities for the information age*. An ERIC Information Analysis Product, Syracuse, NY: ERIC Clearinghouse on Information Resources.

Koper, R., & Tattersall, C. (Eds.). (2005). *Learning design: A handbook on modelling and delivering networked education and training*. Berlin: Springer.

Kozma, R. (1994). Will media influence learning? Reframing the debate. *Educational Technology Research and Development, 42*, 7–19.

Kress, G. (2003). *Literacy in the new media age*. London: Routledge.

Kulik, J., Kulik, C., & Cohen, P. (1980). Effectiveness of computer-based college teaching: a meta-analysis of findings. *Review of Educational Research, 50*, 525–544.

Lajoie, S. (Ed.). (2000). *Computers as cognitive tools: No more walls – theory change, paradigm shifts, and their influence on the use of computers for instructional purposes*. Mahwah, NJ: Lawrence Erlbaum Associates.

Lajoie, S., & Derry, S. (Eds.). (1993). *Computers as cognitive tools*. Hillsdale, New Jersey: Lawrence Erlbaum Associates.

Latchem, C., & Lockwood, F. (Eds.). (1998). *Staff development in open and flexible learning*. London: Routledge.

Laurillard, D. (1984). Learning from problem-solving. In F. Marton, D. Hounsell, & N. Entwistle (Eds.), *The experience of learning*. Edinburgh: Scottish Academic Press.

Laurillard, D. (1987). The different forms of learning in psychology and education. In J. Richardson, M. Eysenck & D. Warren Piper (Eds.), *Student learning: Research in education and cognitive psychology* (pp. 198–207). Buckingham: Open University Press.

Laurillard, D. (1993). *Rethinking university teaching: A framework for the effective use of educational technology*. London: Routledge.

Laurillard, D. (2001). The E-University: What have we learned? *International Journal of Management Education*. Available at: http://www.heacademy.ac.uk/assets/bmaf/documents/publications/IJME/Vol1no2/Laurillard_The_E-University.pdf

Laurillard, D. (2002). *Rethinking university teaching: A conversational framework for the effective use of educational technology* (2nd ed.). London: Routledge Falmer.

Lave, J., & Wenger, E. (1991). *Situated learning: Legitimate peripheral participation*. Cambridge: Cambridge University Press.

Lewis, R. (2002). The hybridisation of conventional higher education: UK perspective. *The International Review of Research in Open and Distance Learning, 2*. Available at: http://www.irrodl.org/index.php/irrodl/article/viewArticle/58

Li, N., & Kirkup, G. (2007). Gender and cultural differences in Internet use: a study of China and the UK. *Computers & Education, 48*, 301–317.

Li, N., Kirkup, G., & Hodgson, B. (2001). Cross-cultural comparison of women students' attitudes toward the Internet and usage: China and the United Kingdom. *CyberPsychology & Behavior, 4*, 415–426.

Lippincott, J. K. (2006). Linking the information commons to learning. In D. Oblinger (Ed.), *Learning spaces*. Washington, DC; Boulder, CO: Educause.

Lockwood, F., & Gooley, A. (Eds.). (2001). *Innovation in open and distance learning: Successful development of online and web-based learning*. London: Routledge Falmer.

Lockwood, F., & Latchem, C. (2004). Staff development needs and provision in commonwealth countries: findings from a Commonwealth of Learning Training Study. *Distance Education. 25*, 159–173.

Lombardi, M. M., & Wall, T. B. (2006). Perkins Library: Duke University. In D. Oblinger (Ed.), *Learning spaces*. Washington, DC, Boulder, CO: Educause.

Long, P. D. (2006). The brain and sciences complex. In D. Oblinger (Ed.), *Learning spaces*. Washington, DC, Boulder, CO: Educause.

Lowry, C. H. (1994). Nurses' attitudes toward computerised care plans in intensive care: part 2. *Intensive and Critical Care Nursing, 10*, 2–11.

Loyens, S. M., Rikers, R. M., & Schmidt, H. G. (2006). Students' conceptions of constructivist learning: a comparison between a traditional and a problem-based learning curriculum. *Advances in Health Science Education, 11*, 365–379.

Ludwig, L., & Starr, S. (2005). Library as place: results of a delphi study. *Journal of the Medical Library Association, 93*, 315–326.

Lynch, D. (2006). *Boyer Hall*. In D. Oblinger (Ed.), *Learning spaces*. Washington, DC, Boulder, CO: Educause.

Marton, F. (1981). Phenomenography: describing conceptions of the world around us. *Instructional Science, 10*, 177–200.

Marton, F. (1992). Phenomenography and 'the art of teaching all things to all men'. *Qualitative Studies in Education, 5*, 253–267.

Marton, F., & Booth, S. (1997). *Learning and awareness*. Mahwah NJ: Lawrence Erlbaum Associates.

Marton, F., Dall'Alba, G., & Beaty, E. (1993). Conceptions of learning. *International Journal of Educational Research, 19*, 277–300.

Marton, F., Hounsell, D., & Entwistle, N. (1997). *The experience of learning, implications for teaching and studying in higher education* (2nd ed.). Edinburgh: Scottish Academic Press.

Marton, F., & Säljö, R. (1976a). On qualitative differences in learning I. Outcome and process. *British Journal of Educational Psychology, 46*, 4–11.

Marton, F., & Säljö, R. (1976b). On qualitative differences in learning II. Outcome as a function of the learner's conception of the task. *British Journal of Educational Psychology, 46*, 115–127.

Marton, F., & Tang, M. (2006). On some necessary conditions of learning. *Journal of the Learning Sciences, 15*, 193–220.

Mason, R., & Kaye, A. (Eds.). (1989). *Mindweave: communication, computers and distance education*. Oxford: Pergamon.

Mayer, R. E., & Wittrock, M. C. (1996). Problem-solving transfer. In D. Berliner & R. Calfee (Eds.), *Handbook of educational psychology* (pp. 47–62). New York: Simon & Schuster Macmillan.

McConnell, D. (2000). *Implementing computer supported cooperative learning*. London: Routledge.

Meacham, J. (1994). Discussions by E-mail: Experiences from a large class on multiculturalism. *Liberal Education, 80*, 36–39.

Michael-Barber, J. (2006). Peter H. Armacost Library: Eckerd College. In D. Oblinger (Ed), *Learning spaces*. Washington, DC, Boulder, CO: Educause.

Mora, F., Segovia, G., & del Arco, A. (2007). Aging, plasticity and environmental enrichment: structural changes and neurotransmitter dynamics in several areas of the brain. *Brain Research Reviews, 55*, 78–88.

Morrison, D., & Collins, A. (1996). Epistemic fluency and constructivist learning environments. In B. Wilson (Ed.), *Constructivist learning environments* (pp. 107–19). Englewood Cliffs, NJ: Educational Technology Press.

Naidu, S. (Ed.). (2003). *Learning and teaching with technology: Principles and practices.* London: Kogan Page.

Nardi, B., & O'Day, V. (1999). *Information ecologies: Using technology with heart.* Cambridge, MA: MIT Press.

NCIHE. (1997). *Higher education in the learning society (Report of the National Committee of Inquiry into Higher Education: The Dearing Report).* London: HMSO.

Newell, A., & Simon, H. A. (1972). *Human problem solving.* Englewood Cliffs, NJ: Prentice Hall.

Newman, J. H., & Turner, F. M. (1996). *The idea of a university.* USA: Yale University Press.

Ng, C., & Cheung, W. (2007). Comparing face to face, tutor led discussion and on-line discussion in the classroom. *Australasian Journal of Educational Technology, 23,* 455–469.

Nicol, D. J., & Coen, M. (2003a). A model for evaluating the institutional costs and benefits of ICT initiatives in teaching and learning in higher education. *Association for Learning Technology Journal, 11*(2), 46–60.

Nicol, D. J., & Coen, M. (2003b). The importance of cost–benefit analysis: a response. *Association for Learning Technology Journal, 11*(3), 122–124.

Norman, D. (1999). Affordance, conventions and design. *Interactions, 6,* 38–43.

Norman, G. R., & Schmidt, H. G. (1992). The psychological basis of problem-based learning: a review of evidence. *Academic Medicine, 67,* 55–565.

Norman, G. R., & Schmidt, H. G. (2000). Effectiveness of problem-based learning curricula: theory, practice and paper darts. *Medical Education, 34,* 721–8.

Nussbaum, M. C. (1997). *Cultivating humanity: A classical defense of reform in liberal education.* Cambridge, MA: Harvard University Press.

Oblinger, D. (Ed.) (2006a). *Learning spaces.* Washington, D.C.: Boulder, CO, Educause.

Oblinger, D. (2006b). Learning how to see. In D. Oblinger (Ed.), *Learning spaces.* Washington, DC, Boulder, CO: Educause.

Oblinger, D., & Hawkins, B. (2006). The myth about no significant difference. *Educause Review, 41,* 14–15.

Oblinger, D., & Oblinger, J. L. (2005). *Educating the net generation.* Boulder, CO, Educause. Available at: http://www.educause.edu/educatingthenetgen/5989

OECD. (2005). *E-Learning in tertiary education: Where do we stand?* Paris: Centre for Educational Research and Innovation (CERI), Organisation for Economic Cooperation and Development.

Ohlsson, S. (1995). Learning to do and learning to understand. In P. Reimann, & H. Spada (Eds.). *Learning in humans and machines* (pp. 37–62). Oxford: Pergamon.

Oliver, B., & Goerke, V. (2007). Australian undergraduates' use and ownership of emerging technologies: implications and opportunities for creating engaging learning experiences for the Net Generation. *Australasian Journal of Educational Technology, 23,* 171–186.

Oliver, M., & Trigwell, K. (2005). Can 'blended learning' be redeemed? *E-Learning, 2,* 17–26.

Oliver, R., Harper, B., Hedberg, J., Wills, S., & Agostinho, S. (2002). Formalising the description of learning designs. In A. Goody, J. Herrington, & M. Northcote (Eds.), *Quality conversations: Research and development in higher education, Vol. 25* (pp. 496–504). Jamison, ACT: HERDSA.

Oliver, R., & Herrington, J. (2000). Using situated learning as a design strategy for Web-based learning. In B. Abbey (Ed.), *Instructional and cognitive impacts of Web-based education* (pp. 178–191). Hershey, PA: Idea Publishing Group.

Palfrey, J., & Gasser, U. (2008). *Born digital: Understanding the first generation of digital natives.* New York: Basic Books.

Palloff, R. M., & Pratt, K. (1999). *Building learning communities in cyberspace: Effective strategies for the online classroom.* San Francisco: Jossey-Bass.

Palloff, R. M., & Pratt, K. (2003). *The virtual student: A profile and guide to working with online learners.* San Francisco: Jossey-Bass.

Papert, S. (1980). *Mindstorms: Children, computers and powerful ideas.* Brighton: Harvester.

Patron, L., Ellis, R. A., & Barrett, B. (forthcoming). University teacher approaches to design and teaching of case studies using ICTs: virtual 'field trips'. *PROSPECTS, Journal of Comparative Education, 4,* 1–3.

Pea, R. (1993). Practices of distributed intelligence and designs for education. In G. Salomon (Ed.), *Distributed cognitions: Psychological and educational considerations* (pp. 47–87). Cambridge: Cambridge University Press.

Phipps, R., & Merisotis, J. (1999). *What's the difference: A review of contemporary research on the effectiveness of distance learning in higher education.* Washington DC: The Institute for Higher Education Policy.

PKAL (2007). About project kaleidoscope. Available online: http://www.pkal.org/collections/About.cfm

Prensky, M. (2001a). Digital natives, digital immigrants. *On the Horizon, 9*, 1–6.

Prensky, M. (2001b). Digital natives, digital immigrants, part II: do they really think differently? *On the Horizon, 9*, 1–6.

Prosser, M., & Trigwell, K. (1999). *Understanding learning and teaching: The experience in higher education.* Buckingham: SRHE/Open University Press.

Prosser, M., Trigwell, K., & Taylor, P. (1994). A phenomenographic study of academics' conceptions of science learning and teaching. *Learning and Innovation, 4*, 217–231.

Ramsden, P. (1979). Student learning and perceptions of the academic environment. *Higher Education, 8*, 411–28.

Ramsden, P. (1991). A performance indicator of teaching quality in higher education: the course experience questionnaire. *Studies in Higher Education, 16*, 129–150.

Ramsden, P. (1993). Theories of learning and teaching and the practice of excellence in higher education. *Higher Education Research and Development, 12*, 87–98.

Ramsden, P. (2002). *Learning to teach in higher education.* (2nd ed,). London: Routledge.

Ramsden, P. (2008). *The future of higher education: Teaching and the student experience.* London: Department for Innovation, Universities and Skills.

Reeves, T. C., Benson, L., Elliott, D., Grant, M., Holschuh, D., Kim, B., Kim, H., Lauber, E., & Loh, S. (2002). Usability and instructional design heuristics for e-learning evaluation. *World Conference on Educational Multimedia, Hypermedia, and Telecommunications, 1*, 1615–1621.

Roberts, G. (2003). Teaching using the web: conceptions and approaches from a phenomenographic perspective. *Instructional Science, 31*(1/2), 127–150.

Roberts, S. (2003). Campus communications and the wisdom of blogs. *Syllabus, 17*, 22–25.

Robertson, I. (2000). Imitative problem solving: why transfer of learning often fails to occur. *Instructional Science, 28*, 263–289.

Rogers, E. M. (1995). *The diffusion of innovations* (4th Ed.). New York: Free Press.

Romainville, M. (1994). Awareness of cognitive strategies: The relationship between university students' metacognition and their performance. *Studies in Higher Education, 19*, 359–366.

Salaway, G., Caruso, J., & Nelson, M. (2007). *The ECAR study of undergraduate students and information technology, 2007.* Washington, DC and Boulder, CO: Educause.

Säljö, R. (1979). Learning in the learner's perspective. I. Some common sense conceptions. Reports from the Department of Education, University of Göteborg, No. 76.

Säljö, R. (1988). Learning in educational settings: methods of inquiry. In P. Ramsden (Ed.), *Improving learning: New perspectives* (pp. 32–48). London: Kogan Page.

Säljö, R. (1995). Mental and physical artifacts in cognitive processes. In P. Reimann & H. Spada (Eds.), *Learning in humans and machines: Towards an interdisciplinary learning science.* Oxford: Pergamon/Elsevier Science.

Säljö, R. (1999). Learning as the use of tools: a sociocultural perspective on the human-technology link. In K. Littleton & P. Light (Eds.), *Learning with computers: Analysing productive interaction* (pp. 144–161). London: Routledge.

Salmon, G. (2001). *E-moderating: The key to teaching and learning online.* London: Kogan Page.

Salmon, G. (2002). *E-tivities: The key to active on-line learning.* London: Routledge Falmer.

Salomon, G. (Ed.). (1993). *Distributed cognitions: Psychological and educational considerations.* Cambridge: Cambridge University Press.

Salomon, G., Perkins, D., & Globerson, T. (1991). Partners in cognition: extending human intelligence with intelligent technologies. *Educational Researcher, 20*, 2–9.

Sawyer, K. (2006). Introduction: the new science of learning. In K. Sawyer (Ed.), *The Cambridge handbook of the learning sciences* (pp. 1–18). Cambridge: Cambridge University Press.

Scardamalia, M., & Bereiter, C. (1994). Computer support for knowledge building communities. *Journal of the Learning Sciences, 3*, 265–283.

Scardamalia, M., & Bereiter, C. (2006). Knowledge building: theory, pedagogy and technology. In K. Sawyer (Ed.), *The Cambridge handbook of the learning sciences* (pp 97–115). Cambridge: Cambridge University Press.

Schrire, S. (2006). Knowledge building in asynchronous discussion groups: going beyond quantitative analysis. *Computers and Education, 46*, 49–70.

Schwartz, D., & Bransford, J. (1998). A time for telling. *Cognition and Instruction, 16,* 475–522.

Scott, P. (1995). *The meanings of mass higher education.* Buckingham: Open University Press.

Scottish Funding Council [SFC], (2006). *Spaces for learning: a review of learning spaces in further and higher education.* Available at: http://www.sfc.ac.uk/information/information_learning/Spaces_for_Learning_report.pdf

Sfard, A. (1998). On two metaphors for learning and the dangers of just choosing one. *Educational Research, 27,* 4–12.

Shavelson R. J. (2002). *Scientific research in education.* Center for Education, Division of Behavioral and Social Sciences and Education, National Research Council. National Academies Press.

Shoenfeld, A. H. (1999). Looking toward the 21st century: challenges of educational theory and practice. *Educational Researcher, 28,* 7, 4–14.

Shuell, T. (1986). Cognitive conceptions of learning. *Review of Educational Research, 56,* 411–436.

Shuell, T. (1992). Designing instructional computing systems for meaningful learning. In M. Jones & P. Winne (Eds.), *Adaptive learning environments.* New York: Springer Verlag.

Simons, R. J., Linden, J. V. D., & Duffy, T. (Eds.). (2000). *New learning.* Dordrecht: Kluwer Academic Publishers.

Singley, M., & Anderson, J. (1989). *The transfer of cognitive skill.* Cambridge, MA: Harvard University Press.

Smith, A., & Webster, F. (1997). *The postmodern university.* Buckingham: Open University Press.

Space Management Group [SMG]. (2006a). *UK Higher Education Space Management Project: Managing space: a review of English further education and HE overseas.* Available at: http://www.smg.ac.uk/resources.html

Space Management Group [SMG]. (2006b). *UK Higher Education Space Management Project: Space utilisation: practice, performance and guidelines.* Available at: http://www.smg.ac.uk/resources.html

Spot+ (2004). *SPOTplus – student perspectives on technology in teaching and learning in European universities.* University of Erlangen, www.spotplus.odl.org

Star, S., & Ruhleder, K. (1996). Steps toward an ecology of infrastructure: design and access for large information spaces. *Information Systems Research, 7,* 111–134.

Sternberg, R. J., & Horvath, J. A. (1999). *Tacit knowledge in professional practice: Researcher and practitioner perspectives.* Mahwah, NJ: Lawrence Erlbaum Associates.

Steward, J. (2006). The concept and method of cultural ecology. In H. Moore & T. Sanders (Eds.), *Anthropology in theory: Issues in epistemology* (pp.100–107). Oxford: Blackwell.

Strijbos, J.W., Kirschner, P., & Martens, R. (Eds.). (2004). *What we know about CSCL and implementing it in higher education.* Boston: Kluwer.

Stubbs, M., Martin, I., & Endlar, L. (2006). The structuration of blended learning: putting holistic design principles into practice. *British Journal of Educational Technology, 37,* 163–175.

Suchman, L. (1987). *Plans and situated actions: The problem of human-machine communication.* Cambridge: Cambridge University Press.

Suchman, L. (2007). *Human-machine reconfigurations: Plans and situated actions* (2nd ed.). Cambridge: Cambridge University Press.

Sweller, J. (1988). Cognitive load during problem solving: Effects on learning. *Cognitive Science, 12,* 257–285.

Sweller, J. (2004). Instructional design consequences of an analogy between evolution by natural selection and human cognitive architecture. *Instructional Science, 32,* 9–31.

Szczepanski, J. (1968). The future of the nineteenth century idea of a university. *Minerva, 6,* 419–423.

Tapscott, D. (2008). *Grown up digital: How the net generation is changing your world.* New York: McGraw Hill.

Taylor, R., Barr, J., & Steele, T. (2002). *For a radical higher education: After postmodernism.* Buckingham: SRHE/Open University Press.

Tegegne, T., & Chen, C. (2003). Student use of internet in China: a study on Huazhong University of Science and Technology. *Pakistan Journal of Information and Technology, 2,*(1), 25–29.

Tertiary Education Facilities Management Association [TEFMA] (2006). *2005 Higher Education Facility Management Association of South Africa.*

Tisdell, E. J., Strohschen, G. I. E., Carver, M. L., Corrigan, P., Nash, J., Nelson, M., Royer, M.,

Strom-Mackey, R., and O'Connor, M. (2004). Cohort learning online in graduate higher education: constructing knowledge in cyber community. *Educational Technology & Society*, 7, 115–127.

Tobias, S. (1994). Interest, prior knowledge, and learning. *Review of Educational Research*, 64, 37–54.

Tobias, S., & Duchastel, P. (1974). Behavioral objectives, anxiety, and sequence in CAI. *Instructional Science*, 3, 231–242.

Trigwell, K., & Prosser, M. (1997). Towards an understanding of individual acts of teaching and learning. *Higher Education Research & Development*, 16, 241–252.

Trigwell, K., Prosser, M., & Taylor, P. (1994). Qualitative differences in approaches to teaching first year university science. *Higher Education*, 27, 75–84.

Trow, M. (1973). *Problems in the transition from elite to mass higher education*. Berkeley, CA: Carnegie Commission on Higher Education.

Turner, P. (2005). Affordance as context. *Interacting with Computers*, 17, 787–800.

van Hooft, S. (1999 and 2005). Socratic dialogue as collegial reasoning. *Ethics and Justice*, 2, 21–29 (electronic journal available at: http://www.ethics-justice.org/). Subsequently published in Nigel Sanit (Ed.), *Motivating science: Science communication from a philosophical, educational and cultural perspective* (pp. 217–228). Luton: The Pantaneto Press, 2005.

Varma, S., & Schwartz, D. (2008). How should educational neuroscience conceptualise the relation between cognition and brain function? Mathematical reasoning as a network process. *Educational Research*, 50, 149–161.

Veerman, A. L. (2000). *Computer-supported collaborative learning through argumentation*. Enschede: Print Partners Ipskamp. Available at: http://eduweb.fss.uu.nl/arja/

Vermunt, J. D. (1998). The regulation of constructive learning processes. *British Journal of Educational Psychology*, 68, 149–171.

Vermunt, J., & van Rijswik, F. (1988). Analysis and development of students' skill in self-regulated learning. *Higher Education*, 17, 647–682.

Walton, G. (2006). Learners' demands and expectations for space in a university library: outcomes from a survey at Loughborough University. *New Review of Academic Librarianship*, 12, 133–149.

Weaver, M. (2006). Exploring conceptions of learning and teaching through the creation of flexible learning spaces: the learning gateway, a case study. *New Review of Academic Librarianship*, 12, 109–125.

Webster, J. (1999). Campus planning and architectural design. A.A.J. Conference.

Wedge, C. C., & Kearns, T. D. (2005). Creation of the learning space: Catalysts for envisioning and navigating the design process. *Educause Review*, 40, 32–38. Available at: http://www.educause.edu/ir/library/pdf/erm0541.pdf

Weick, K., & Sutcliffe, K. (2007). *Managing the unexpected: Resilient performance in an age of uncertainty* (2nd Ed.). New York, USA: John Wiley & Sons, Inc.

Weinstein, C. S. (1981). Classroom design as an external condition for learning. *Educational Technology*, 21, 12–19.

Whipp, J. (2003). Scaffolding critical reflection in online discussions. *Journal of Teacher Education*, 54, 4, 321–333.

Wild, F., Modritscher, F., & Sigurdarson, S. (2008). Designing for change: mash-up personal learning environments. *elearningpapers*, 9.

Winne, P., & Marx, R. (1982). Students' and teachers' views of thinking processes for classroom learning. *The Elementary School Journal*, 82, 493–518.

Wisner, A. (1995a). Understanding problem building: ergonomic work analysis. *Ergonomics*, 38, 595–605.

Yinger, R., & Hendricks-Lee, M. (1993). Working knowledge in teaching. In C. Day, J. Calderhead & P. Denicolo (Eds.), *Research on teacher thinking: Understanding professional development* (pp. 100–123). London: Falmer.

Zastrocky, M., Harris, M., & Lowendahl, J. (2007). *E-learning for higher education: Course management systems*. Stanford, CA: Gartner Research.

Zhang D. (2002). Media structuration – towards an integrated approach to interactive multimedia-based e-learning. Unpublished Ph.D. dissertation, The University of Arizona.

Zhao, Y., & Frank, K. (2003). Factors affecting technology use in schools: an ecological perspective. *American Educational Research Journal*, 40, 807–840.

Index